GREAT

TRAVEL THE WORLD'S MOST SPECTACULAR ROUTES

JOURNEYS

CONTENTS

❧

GREAT JOURNEYS, SMART TRAVEL

Why do we travel? To broaden our minds? To get away from ourselves and other people (or conversely to 'find' ourselves)? To undergo rites of passage before embarking on the next stage of our lives? To celebrate our union with the planet and all its peoples? Often enough today, we travel simply because we can. Cheap and plentiful airfares have shrunk the globe, making it easier to jump on a plane and lie on a beach halfway across the world. The idea of the authentic, all-consuming 'classic' journey is something different though, isn't it? Isn't that what we really mean when we talk of travel broadening the mind? Aren't we talking about those bygone days when we really were out of our comfort zones, when we lingered with travel?

Many of the trips, voyages and expeditions we've collected here have little to do with tourism or travel in the modern sense. In fact, quite a few are a product of the rise of civilisation itself, when new lands were forged and new knowledge cultivated as a consequence; journeys undertaken at a time when, unlike now, most of the world was unknown and seemingly unknowable. That's not to say that you won't find a relaxing ocean-side drive in this book as well.

Marco Polo brought back to Venice tales of lands no one had ever dreamt of, places so exotic and otherworldly that his recounting of his adventures rendered him a prophet without honour, branded a liar by his own people. As JG Ballard wrote, Marco was ostensibly the 'first tourist', setting the stage for many Grand Tours and Grand Packages to come, inspiring legions of travellers to seek out new lands, to travel for travel's sake. Many of our great journeys are the product of

this adventurous spirit, of the thrill of divesting oneself of the trappings of modern life and simply experiencing the world in its infinite variety and beauty, letting the journey unfold.

Each journey is epic – epic in scale, physicality, significance, or scenery, sometimes all at once. When you've stared down the mighty fjords and glaciers of Norway, you might think everything else pales into insignificance. For those with a spiritual bent, the Shikoku Pilgrimage and Buddha's odyssey are designed to achieve enlightenment and transcend earthly limitations, while Muslims undertaking the pilgrimage to Mecca believe that the journey will divest them of prior sins while showing the way to a more fulfilling life. These quests are about the desire to understand our place in the universe, and, in some ways, so are the world-beating missions from the Golden Age of exploration, which tested the claims of unassailable and unobtainable lands because these voyagers felt that to stay at home and never try to find out what lies beyond would mean stagnation, a devolution of the human spirit rather than evolution.

Today, the spirit of great exploration is not dead, merely displaced. After all, no one rides the *Royal Scotsman* luxury train around the Scottish Highlands with the express intent of advancing the human race. Well, maybe not consciously... Nostalgia, in the case of the *Scotsman* and pretty much every classic train journey, is a more accurate way to describe the engine that drives such voyages, and that's part of their own peculiar 'greatness' – the trains are slow and they take their time, and they can instantly transport you back to an era when

much travel for pleasure was painstakingly enabled by rail.

Elsewhere, curiosity is one of the strongest motivating factors. It seems hardwired into the collective consciousness, as we are essentially migratory, also social creatures and many of our great journeys were – and are – undertaken to satisfy our social, curious urges. We want to connect with other lands, other peoples, to imbibe the rituals of another culture so that we may alloy them with the things in our own world that we cherish. Other journeys are one-offs and can be admired as virtually unrepeatable achievements. Realistically, not many of us will have the wherewithall to recreate Amelia's Earhart's incredible plane journey around the globe, although reading about it should be no less inspirational as we recreate in our minds what it must have been like for her to travel so far and wide, and what it must have felt like to stumble at the very last hurdle.

That's the real key to this book: inspiration. Above all, we aim to instil that sense of great exploration that many feel has been buried by the modern world. Of society today, it's often said that we are 'time poor', that no one seems to possess the time to do anything of lasting duration, which explains the rise of 'slow travel', 'slow food' and other 'slow' movements designed to restore what has supposedly been leached away by a world in which everything is within easy reach. Think of this book then as your own personalised guide to slow travel. You can pick and choose which journeys you will actually undertake and which you will simply read about, allowing the latter to linger in soft-focus in the imagination as wondrous feats from bygone ages. With the former, you may not be able to conquer the world like, say, Alexander the Great did, but you can certainly travel from his birthplace, Pella, in Greek Macedonia, to Alexandria in Egypt, the city he founded, savouring Alexandrian sights along the way.

In recent times, there has been a rash of scientific evidence for the therapeutic value of travel. This evidence suggests that getting away from it all opens up neural pathways that help to beat stress, stave off Alzheimer's and produce positive and effective thinking. When overseas, the act of having to cope with a linguistic problem of translation or a confusing transport timetable forces us to think in new and unexpected ways. The thrilling disorientation of arriving in a foreign land and grappling with its mysteries and complexities seems to unlock a hidden dimension of creativity, as our brains rewire in an attempt to acclimatise. As a knock-on benefit, we are now able to solve the problems in our lives that, when we first left home, seemed insurmountable. Thousands of kilometres away, we can view them as if through the wrong end of a telescope – small and insignificant; easier to grasp, ruminate upon and solve for the perversely liberating distance that has been placed upon them. No wonder so much great literature was derived from partaking of a classic journey or two: the Shelleys on the Grand Tour; Theroux in the Pacific and on the Trans-Siberian; Stevenson in Cévennes; Conrad's *Heart of Darkness*. No wonder many future leaders, Che Guevara foremost, returned from their own great journey with ideas that would change the world.

You might think that travelling as far and as uncomfortably as possible would increase the chances of all that happening, but positive disorientation of the kind we're talking about does not have to be achieved solely through discomfort or endurance. It can come from a confrontation with sheer beauty: the fjords; the soaring Three Gorges on the Yangtze; the indescribable magic of the Copper Canyon; the majesty of the mightiest rivers – the Nile, the Mekong, the Ganges, the Amazon.

So, as you thumb through this book and perhaps plan a journey or two, be comforted by the thought that when you return from your adventure you'll doubtless have confirmed what we knew all along: that by travelling – by doing it right, by foregoing convenience for substance – you'll have become a smarter, more well-rounded human being.

OVERLAND

GREAT JOURNEYS

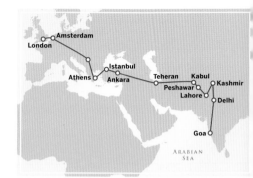

THE HIPPY TRAIL

THIS IS THE ROSETTA STONE – THE JOURNEY UPON WHICH LONELY PLANET FOUNDERS TONY AND MAUREEN WHEELER CUT THEIR TEETH. IT'S THE NOTORIOUS 'HIPPY TRAIL', THE OVERLAND ROUTE THROUGH ASIA, WHERE IN THE EARLY 1970S TRAVELLERS SOUGHT DRUGS, SEX, GURUS AND ADVENTURE.

10

In the 1960s and '70s, with free love coursing through the air, so-called 'hippies' travelled overland, seemingly en masse, from Europe to southern Asia through Pakistan, Afghanistan, India, Nepal, Turkey and Iran. It was all about dropping out of straight society, getting high and enjoying good times. Hippies took to this route because it could be travelled cheaply (mainly via hitchhiking, buses and trains) and was as far away from the evil capitalist West as possible. Of course, there was also plenty of mystique attached to these far-flung lands – highly desirable to people looking for spiritual enlightenment at the same time as a good time.

Usually, the European capitals of free love and dope, London and Amsterdam, would be the starting point for the journey. An ideal route from there would go down through Europe via Yugoslavia, Bulgaria or Greece into Turkey and Istanbul. From Istanbul, permutations were varied, but a typical path went to Ankara, then through Iran to Tehran, to Kabul in Afghanistan, through the Khyber Pass to Peshawar and Lahore in Pakistan, and then on to Kashmir, Delhi and Goa in India.

Lonely Planet's very first guidebook, Across Asia on the Cheap, was all about doing the hippy trail. In Tony and Maureen's case, they bought a clapped-out minivan for £65 in London and drove it to Kabul before pressing on to Australia across the Balkans, Turkey, Iran, Pakistan, India, Nepal, Thailand, Malaysia and Indonesia by any and all means possible. After selling the van in Afghanistan, they pressed on via chicken buses, trains and hitched rides in trucks, arriving nine months later in Sydney with no money to their name.

Today, the hippy trail is undergoing a revival with the rise in popularity of low-cost airlines and more accessible travel. But these days no one is 'dropping out' – the 'hippies' in these modern-day trails are invariably urban professionals.

ESSENTIAL EXPERIENCES

* **Relaxing on Paradise Beach in Mykonos, Greece, famous on the '60s trail for its hedonistic blend of free love and unfettered carousing; now backpackers have replaced the hippies.**

* Kicking back in Pai, northern Thailand, a cool, moist town nestled in a corner of a mountain valley. The hippy trail is alive and well with a New Age music and art scene co-existing with the local Shan, Thai and Muslim Chinese residents.

* **Discovering the amazing beach at hedonistic Kuta in Bali, a popular stop on the original trail.**

* Surveying the distant Himalaya at sunrise after trekking up to the rim of the Kathmandu Valley.

DISTANCE - APPROXIMATELY 7500KM | **COUNTRIES COVERED** - ENGLAND, THE NETHERLANDS, GREECE, BULGARIA, TURKEY, IRAN, AFGHANISTAN, NEPAL, INDIA | **IDEAL TIME COMMITMENT** - TWO TO THREE MONTHS | **BEST TIME OF YEAR** - ANY TIME YOU FEEL THE NEED TO GET AWAY FROM IT ALL | **ESSENTIAL TIP** - CHECK THE LATEST SECURITY WARNINGS BEFORE TRAVELLING TO AFGHANISTAN

MATALA

In the early 1970s, Matala in Crete, Greece, on the south coast 11km southwest of Phaestos, was a favourite on the trail. Hippies would sleep like troglodytes in the sandstone caves that pockmark the giant overhanging rock slab at water's edge, disregarding the fact that they were originally used as Roman tombs in the 1st century AD. Matala still attracts people tuned in to the hippy ideal, although it's become rather more 'civilised' since the heady days of the overland trail. Today it has morphed into a low-key vacation settlement, although there's still a beautiful sandy beach below the caves.

POKHARA

The original hippies were actually trailblazers in their desire to escape society: aside from the odd explorer, in the 1970s they were the first Westerners to reach Pokhara in Nepal, beneath the Annapurna mountain range. With its lakeside setting, chilled-out pace and abundant marijuana, it made the ultimate end-point for the south Asian portion of the overland trail. Later, it became a popular mountain resort with many hotels and shops until the Maoist conflict enforced a decade-long slump. In recent times it's returned to normal, with tourists once again arriving.

THE JOURNEY TODAY

You've crossed the Iranian border near Mashhad into Afghanistan and you're heading to the old Silk Road city of Herat. There, you drink in views from the imposing Citadel before gazing at the fabulous mosaic tiling of the Friday Mosque. After a few days, you chart a course for the northeast. Reality bites now, with Afghanistan's volatile political situation and explosive security requirements forcing you to travel by air. While it's not an entirely 'overland' trail anymore, the thrill remains.

At Mazar-e Sharif discover Afghanistan's holiest site, the blue domes of the Shrine of Hazrat Ali. Nearby are the equally evocative ruins of Balkh, with its crumbling city walls and ancient mosques. Once known as the 'Mother of Cities', it's probably the oldest in the country. Back on the bus, you make for Kabul, watching the plains gradually rise into the Hindu Kush mountains.

Across the Salang Pass, the main route between north and south Afghanistan, the road surface is better than normal but the traffic is hellfire crazy. Hang on as your driver skilfully negotiates the tricky, moving hazards all around. Arriving at the Afghan capital, Kabul, you can unwind and take in the many unique sights including Mughal gardens, mine museums and the infamous Chicken Street, a crucial node on the original trail, and where all kinds of handicrafts are still available today: jewellery, carpets, lapis lazuli, and even 'antique' muskets.

With all that behind you, you're on your way in a hired taxi to the Pakistan border, ready to leave Afghanistan through the Khyber Pass, the gateway to the Indian subcontinent, and the next stage of the adventure that is your reconstructed, updated version of the hippy trail.

SHORTCUT

If you're pressed for time, an Afghan sojourn (as outlined in the previous section) should satisfy your inner hippy. First you have to get yourself to the country using the standard trail methodology – 'by any means possible' – then allow yourself two to three weeks to fully enjoy the tour.

DETOURS

Allow a few days for a side trip to Bamiyan where the Taliban-destroyed Buddha statues have left a gaping hole in what remains one of Afghanistan's most beautiful valleys. A short drive away are the gorgeous, glittering blue lakes of Band-e Amir, arguably Afghanistan's most astounding natural sight, hidden in the Koh-e Baba at an altitude of 2900m. A series of six linked lakes, their deep blue waters sparkle like otherworldly jewels against the dusty mountains surrounding them.

13

OPENING SPREAD You need good balance to sell bread at Kabul's market bazaars. **LEFT** Nothing less than a retinal feast: a Kathakali dancer in full costume, Kerala, India. **ABOVE (L)** In Mazar-e-Sharif, Afghanistan, a pilgrim passes the Shrine of Hazrat Ali. **ABOVE (R)** Matala's famous hippy caves.

ARMCHAIR

❋ *Magic Bus: On the Hippie Trail from Istanbul to India* (Rory MacLean) An absorbing account of the author's 2008 quest to retrace the original trail, with many interesting insights on political and cultural changes in the various countries.

❋ *On the Road Again* (Simon Dring) A 1995 account of the author's retracing of the overland trail he took in the 1960s.

❋ *Across Asia on the Cheap* (Tony Wheeler) Lonely Planet's first guidebook, if you can find it, is worth reading for the amusing hippy slang peppered throughout and the fervour surrounding the journey.

❋ *Once While Travelling: The Lonely Planet Story* (Tony & Maureen Wheeler) This 2005 joint autobiography details the original overland journey that became the basis for that first guidebook.

CAIRO TO CAPE TOWN

AFRICA, TOP TO BOTTOM: A FEET-ITCHING PROSPECT OF LIONS AND HIPPOS AND 3000-YEAR-OLD RUINS, SUN-KISSED SAVANNAH AND TROPICAL DOWNPOURS, BORDER BULLIES, BURST TYRES, BUG BITES AND BUSH CAMPS – AND A LARGE DOSE OF THE UNEXPECTED.

14

On 19 July 1913, the New York Times announced that Captain Kelsey and team were ready to sail from England to Cape Town, in order to make their way to Cairo by automobile. The men anticipated their epic road trip, which included 'visiting little-known districts...[to gauge] suitability for European habitation, and the temper of the natives', would take one year. It did not. Kelsey followed a wounded leopard into the bush in Zimbabwe and was mauled to death.

Back in the 1890s, British imperialists dreamed of a highway linking their Empire from Egypt to South Africa, through what are now North Sudan, South Sudan, Kenya, Malawi, Zambia, Zimbabwe and Botswana, with the hope that the Germans would allow passage through their colony of Tanzania. The highway still doesn't quite exist – not as a single road – but that hasn't stopped explorers completing the traverse, or, latterly, adventurous travellers.

There's no set-in-stone Cairo to Cape Town – political machinations and all-out wars have variously closed sections and opened others. That said, many travellers blaze a similar trail, meandering from Egypt, through North Sudan and South Sudan, into Ethiopia, Kenya, side-stepping to Uganda and Rwanda, then Tanzania, Malawi, Mozambique, and possibly Zambia, Zimbabwe, Botswana and Namibia, before South Africa and the continent's end.

But even if there was a main highway, would you want to follow it? The fun is in Africa's 'backstreets', the dirt tracks that lead to parks a-roar with game, to ancient ruins semi-submerged in sand, to beaches where fishermen cast nets off wooden outriggers, to sleeping volcanoes, rock-hewn churches and flamingo-filled lakes. It's a landmass of extremes, best appreciated by seeing the lot. Just watch out for the leopards...

ESSENTIAL EXPERIENCES

* **Wondering at the architectural acuity of the ancient Egyptians: at Giza, Luxor and Abu Simbel.**

* Visiting Meroe, North Sudan's lesser-known – and less-visited – desert-set pyramids.

* **Seeing the cow-running rituals and lip-plated ladies of Ethiopia's Omo Valley tribes.**

* Penetrating Bwindi Impenetrable National Park for intimate encounters with Uganda's mountain gorillas.

* **Pausing to climb 5985m Mt Kilimanjaro, Tanzania – the rooftop of Africa.**

* Swimming with whale sharks off the Swahili-coast island of Zanzibar.

* **Watching rainbows shimmer at Victoria Falls before rafting along the hippo-infested Zambezi.**

* Paddling a mokoro (dugout canoe) along the wild tributaries of the Okavango Delta, Botswana.

* **Wine-tasting by bicycle between the vineyards of Stellenbosch, South Africa.**

DISTANCE - AROUND 12,000KM | COUNTRIES COVERED - EGYPT, NORTH SUDAN, SOUTH SUDAN, ETHIOPIA, KENYA, TANZANIA, MALAWI, BOTSWANA, UGANDA, ZAMBIA, ZIMBABWE, SOUTH AFRICA | **IDEAL TIME COMMITMENT** - FOUR TO SIX MONTHS | **BEST TIME OF YEAR** - OCTOBER DEPARTURE **ESSENTIAL TIP** - KEEP LOTS OF EMPTY PAGES IN YOUR PASSPORT FOR BORDER STAMPS.

CAIRO TO CAPE BY RAIL?

Cecil Rhodes had a grand plan: to link British interests in Africa by train. It didn't work; there's no trans-Africa railway. But you can (slowly) cover much of the continent this way. In Egypt, locomotives link Cairo to Aswan, where a ferry to North Sudan meets a train to Khartoum. Things are sketchy in Ethiopia and Kenya (use buses), though trains connect Nairobi to coastal Mombasa. From Dar es Salaam, Tanzania, you can ride uninterrupted into Zambia via Victoria Falls on the *Pride of Africa* (p46), and on to Zimbabwe and South Africa; here the luxury *Blue Train* (p74) awaits, as do the cheaper long-distance Shosholoza Meyl trains.

▦ THE JOURNEY TODAY

Your backside is bruised, your neck jarred from a multitude of mini-whiplashes. You smell. Your truck-mates smell. It's hot in this tin box, and you've been wearing the same clothes for about three months. Your malaria tablets are making your skin sun-sensitive, your camera's innards have been invaded by Saharan sand, and tonight it's your turn (again) to cook dinner for 20 on a wilderness campfire. But you're in absolute heaven. Outside all of Africa is passing by – ladies in rainbow wraps, men on bicycles, trundling bullock carts, and boys toting stick bundles bigger than themselves.

The view varies enormously as you top-to-toe this continent, though some stretches haven't changed for millennia: big skies over grassy savannah, mud-hut villages nibbled by goats, the ancient awe of the pyramids. Other things change constantly. The biggest challenge is negotiating borders and political powder-kegs. For instance, the Egypt–North Sudan border must be crossed by ferry, not road, and South Sudan is usually avoided by detouring east from Khartoum into Ethiopia, where roads are deemed safer, though they are still bone-jarringly bad.

Travelling on a tour operator–arranged overland truck is the easiest way – transport is sorted and most logistics and red tape issues are handled for you. It can be cheaper too, as meals are communal, travel expenses shared and highlights efficiently, if speedily, ticked off – a safari here, a Maasai village there, snorkel in the Indian Ocean – but can you cope being cooped up with strangers for weeks? Many independent travellers have driven, caught a bus or even walked the Cairo to Cape Town trail.

Either way, this is a journey that's far more than the sum of its varied parts.

ARMCHAIR

✳ **Africa: A Biography of a Continent** (John Reader) Very readable history of the continent, from geological creation to 20th-century.

✳ **Into Africa** (Martin Dugard) The legend of explorers Sir Henry Stanley and David Livingstone retold in vivid fashion.

✳ **African Ceremonies** (Angela Fisher & Carol Beckwith) A glossy tome of arresting images, documenting rituals, rites and traditions across the continent.

✳ **The Shadow of the Sun** (Ryszard Kapuscinski) A series of vignettes from the veteran Polish foreign correspondent, documenting his life in, and views on, Africa.

✳ **The Kingdon Field Guide to African Mammals** (Jonathan Kingdon) Detailed animal reference book – the ultimate safari companion.

✳ **Dark Star Safari** (Paul Theroux) The author travels from Cairo to Cape Town, avoiding tourist hot-spots to get under Africa's skin.

SHORTCUT

Get a trans-Africa flavour by following a short chunk of the journey, best done with an overlanding company so you don't need to worry about practicalities and delays. Nairobi to Victoria Falls, taking in Lake Malawi and Zimbabwe, can be done in four weeks, allowing time to stop at national parks and Swahili islands; Victoria Falls to Cape Town, via Botswana's Okavango Delta and Namibia's dunes, could be done in three weeks.

DETOUR

Change your plan of attack to see, quite literally, another side to Africa. Start from Tangier – north Morocco's superbly seedy port is only a ferry-hop from Europe, and the gateway to West Africa. On the continent's Atlantic edge, the emphasis is not on wildlife but on humans, from desert nomads to slave-trade reminders to world-class musicians in the nightclubs of Senegal. From Morocco, head south via the medieval medina of Fès and the Atlas Mountains, into the Sahara and little-visited lands such as Mali, Burkina Faso, Benin (for voodoo), and Cameroon. Angola, long a war-torn country, has finally reopened, allowing passage into Namibia, and beyond that, Cape Town.

CORBIS | PHOTOLIBRARY

OPENING SPREAD The mighty Egyptian Pyramids of Giza in all their otherwordly glory. **ABOVE** Cape Town's delectable Clifton Beach. **BELOW** The awe-inspiring sight of a flock of blue wildebeest on migration in Tanzania.

THE ANIMAL OVERLAND

Cairo to Cape Town is a long journey but, en route, you'll pass another epic exodus. Every year, 1.5 million wildebeest, 500,000 Thomson's gazelle and 200,000 zebra trudge their way around the Serengeti–Masai Mara ecosystem, following the good grazing – and creating one of the world's greatest natural spectacles. Plan your overland expedition to take in the right part of Kenya or Tanzania at the right time to witness this mass movement: highlights include the calving season in the southern Serengeti (January to March) and the crossings of the Grumeti and Mara Rivers (June to September), where hungry crocs and salivating lions lay in wait.

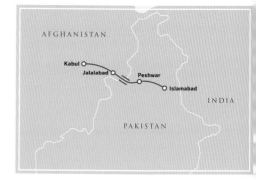

THE KHYBER PASS

UP THE KHYBER! NEAR JALALABAD, AN IMPORTANT CITY FOUNDED BY THE
MUGHALS AS A WINTER RETREAT, THE KHYBER PASS IS THE AGE-OLD GATEWAY
TO THE INDIAN SUBCONTINENT. GETTING A PASSPORT STAMP HERE AS YOU
SLIP BETWEEN AFGHANISTAN AND PAKISTAN IS AN EVOCATIVE EXPERIENCE.

18

The road from Torkham to the Pakistani city of Peshawar moves across
the pass, stretching for 50km through the Hindu Kush and linking
Afghanistan to the Indian subcontinent. The Khyber isn't at the border
but weaves through the Suleiman Range for many kilometres. It's a long,
winding, barren passage, and for many travellers one of the world's most
famous and strategically important mountain passes, attractive not so
much for the views but rather the idea of it. For centuries, the pass has
divided and linked empires and peoples, marking a watershed between
Central Asia and the subcontinent. Consider those drawn here, and those
who have wanted to conquer it: Darius the Great, Buddhist travellers,
Scythian warriors. This is where Babur drove his army through on his
way to set up the Mughal empire. It's also the pass that throughout
history Afghans have used to plunder the riches of India. In a land with
more strategic and important passes than most, none have quite the
same level of romance and historical allure: the Khyber Pass is saturated
in tales of honour, hospitality and revenge.

During the time of the British Empire, the Khyber became a key
strategic pawn. Of course, the British weren't keen on letting the Afghans
have this advantage, so they reinforced the pass with forts to ensure that
Peshawar and the Khyber stayed on their side of the border. But the pass,
somehow, always managed to get the better of them, and they had to buy
off the local Pashtun tribes to stop them raiding British convoys. Even
today, the Pakistani government only controls the main highway – step
off the tarmac and you're in tribal land. Indeed, the local Afridi Pashtuns
have built a second road through the pass, away from the highway, to
allow them to continue their traditional smuggling unimpeded, carrying
everything from opium to DVD players.

ESSENTIAL EXPERIENCES

❋ **Photographing Jamrud Fort, built by
the Sikhs in 1823 to mark the western
edge of their empire (one of the few to
expand westward to the Khyber), with its
stone arch marking the formal entrance
to the pass.**

❋ Taking in the sight of the Ali Masjid and the
commanding Ali Masjid Fort above it.

❋ **Absorbing the history of Shahgai Fort,
another British legacy. Built in the 1920s,
it's now occupied by the Frontier Force and
closed to the public.**

❋ Reflecting upon the ruins of the Sphola Stupa
on a promontory overlooking the road and
dating from Kushan times.

DISTANCE - 53KM | COUNTRIES COVERED - PAKISTAN, AFGHANISTAN | **IDEAL TIME COMMITMENT** - ONE DAY | **BEST TIME OF
YEAR** - MAY TO OCTOBER FOR THE BEST WEATHER | **ESSENTIAL TIP** - CHECK TRAVEL WARNINGS FOR THE REGION BEFORE YOU GO.

ALI MASJID

Near the pass's narrowest point, 15km from Jamrud, is Ali Masjid (Ali Mosque), which has an interesting history. Above the mosque, Ali Masjid Fort commands a view over this strategic sector of the pass, with a small cemetery containing the graves of British soldiers who fell in the Second Anglo-Afghan War. Before the pass was widened to 3m, it was said to have been too narrow for two fully laden camels to pass each other. The valley walls bear insignias of regiments that have served here.

THE JOURNEY TODAY

Why is it that you feel like a character in a Kipling novel? Is it the charged anticipation that wells up inside you as you collect your permit and armed escort? The queasy nervousness, offset by mounting excitement, as you pass the sign that says 'Foreigners not permitted beyond this point'? The spine-tingling sensation as you enter the Tribal Areas? Or the realisation that soon you will be passing by Afridi homes, Buddhist ruins and old forts, a combination designed to tip your excitement levels into the stratosphere?

You have arrived in the broiling summer, to this region that harks back to a time when Afghanistan was a Buddhist nation, with its monasteries and prayer wheels. You've passed through the trademark stone arch over the road that signifies the entrance to the pass, and now, as your hired guard informs you, Pakistani law no longer applies – it's tribal law all the way. That's why he's here with you: as protection. You drive further along to about 6km from Jamrud, where the road climbs in a series of switchbacks and there are excellent views back east over the road. You marvel at the Khyber railway winding its way through numerous tunnels and the massive Pashtun houses that pepper the hills. You're amazed at the scattered concrete known as 'dragon's teeth', obstacles on the valley floor designed to stop German tanks, set up by war-era Brits fearful of a Nazi invasion of India.

Further on, you come across the ruined Sphola stupa in a broad valley by the village of Zarai. Dating from Kushan times, it's a poignant reminder of the region's past, something you reflect on further when you reach Landi

Kotal at 1200m. Once known as the archetypal 'contraband city', the labyrinthine bazaar still features several gun shops nestled next door to vegetable sellers and toy dealers. But that's the Khyber all over: incongruous, yet explosive, with a deep, often divisive history that won't be denied.

SHORTCUT

As the Khyber Pass is only 53km long and heavily controlled (trails off the main road can only be used by locals), it's not really possible to abbreviate the journey. Just sit back and enjoy the ride.

DETOUR

The Khyber Railway, built by the British in 1925, is a great alternative trip. An incredible feat of engineering, with 34 tunnels and 92 bridges and cuttings, it's so steep that two engines are needed to push and pull the train up 600m in 30km. There are no public services, although the train can be chartered. It travels with armed guards and stops at Peshawar airport and Shahgai Fort before pulling in at Landi Kotal four hours later.

OPENING SPREAD Suffused in golden light: the Seraj-ul-Emorat (Light of Buildings) Palace in Jalalabad. **ABOVE** A scene as rich, as timeless as the pass itself: Jamrud Fort and the gateway to the Khyber. **RIGHT** Local culture and produce on display: a colourful Peshawar street scene.

ROBERT HARDING | PHOTOLIBRARY

ARMCHAIR

✳ **King of the Khyber Rifles** (1953) This film, starring Tyrone Power and Terry Moore, is about anti-Pashtun prejudice in a British garrison near the Khyber.

✳ **The Man Who Would Be King** (1888) Kipling's book, filmed in 1975 by John Huston, is set in 19th-century India and follows the travails of two ex-British soldiers who journey through the Khyber Pass into Kafiristan.

✳ **Carry On... Up the Khyber** (1968) This entry in the venerable British comedy franchise parodies Kipling. Taking place in British India, it features an anti-British uprising and a storming of the pass.

✳ **Kandahar** (2001) This film by Iranian director Mohsen Makhmalbaf is about an Afghan exile returning to the country to save her friend from suicide. Apparently, even George W Bush saw it.

THE PASHTUN MORAL CODE

For the local Pashtun population in Peshawar, Pashtunwali, the Pashtun moral code, traditionally takes precedence over external laws and acts as a constitution for Pashtun society. It's often taken by the West to be merely a form of tribal extremism, but in reality it provides an open and democratic code for managing tribal affairs within the Pashtun feudal society. The key concepts are *siali* (individual equality), *nang* (honour) and *melmastia* (hospitality), while group decisions are a matter for the *jirga* (council of elders).

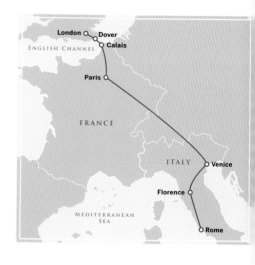

THE GRAND TOUR

FOLLOW IN THE FOOTSTEPS OF THE PRETTY, BRIGHT YOUNG THINGS OF THE 17TH AND 18TH CENTURIES, WHO TRAVELLED AROUND EUROPE TO GAIN WORLDLY KNOWLEDGE...AND WHO ENJOYED JUST AS MUCH HEDONISTIC PARTYING AS MANY TOURISTS TODAY.

In today's terms, the Grand Tour can be considered the prototype of the gap year: an extended bout of travel that served as a rite of passage, undertaken by young people who desired to see the world before they 'grew up' and became responsible adults. The tradition began in the mid-17th century, reached a peak in the 18th century and survived for two more centuries until rail travel and the rise of commercial tourism killed it off. Back then, it was mainly wealthy, upper-class males from Britain who took the tour, which could last anywhere from a few months to four years. Travel was time-consuming, difficult and expensive, and so it became the natural preserve of the privileged classes. Often, the real reason to undertake it was to have the Mother of All Flings before accepting the role of stately member of the aristocracy.

Aside from broadening their world view, the Tour was the only way for the cultural elite to consume the art and music that they held dear, namely the traditions of antiquity and the Renaissance. While Italy was a favoured destination, with Rome, Florence and Naples major stops of importance, Paris was the most popular city, being easily accessible from England and sharing many confluences with English culture (French, for example, was the second language of rich folk of the era). And while imbibing classical culture was a prime motivation, often it would be forgotten for weeks, even months on end, as the Tourists settled into the way of life of their city of choice, carousing with the locals in an explosion of hedonistic pleasure-seeking.

Typically, the Grand Tourist would cross the English Channel from Dover to Calais and then continue on to Paris. From there, the route might cross the Alps to Italy or traverse the Mediterranean Sea. Occasionally, the Tour would detour to Portugal, Spain, Germany, Eastern Europe or the Baltics, although the principal interest always remained the classic Romantic cities.

ESSENTIAL EXPERIENCES

* ❋ **Savouring Paris's néo-bistro craze: small, casual dining under the tutelage of talented master chefs.**
* ❋ Finding new and unique ways to enjoy the monumental Eiffel Tower.
* ❋ **Tossing coins into Rome's Trevi Fountain, like many Grand Tourists must have done centuries ago.**
* ❋ Visiting Rome's fabled Spanish Steps at the Piazza di Spagna, famous meeting point for Grand Tourists, eminent citizens and Rome's most desirable men and women.
* ❋ **Marvelling at Florence and Venice, which at times seem more like incredible, virtual outdoor museums than cities.**

DISTANCE - APPROXIMATELY 1800KM | **COUNTRIES COVERED** - FRANCE AND ITALY | **IDEAL TIME COMMITMENT** - ONE TO TWO MONTHS | **BEST TIME OF YEAR** - APRIL TO JUNE, BEFORE THE TOURIST FLOOD | **ESSENTIAL TIP** - ALLOW TIME FOR DISTRACTIONS.

ROME'S ANCIENT WONDERS

If you want to ruminate on the ancient wonders of Rome as the Grand Tourists did, these are the must-see attractions. Top of the list is the Colosseum, Rome's most iconic ancient site, so evocative you can almost hear the roar of the crowd. At Palatine, you can dream about the lives of ancient emperors, while the frescoes in Palazzo Massimo alle Terme afford privileged glimpses into the interior decor of wealthy, ancient Romans. As for the Pantheon, well, it's hard to believe it has been standing for several millennia – it's simply mind-blowing. Then there's the Mithraic temple beneath San Clemente: mystical, mysterious and wonderful.

PARISIAN SUPPER CLUBS

If you take your Grand Tour in Paris and want to recreate the decadent carousing of the Tourists, try the city's sumptuous supper clubs. Jim Haynes' Sunday dinner in a belle époque atelier is the original, but as in so many other world-class cities, supper clubs are popping up everywhere in Paris. While some of the clubs are more about socialising and perhaps even landing a date, many of the newer clubs focus on multicourse gastronomic meals or visiting the hip *adresse* (restaurant) of the moment with a local food celebrity.

■ THE JOURNEY TODAY

You have arrived in Italy, following in the footsteps of the Grand Tourists. Although you're not an aristocrat, you plan to do the Italy portion of the Grand Tour – Milan to Palermo – in one month, seeing everything the Tourists would have. This means large doses of ancient and classical architectural and culinary delights, Romanesque ruins, medieval sites and baroque palaces.

From Milan you head north and east to the glittering Lombard lakes, elegant Verona and, most glorious of all, Venice, the enchanting lagoon city. In Bologna you sample amazing cuisine before making your way to Florence, where you take in the incredible Renaissance art at the Uffizi Gallery.

From Florence you plan to make your way further south, but you encounter the same impasse that regularly afflicted the Grand Tourists: you become addicted to the city's magnetism and charm. Many elements conspire to keep you in Florence: designer boutiques and artisan workshops; buzzing cafes and bars; vine-laden hills and terrace restaurants just outside of town. Not to mention the gelato – possibly Italy's creamiest, most flavourful and freshest. And you haven't even begun to explore the literary haunts of Byron, the Shelleys, the Brownings, Dostoevsky and Henry James, who all thrived in this city of cities. After two weeks in Florence, you still haven't seen it all, so how on Earth will you fit in the rest of your schedule, which includes wondrous Pisa, enchanting Perugia, chaotic Naples, sizzling Sicily and fascinating Palermo? Simple. You'll just have to do as the Grand Tourists did: just keep going for as long as it takes.

■ SHORTCUT

For a whistle-stop Grand Tour, imbibe the three great Italian destinations: Rome, Venice and Florence. Try three days in each city, beginning in Rome, home to St Peter's, the Sistine Chapel and the Colosseum, then head to Florence, Italy's Renaissance jewel. Finally, Venice, to explore the city's waterways and architectural grandeur.

■ DETOUR

When Grand Tourists diverted to Spain, Barcelona was the most popular destination. To appreciate the cultural delights they enjoyed, visit Museu Nacional d'Art de Catalunya, with its 11th- and 12th-century murals, woodcarvings and altar frontals. Gathered from decaying churches in northern Catalonia last century, this is among Europe's best collections of Romanesque art. The two outstanding items are an image of Christ in majesty from 1123 and an apse image of the Virgin Mary and child from the nearby Esglesia de Santa María de Taüll.

25

OPENING SPREAD Venice's beautiful Grand Canal from Ponte di Rialto. **ABOVE** Like a wormhole into the distant past: Rome's Temple of Saturn and Arch of Septimius Severus. **LEFT** No introduction necessary: the Eiffel Tower.

ARMCHAIR

❋ **Continental Drifter** (Tim Moore) The author's musings, published in 2002, on the origins of the Grand Tour while recreating it himself, albeit with a modern twist: sleeping rough in a vintage Rolls Royce and wearing a crumpled velvet suit.

❋ **Dreams, Waking Thoughts and Incidents; In a Series of Letters, from Various Parts of Europe** (William Thomas Beckford) The English novelist Beckford (1760–1844) published his second book in 1783, based on his Grand Tour throughout Italy the previous year.

❋ **Brian Sewell's Grand Tour** (2006) In this 10-part TV series, art historian Sewell traced the Grand Tour by car, travelling through Rome, Florence, Vesuvius, Naples, Pompeii, Turin, Milan, Cremona, Siena, Bologna, Vicenza, Paestum, Urbino, Tivoli and Venice.

ISTANBUL TO CAIRO

A CLASSIC OVERLAND TRIP ENCOMPASSING A MAELSTROM OF EXPERIENCES, SANDWICHED BETWEEN TWO VIBRANT CITIES, ISTANBUL AND CAIRO. EN ROUTE YOU'LL SAVOUR SUMPTUOUS MEDITERRANEAN COAST INSET WITH RISING MOUNTAINS, AND VAST TRACTS OF WINDSWEPT, SUN-BEATEN DESERT.

26

The Istanbul to Cairo route is a favourite for novice backpackers and seasoned travellers alike, and the reasons for that are not hard to divine. Firstly, Istanbul straddles two continents, making it an excellent entry point into the Middle East. From there, the route snakes its way down through Turkey, which has an abundance of historical riches including the Gallipoli peninsula and the poignant Anzac battlefields; the amazing Istanbul; Ephesus, with its marvellous Roman remains; and Cappadocia's extraordinary fairy chimneys. The route then enters Syria and the stimulating bazaar at Aleppo, not to mention the stunning city of Damascus. Many travellers follow their nose to Jordan, where there is so much to enjoy: the ruins of Petra, for example, or the chance to float in the Dead Sea. A detour to Jerusalem is always worthy regardless of your religious views, while snorkelling in the Red Sea provides more of an earthly thrill. Crowded Cairo is the end point and a trip to the Pyramids the icing on the cake.

The route is versatile and exciting and can encompass many different adventures: diving among spectacular marine scenery, trekking through waves of sand dunes, spending days adrift on a small Nile felucca or whiling away nights at old colonial drinking dens and pounding Mediterranean nightclubs. There are five millennia of history and culture here, including the pyramids and the rock-cut city of Petra, the desert oasis ruins of ancient Palmyra and the gigantic columns of the Roman temple at Baalbek. Every town and city, valley and hillside seems like it's a living museum: the field that saw Ramses triumph over the Hittites; the site where Alexander the Great sought the advice of the Oracle; the location where Cleopatra bathed; the route walked by Christ; the spot where Napoleon put ashore.

ESSENTIAL EXPERIENCES

✳ **Overdosing on classic historical wonders: the pyramids in Cairo and Petra; Palmyra and the Crusader castle of Krak des Chevaliers in Syria; Ephesus in Turkey; the Aya Sofia in Istanbul; the Dome of the Rock and the Western Wall in Jerusalem.**

✳ Doing the rounds of essential museums: Cairo's Egyptian Museum, which contains some of the most amazing artefacts in the world; the Topkapi Palace in Istanbul and Azem Palace in Damascus; the Israel Museum in Jerusalem; and the Diaspora Museum in Tel Aviv.

✳ **Kicking back on sumptuous beaches: Patara in Turkey; Eilat on the Red Sea; Netanya, Tel Aviv, Bat Yam and the Sinai Peninsula.**

✳ Enjoying the nightlife in Tel Aviv, Istanbul and Cairo.

DISTANCE - 1200KM | **COUNTRIES COVERED** - TURKEY, SYRIA, LEBANON, JORDAN, ISRAEL, EGYPT | **IDEAL TIME COMMITMENT** - SIX TO EIGHT WEEKS | **BEST TIME OF YEAR** - SEPTEMBER TO NOVEMBER, MARCH TO MAY | **ESSENTIAL TIP** - SYRIA DENIES ENTRY TO ANYBODY WITH AN ISRAELI PASSPORT-STAMP; TRAVEL FROM ISTANBUL TO CAIRO FOR A DETOUR THERE AFTER SYRIA.

PETRA

Anyone on the Istanbul to Cairo route should prioritise a visit to Jordan's ancient city of Petra. Hewn from towering rock walls of multicoloured sandstone, the imposing facades of its great temples and tombs are an enduring testament to the vision of the desert tribes who sculpted them. Almost as spectacular as the monuments themselves are the countless shades and Neapolitan swirls formed in the rock. Petra is often called the 'Rose Red City' but even this hardly does justice to the extraordinary range of colours that blend as the sun makes its daily passage over the site.

THE JOURNEY TODAY

You've travelled to Egypt overland from the north, and the first place you hit is the Sinai Peninsula. You snorkel the spectacular Sinai coast and hit the superb beaches. From southern Sinai you go to Cairo, visit the pyramids and catch a train down to see the Pharaonic splendours gathered around the Upper Egyptian centres of Luxor and Aswan. From Upper Egypt, you travel straight up the Nile Valley. Egypt really is the most extraordinary place, you reflect, recalling the words of the ancient Greek historian, Herodotus: 'Concerning Egypt, I will now speak at length, because nowhere are there so many marvellous things, nor in the world besides are there to be seen so many things of unspeakable greatness'.

The pyramids leave an indelible mark on you, as do the immense, awe-inspiring temples and monuments left by the Pharaohs, the legacy of the Greeks and Romans, the churches and monasteries of the early Christians and the incredible art and architectural legacy of early Islam.

Back in Cairo, at the end of your Egyptian sojourn, you relax in a busy coffee house at dusk, as the voice of Egyptian diva, Umm Kolthum, wafts around you. You people-watch out onto the busy street, fascinated by the day-to-day machinations of Egyptian society and culture, which seem to provide just as much intrigue and magic as the country's historical treasures.

It is this latter thought that stays with you as you catch a ferry to some small family restaurant on the far bank of the Nile, thinking that the street scenes are almost as exciting as the pyramids themselves.

SHORTCUT

If time is pressing, two weeks should be enough to enjoy two countries along the way: Egypt and Jordan, say, or Jordan and Israel, or Syria and Lebanon. Turkey alone would probably need the whole two weeks.

DETOUR

In Turkey, many overlanders cross the Sea of Marmara in a hurry to get to the coast. Meanwhile, travellers who only have eyes for Gallipoli journey down through Thrace to the Gallipoli peninsula. Both sets of adventurers miss out on Bursa, a key city on the original Silk Route and a wonderful stopover. It's easily reached from Istanbul and is a complete contrast to the coastal regions with a very Turkish feel. Bursa's big attraction, now and historically, is the thermal springs at Çekirge. The city is also famous as the place where the oh-so-savoury Iskender kebab was invented and as the birthplace of Karagöz shadow puppets.

OPENING SPREAD Petra's dizzying, towering, rose-red rock walls. **ABOVE (L)** Too good to be true: Kaputa beach near Kas, Turkey. **ABOVE (R)** Cairo's bustling Khan al-Khalili (Great Bazaar). **LEFT** The sumptuous dome interior of the Hagia Sophia Church (Church of Divine Wisdom), Istanbul.

RICHARD I'ANSON | LONELY PLANET IMAGES ©

ARMCHAIR

* ***The Spy Who Loved Me (1977)** and **Death on the Nile** (1978)* Egypt's enormous Amun Temple Enclosure contains the famous hypostyle hall, as featured in both films.

* ***From the Holy Mountain*** (William Dalrymple) This book is an ambitious attempt to revisit the roots of Christianity in the troubled spots of eastern Turkey, Lebanon, Palestine and middle Egypt.

* ***Lawrence of Arabia*** (1962) In David Lean's film, Der'a in Jordan is where Lawrence (played by Peter O'Toole) is captured while in disguise.

* ***Star Wars*** (1977) Selime, at the northern end of the Ihlara Valley, is where some scenes for the original *Star Wars* were filmed.

* ***The Pillars of Hercules*** (Paul Theroux) Author Theroux's exploratory jaunt around seaside Turkey, Syria, Israel and Egypt.

NORTH CAPE TO GIBRALTAR

FROM EUROPE'S NORTHERNMOST POINT, LAPLAND'S NORTH CAPE, TO ITS SOUTHERNMOST, GIBRALTAR, IT IS OVER 5000KM. THIS IS ONE OF EARTH'S GREAT CYCLING ROUTES, AS MANY HAVE DISCOVERED, REPORTING BACK WITH THRILLING TALES OF BIKING THROUGH EUROPE'S GREATEST LANDSCAPES.

30

North to south, Europe stretches from the North Cape in Norway to Gibraltar at the foot of Spain. This fabled route provides the coordinates for a thrilling journey that many people undertake simply to say they've done it – once you've travelled from as far north to as far south as possible, there's nowhere else to go. Of course, what happens in between is very exciting too, as you pass through some of the great countries of continental Europe. Numerous cars make the trip, but many cyclists are also drawn to it because of the variety and challenge of the physical landscape. Consider the scenery: the Norwegian fjords; the Swedish forest; Germany's Bergisches Land; the Ardennes mountains in Belgium; the Pyrenees through Spain and France; Spain's Costa del Sol and Sierra Nevada; the Rock of Gibraltar.

How long it takes depends on how much sightseeing you do and, if cycling, how fit you are. Erik Straarup, who cycled from North Cape to Gibraltar in a staggering 18 days, set a world record by travelling over 300km daily. He chose the shortest route through Spain and France, avoiding the Mediterranean coast, but for most, the dramatic coastline is one of the main reasons to do this trip. Luckily, the cycling organisation EuroVelo has developed a series of long-distance cycling routes across Europe that cling to the coast.

EuroVelo route 1 (EV1) hugs the Norwegian coastline from North Cape to Bergen, connecting at the latter with EV12. If you follow EV12 to Göteborg, you can get a ferry across to Denmark, where the route continues along the Danish coast through Germany, the Netherlands and Belgium. EV12 then connects with EV5 to go inland through Luxembourg, France, Switzerland and Italy. Finally, EV5 crosses with EV8 in Italy, the latter taking you right along the incredible Mediterranean coastline through France, Monaco and Spain, and into Gibraltar.

ESSENTIAL EXPERIENCES

✳ **Hiking to Europe's true northernmost point, Knivskjellodden, 9km from North Cape.**

✳ Cycling through some of the most dramatic countryside you're likely to see: the Norwegian fjords.

✳ **Beetling along Spain's Costa del Sol, strewn along the seaboard from Malaga almost to Gibraltar, and chuckling at its deviant depiction in JG Ballard's novel *Cocaine Nights*.**

✳ Making your way through the Pyrenees (see p298), those wild peaks packed with historic ski stations, isolated valleys, subterranean caves and snow-dusted mountaintops.

✳ **Pulling into the Rock, looking out across the Strait of Gibraltar and, feeling superhuman after all that exertion, wondering if you could swim to Morocco.**

DISTANCE - AROUND 5500KM | **COUNTRIES COVERED** - NORWAY, SWEDEN, DENMARK, GERMANY, THE NETHERLANDS, BELGIUM, LUXEMBOURG, FRANCE, SWITZERLAND, ITALY, MONACO, SPAIN | **IDEAL TIME COMMITMENT** - ONE TO TWO MONTHS | **BEST TIME OF YEAR** - ANY TIME | **ESSENTIAL TIP** - TAKE YOUR TIME!

GIBRALTAR

The British colony of Gibraltar, surrounded by
Spain and the Strait of Gibraltar, is a fascinating,
contradictory place. It looks English, with
bobbies on the beat, red postboxes and other
reminders of 1960s England, but it's actually
a multicultural marvel with Genoese, Spanish,
North African and other elements that have
made it enormously prosperous. The main
attraction is the stupendous Rock, an immense
limestone ridge rising to 426m with sheer cliffs
on the northern and eastern sides. Of course,
Gibraltar's location and highly defensible
nature have made it most desirable to military
strategists throughout history, giving it much
of its weirdly thrilling charge.

■ THE JOURNEY TODAY

It's cold, getting dark, and you're cycling out from North Cape. Today you've been going for 150km nonstop and your tired, feverish mind is playing tricks. 'See that craggy mountain peak topped with snow in the distance,' you ask yourself. 'Yes,' you reply. 'It looks like Margaret Thatcher's head perched atop an ice-cream cone...' Welcome to the surreal world of the long-distance cyclist.

You stop, set up camp. The pure Norwegian air cleanses your mind of ridiculous thoughts. With darkness enveloping you inside your tent, you think about your trip through the long, narrow Nordland region and how you saw the Northern Lights slashing across the night sky. You recall the reindeer that almost knocked you off your bike as it stood in the middle of the road. You jammed on the anchors and almost went over the handlebars after it didn't move like you thought it would. That wasn't a hallucination – it was real. You apologised to the creature for getting in its way, and with that memory, you finally drift off to sleep.

It's morning. Conditions are brewing – there's going to be a killer headwind. You saddle up. There are hills ahead of you. You cycle on for hundreds of kilometres more. Days pass, through the Arctic Circle and into Sweden. Mosquitoes bite you as if you're the tastiest morsel alive. You're covered in welts. You have wind burn. You've not washed for a week. Your face itches. You took a wrong turn and got hopelessly lost. You've had more than enough flat tyres and your inner tubes are as patched up as an Egyptian mummy. It's hard, slow work but as you look out at the remote, rugged and indescribably beautiful Swedish forest, you know you wouldn't trade places with anyone else in the world.

ARMCHAIR

※ **Black Eyes** (1987) Film by Russian director Nikita Mikhalkhov set in the spectacular landscapes around Kjerringøy in Nordland, probably about as close to North Cape as any feature film has got.

※ **The Living Daylights** (1997) The opening scene of this James Bond actioner was filmed in Gibraltar.

※ **A Vision of Battlements** (Anthony Burgess) A 1965 novel about a British soldier in Gibraltar.

※ **Gil Braltar** (Jules Verne) This 1887 novel, and Verne's short story 'The Day of an American Journalist in 2889', are satirical takes on British colonialism in Gibraltar.

※ **Cocaine Nights** (JG Ballard) A darkly subversive novel about a travel writer lured to Gibraltar by the incarceration of his brother.

SHORTCUT

Some EuroVelo cycling routes can take you through sections of the journey, if the entire 5500km seems daunting. If you just want to see northern Europe, EV1 goes from North Cape to Bergen and Stavenger. EV7 and EV10 go from North Cape to Stockholm, Göteborg or Malmö. EV7 and EV11 both go from North Cape through Lapland to Helsinki, either inland or via the Finnish coast. For southern Europe, EV8 goes from Gibraltar along the Spanish and French Mediterranean coast and into Italy.

DETOUR

North Cape is not Europe's true northernmost point – that honour actually belongs to Knivskjellodden, an 18km round-trip hike from North Cape. Although inaccessible by vehicle, it's preferred by many who find the Cape too touristed. Hike to the tip of this promontory from a marked car park 6km south of the North Cape tollbooth. Wear hiking boots – it gets mucky after precipitation. Knivskjellodden is not as spectacular as the Cape, but it's still a great view, and you'll have the satisfaction of knowing you really have reached the extreme north.

JEAN-PIERRE LESCOURRET | LONELY PLANET IMAGES ©

OPENING SPREAD An imposing sight: the Rock of Gibraltar rising high above the low clouds. **ABOVE** It doesn't get any better: cruising through sublime Geiranger fjord. **BELOW** Noon in Nordland: and the sun is rising for the last few days before the polar night.

NORDLAND

While in northern Norway, make the most of it: don't just stick to the main roads and cycling routes. In Nordland, the country's north, you're spoilt for spectacular choice after choice. Indulge yourself on the Kystriksveien coastal route, try some ferry hopping or detour to glaciers and offshore islands. Lofoten is a necklace of offshore islands with razor-sharp peaks and Caribbean-coloured bays. Further north, Andenes, at the northern tip of Andøya, has Norway's best whale-watching. The stunning inland Arctic Highway, lightly trafficked, is another option.

LA RUTA MAYA (THE MAYA ROUTE)

FOR MILLENNIA THE MAYAN CIVILISATION SPREAD OVER JADE HILLS AND TANGLED JUNGLE, FLOURISHED ON SUGAR-WHITE SAND BEACHES LAPPED BY TURQUOISE LAGOONS, AND LEFT BEHIND PYRAMID CITIES THAT WOULD FASCINATE EVERYONE FROM SPANISH CONQUISTADORES TO GEORGE LUCAS.

34

At its apex, Mayan civilisation extended from the southern Mexican states of Tabasco, Yucatán, Quintana Roo, Campeche and Chiapas, through Belize and Guatemala, with a pinkie in both El Salvador and Honduras. Archaeologists believe the oldest of Maya's pyramids were built in present-day Belize in 2600 BC, but the lunar calendar, for which they have received most publicity, dates back to 3114 BC. The famed stepped pyramids and larger city-states, including Palenque (Chiapas), Tikal (Guatemala) and Copán (Honduras), were built during what scholars define as the Classic period (250–900 AD).

Jade and obsidian were its earliest trade goods, soon supplemented by salt, sea shells and cacao, which they traded with other early Mesoamerican cultures, including the Zapotecs to the north and Tainos to the southeast. The southern lowland cities went into decline and were eventually abandoned in the 8th and 9th centuries, while northern Yucatan cities survived until the Spanish arrived and conquered them. The last surviving city-states fell in 1697.

Initially the Spanish church torched all Mayan texts and art they found, but in the late 18th century Spanish officials began investigating former Maya sites. In 1839, John Lloyd Stephens, an American familiar with those investigations, visited Copán, Palenque and others, with English architect Frederick Catherwood. Their illustrations sparked popular interest worldwide.

Even today, many Maya ruins are hidden by dense jungle, so researchers have turned to satellite imagery that can detect limestone. With more than 70 restored Mayan sites in five countries, there are thousands of ways to tackle La Ruta Maya. We suggest starting at Chichén Itzá on the Mayan Riviera, moving onto Tulum before continuing south into Belize, and then Guatemala, where you'll enjoy mighty Tikal, the charming city of Antigua and Lake Atitlan, before turning back into Mexico to the jungle of Palenque and fabled Uxmal.

ESSENTIAL EXPERIENCES

✳ **Slaloming through the crowds in order to glean the secrets of the Mayan calendar at Chichén Itzá.**

✳ Checking out the enthralling ruins and spectacular beaches in sexy Tulum, the star of the Mayan Riviera.

✳ **Following La Ruta Maya into Belize where you'll glimpse the ancient trading hub of Altun Ha and massive Caracol, tucked away in the jungle.**

✳ Watching the sun drop into the misty jungle from the top of Temple IV in Tikal, arguably the most spectacular site on La Ruta Maya.

✳ **Looking back to the more recent past on a stroll through the sweet cobbled streets of old-town Antigua.**

DISTANCE - 1916KM | **COUNTRIES COVERED** - MEXICO, BELIZE, GUATEMALA | **IDEAL TIME COMMITMENT** - TWO WEEKS
BEST TIME OF YEAR - NOVEMBER TO APRIL | **ESSENTIAL TIP** - GO DURING THE OFF-SEASON (MAY-OCT) TO AVOID CROWDS.

STAR GAZERS

More than a few researchers claim that the Maya are the only pre-telescopic civilisation to demonstrate knowledge of the Orion Nebula as being fuzzy, rather than a pinpoint star. Such anthropologists point to a folk tale that deals with the Orion constellation, and their traditional hearths were oriented toward Orion. The Maya were also very interested in zenial passages – the time when the sun passes directly overhead – which at the latitude of the Mayan civilisation happened twice annually, on a day equidistant between the two solstices. However, according to a recovered record, which anthropologists call the Dresden Codex, Venus was astronomically more important to the Mayans than the sun.

■ THE JOURNEY TODAY

This is a journey best made by mixing air and road travel. The most famous and best restored of the Yucatán Maya sites, Chichén Itzá (Mouth of the Well of the Itzáes) is overcrowded but still impressive, especially after the mysteries of the Maya astronomical calendar are explained in the 'time temples'. The ball court is flanked by temples at either end and bounded by towering parallel walls with stone rings cemented up high. A short drive away, the famed ruins at Tulum are found on a stunning stretch of white sand beach, backed by the Si'an Kaan Biosphere Reserve where you can trek through pristine jungle and stumble on Mayan sites still in the grips of nature.

Belize's Altun Ha, close to Belize City and accessible from Cancun, was an important coastal trading hub and ceremonial centre. The restored portion of Altun Ha has some 300 unexcavated mounds surrounding it. Belize's largest site, Caracol, set in a jungle and not far from Tikal, was found in the 1930s, and excavated in 1985. Its ceremonial centre is dotted with massive pyramids and 20 major plazas. From here you can easily travel to Tikal, the largest of the restored Mayan ruins. At 72m, Temple IV is the highest of the numbered pyramids. Watch the sunset here, amid temples rising above a jungle canopy screeching with howler monkeys, toucans and parrots. You may recognise the view, as Tikal was the setting for the rebel base in *Star Wars IV, A New Hope*.

A short flight from nearby Flores will land you in colonial Antigua, not far from stunning Lake Atitlan. Proceed north from the lake and into the mountains of Chiapas, where you'll find the city of Palenque, noted for its detailed architecture and tremendous stone carvings – particularly in the Temple of Inscriptions. In Campeche, the western flank of the Yucatán peninsula shapes up, and before you reach Merida, the portal to and from the Mayan Riviera, stop in Uxmal for a final fix.

■ SHORTCUT

Cut your Ruta Maya short by sticking to one country – one peninsula even. From Merida you can reach Chichén Itzá, Tulum and Uxmal in one long weekend. With one more day, you can diverge down to Chiapas – where Palenque and the finest Mayan carvings in the empire await.

■ DETOUR

Set in a highland valley surrounded by pine forest, five hours from Palenque, the colonial city of San Cristóbal de las Casas has cobbled streets and markets and a unique ambience. Surrounded by dozens of traditional Tzotzil and Tzeltal villages, San Cristóbal is at the heart of one of the most deeply rooted indigenous communities in Mexico.

36

JEAN-PIERRE LESCOURRET | LONELY PLANET IMAGES ©

OPENING SPREAD & ABOVE (R) The unreal wonderment of the Chichén Itzá Archaeological zone, Yucatán, Mexico. **ABOVE (L)** A Mayan dancer struts his stuff at Xcaret Eco Theme Park, near Playa del Carmen, Mexico.

ARMCHAIR

✳ *2000 Years of Mayan Literature* (Dennis Tedlock) Mayan stories are some of the oldest in the world, and Tedlock was one of the first academics to treat ancient, Mayan-scripted myth as literature.

✳ *Breaking the Maya Code* (Michael D Coe) A true account about the eventual deciphering of the hard-to-crack Mayan language, written by a Yale professor who calls it 'one of the great intellectual adventures of our time'.

✳ *A Forest of Kings* (David Freidel & Linda Schele) Based on deciphered Mayan hieroglyphics and written by two archaeologists, this book tells tales of war, expansion and ritual that defined the Mayan civilisation.

✳ *Apocalypto* (2006) Mel Gibson's film about the decline of the Mayan civilisation and the harrowing escape of a young man trapped for human sacrifice.

RAIL

GREAT JOURNEYS

THE GHAN

DOES 3000KM OF ALMOST ENDLESS OUTBACK SOUND BORING? NOT LIKELY. THIS
TRANS-AUSTRALIA RAIL RIDE IS A JOURNEY OF EPIC PROPORTIONS, AND DRENCHED
IN UNEXPECTED CAMELEER HISTORY, THE EYE-SEARING FLAME OF DESERT
SUNSETS, RESILIENT COMMUNITIES AND A BOUNDING KANGAROO OR TWO.

Darwin to Adelaide is – as they say in the Outback – a bloody long way.
Look at a map: the distance between the cities is nearly 3000km, a
country-wide gulf of yellow-red nothing. No wonder no one was very keen
to cross it. That is, until the Afghan cameleers arrived. From the 1860s
small numbers of immigrants from Asia disembarked with their 'ships of
the desert' and set about opening up Australia's hostile Red Centre. They
did a fine job, and their legacy (aside from the million-odd feral camels
that now plague the Outback) can be felt in one of the greatest train
journeys in the world.

The *Ghan* is a truly epic train ride, connecting the capital cities of
South Australia and the Northern Territory, the crash of the Southern
Ocean and the tropical Timor Sea, via umber mountain ranges, weird
rocks, rainforest and a fair few kangaroos. The railway has existed in its
present form for less than a decade – that's how long it takes to tame a
wilderness this vast – but the first *Afghan Express* left Adelaide back on 4
August 1929. Then, a tremulous crowd gawped as this steam-hauled loco
choo-choo-ed from the city, bound for Alice Springs, 1500km north. The
journey took two days.

Things have changed since then, not least of all the route. The original
tracks proved highly unsuitable, laid in areas prone to flash flooding and
devastation by termite – 10-day delays were not uncommon. In the 1980s
new standard-gauge lines were laid and, in 2004, the line was finally
extended all the way to Darwin. Enter the full *Ghan*, in all its glory.

For glorious it is. Not in an Orient Express–opulence way – though
luxury Platinum Service options exist for a touch of on-board glam. But
even in Coach class the *Ghan* is glorious in scale and scope. You really do
get to watch an entire country – a really big country – glide by.

ESSENTIAL EXPERIENCES

✳ **Ambling between ethnic food-stalls,
indigenous art and fire-throwers at
Darwin's Mindil Beach Night Markets.**

✳ Paddling along the Katherine River,
and cooling off in the pools at Nitmiluk
National Park.

✳ **Riding a stretch of original *Afghan
Express* tracks in a restored loco at
the Old Ghan Historical Railway at
MacDonnell Siding.**

✳ Detouring to Uluru-Kata Tjuta National
Park to learn dot-painting with Aboriginal
artists, to hike Kings Canyon and to catch
the rainbow hues of sunrise and sunset
over Uluru.

✳ **Exploring Adelaide's graceful streets,
before leaving the city for fine tipples
at the vineyards of the nearby
Barossa Valley.**

DISTANCE - 2979KM | COUNTRIES COVERED - AUSTRALIA | **IDEAL TIME COMMITMENT** - EIGHT DAYS | **BEST TIME OF YEAR** - APRIL
TO OCTOBER | **ESSENTIAL TIP** - TAKE A PACK OF CARDS TO HELP GET TO KNOW FELLOW PASSENGERS.

ROAM AROUND THE ROCK

When riding the *Ghan*, it would be rude not to hop off at Alice Springs for a side trip to Uluru, 450km southeast. This hulking lump of rich-red sandstone, soaring 350m above the Outback like Australia's giant 'outie' belly-button, is sacred to the local Aboriginal people. They'd prefer you not to climb it – and there are better options anyway. Scenic flights buzz overhead; the 9.4km Base Walk traces the rock's circumference, revealing spiritual places and secret fissures; and the Sounds of Silence dinner sees pristine waiters serving at sunset, with Uluru views and the low hum of a didgeridoo for atmospheric accompaniment.

RESTAURANT ON WHEELS

Dining on the Ghan has come a long way. In the old days, when delays were common, supplies were sometimes parachuted to the stranded train; one driver even shot goats to feed his marooned passengers. Today, it's less of a life-or-death situation. The Red Diner serves meals and snacks to budget travellers while the Queen Adelaide Restaurant caters to the Gold and Platinum set. Here, there's a nod to the bygone romance of the rails (fancy decor, white linen) with a menu that includes barramundi and kangaroo. Most Australian, however, is a bushtucker walk at Nitmiluk – disembark at Katherine to try the traditional foods of the Jawoyn people.

THE JOURNEY TODAY

You're glad you didn't book a sleeping compartment: there's no way you're going to get any sleep. Not with *that* out of the window – 'that' being the endless, infinity-and-beyondness of the Australian Outback, illuminated by a sky suffering severe celestial measles. There is not a glimmer of light pollution to diminish the stars' sparkle. All in all, the astronomy sideshow plus the train's rhythmic sway have made you feel wide-eyed and hypnotised.

You're not on this train to get from A to B – you're here to plough through the nether regions of a country so big it takes two days to traverse. The plane would have been quicker and cheaper, but where's the fun in that? And few airlines these days offer stop-offs for gorge-canoeing, or feature wallabies bounding by the windows. Besides, the *Ghan* suits all budgets. There are four classes ranging from budget reclining seats up to plush private cabins. Cabin class includes meals in the dining car, and everyone has access to the lounges.

Spectacular sunsets and lightning storms splinter over the bush, but the best bits are the pauses: the train stops at remote stations for leg stretches, and lingers longer at Katherine (4½ hours) and Alice Springs (3½ hours), so those riding the *Ghan* in one go have time to explore – perhaps a camel trek from White Gums Station, a cruise along Katherine Gorge or a helicopter flight over Simpsons Gap. Those with more time can disembark for a few days, then pick up the next *Ghan* – trains run twice weekly from April to October, once weekly otherwise. A four-day stop in Alice would allow the essential Aussie experience – a glimpse of Uluru and a night in a swag under those stars.

SHORTCUT

Without any stop-offs, the *Ghan* takes around 54 hours, including two nights on board, to trundle from Darwin to Adelaide (or vice versa). For a taste of the train without travelling the whole distance, try half the journey: ride from Darwin to Alice (24 hours) to combine tropical Top End and raw Red Centre sights, before flying onwards from Alice Springs Airport.

DETOUR

The *Ghan* stops at Manguri, 900km north of Adelaide, in the wee hours. This isolated, unprepossessing station is the access point for Coober Pedy, opal-mining capital of the world. You'll only be allowed to get off the *Ghan* here if you've prearranged your own transfers to Coober Pedy, 42km away. If you do, this is the place to try your luck digging for gemstones, to explore the mesas and scarps of Breakaways Reserve or check into an underground hotel – many of the town's residents live, eat and pray in subterranean dugouts to escape the blistering sun.

OPENING SPREAD Uluru's natural palette, vibrant in the late-afternoon light. **ABOVE** Floating down the Katherine River, just past the first gorge. **LEFT** As far and as straight as the eye can see: the line stretching from Alice Springs to Darwin.

ARMCHAIR

* ❋ ***Australia By Rail*** (Colin Taylor) Practical guide to travelling the continent by train.

* ❋ ***The Singing Line*** (Alice Thomson) The great-granddaughter of the man who wanted to connect Adelaide to Darwin by telegraph cable retraces his steps across Australia.

* ❋ ***Down Under*** (Bill Bryson) The maestro of modern travel writers turns his pen to Oz, including the journey from Darwin to Alice.

* ❋ ***Australia: A Biography of a Nation*** (RM Crawford) Essential background reading, charting the country's rise from convict colony to aspirational nation.

* ❋ ***The Adventures of Priscilla, Queen of the Desert*** (1994) Three feathered-and-fabulous drag artistes and a silver bus combine in this high-camp romp of a road-trip movie, filmed on location in Alice, Broken Hill and other Outback spots.

THE GLACIER EXPRESS

THIS STRETCH OF SWISS NARROW-GAUGE RAIL RAMBLES THROUGH MEADOWS AND OVER MOUNTAIN PASSES, SKIRTS STONE CASTLES, GINGERBREAD VILLAGES AND THE MATTERHORN, AND RUMBLES OVER 291 BRIDGES AND THROUGH 91 TUNNELS. IT'S ONE OF MOST BEAUTIFUL RAIL JOURNEYS ON EARTH.

42

It might not be as long as the Trans-Siberian, but this classic rail journey makes up for it with a vertical spectacle of stunning proportions. Switzerland has several mountain rail trips, but it is the *Glacier Express*, which runs northeast from Zermatt to St Moritz, that is the most mythical. As Switzerland's Alpine resorts became popular with Europe's rich and famous in the early 20th century, the idea for a train linking Zermatt and St Moritz grew. In 1930, the inaugural steam-train journey between the two Alpine resorts took place and the 7½-hour trip hasn't lost its appeal since.

Starting in Zermatt, the gateway to the Matterhorn, the train winds slowly north down a valley to Brig. From here it swings northeast along the pretty eastern stretch of the Rhône Valley towards the Furka Pass (which it circumvents by tunnel) and descends on Andermatt before again climbing up to the Oberalp Pass, the literal high point of the trip at 2044m. From there it meanders alongside the Vorderrhein River, passing through Disentis/Mustér before arriving in Chur. The main train continues to St Moritz, which has been luring royals, the filthy rich and moneyed wannabes since 1864.

The railway endured the first few years of WWII, but was eventually suspended from 1943 to 1946. It was a seasonal train for the first 50 years because of heavy snow and high-avalanche risk. In fact, each autumn the train's overhead contact wires between Oberwald and Realp were removed and the Steffenbach bridge was dismantled, only to be reassembled in spring. Once the Furka Tunnel was blasted and completed in 1982, the train was able to run year-round and it remains at its most spectacular during winter.

ESSENTIAL EXPERIENCES

* **Watching, awe-struck, as the shark-fin Matterhorn peak soars above Zermatt, signifying the beginning of a spectacular journey.**

* Descending from the snow country into jade valleys where the turquoise Rhône boils over boulders and offers a soothing brand of topographical diversity.

* **Exploring the Goms, and larger towns such as Andermatt, surrounded by mountains and retaining that Alpine village feel. You're in chalet country now.**

* Wandering along the 16th-century cobblestone lanes, past frescoed facades in old Chur.

* **Surrendering to the beautiful bling and luscious powdery slopes of opulent, arrogant, yet still seductive, St Moritz.**

DISTANCE - 275KM | COUNTRIES COVERED - SWITZERLAND | **IDEAL TIME COMMITMENT** - ONE TO TWO DAYS | **BEST TIME OF YEAR** - DECEMBER TO APRIL | **ESSENTIAL TIP** - TAKE THE EASTBOUND TRAIN; IT'S USUALLY LESS CROWDED. BOOK IN ADVANCE IF YOU ARE HEADED WEST FROM ST MORITZ.

MAN OR MATTERHORN?

On 13 July 1865 Edward Whymper led the first successful ascent of the Matterhorn via Hörnli ridge, but the descent was marred by tragedy when four team members crashed to their deaths in a 1200m fall down the North Wall. The catastrophe haunted Whymper, who lamented: 'Every night, do you understand, I see my comrades of the Matterhorn slipping on their backs, their arms outstretched, one after the other, in perfect order at equal distances.' Ironically, the tragedy put Zermatt on the map, and soon other plucky souls came to climb the Matterhorn, and its surrounding giants, including a 20-year-old Winston Churchill, who scaled Monte Rosa (4634m) in 1894.

THE JOURNEY TODAY

You'll board the train in Zermatt, which has starred among Switzerland's glitziest resorts since the 19th century. Today it attracts intrepid mountaineers and hikers, skiers who cruise at snail's pace, spellbound by the scenery, and style-conscious darlings flashing designer togs in the lounge bars. And all are smitten with the Matterhorn, an unfathomable monolith you can't quite stop looking at. Like a shark's fin it rises above the town, like an egotistical celebrity it squeezes into every snapshot, like a diva it has moods swinging from pretty and pink to dark and mysterious.

Close to the Italian border and bisected by the Rhône and Saltina rivers, Brig has been an important crossroads since Roman times. It's here you start to notice the cultural diversity of the *Glacier Express*, as Italian becomes increasingly audible among the otherwise German-dominated chatter in the coach.

The train continues along the Rhône through the Furka Tunnel before descending into Andermatt, a lovely valley village surrounded by mountains.

Considered to be the demarcation point between northern and southern Switzerland, it's accessible by four mountain passes. The eavesdropping twists back from Italian and German into a touch of Romansch, as the rail rises to the wind-chilled Oberalp Pass (2044m), the train's highest point and a pass that separates Graubünden from Uri.

Soon the Vorderrhein River appears by the tracks, and you'll follow it into Chur, Switzerland's oldest city. Here you can saunter the cobblestone lanes of the pedestrianised Old Town, dotted with frescoed 16th-century facades, gurgling fountains and lofty towers before boarding once more and rolling into St Moritz, Switzerland's original winter wonderland and the cradle of Alpine tourism.

ARMCHAIR

* ***Sound of Music*** (1965) Cliché though it may be, it's impossible to have a conversation about the Alps and not hearken back to Julie Andrews and the Von Trapp family singers. These mountains were the family's backyard and were central to this tale of WWII.

* ***Mountains of the Mind*** (Robert Macfarlane) The Alps don't dominate this book about legendary mountain ascents and first person high-country treks, but this journey would be a fine place

to absorb Macfarlane's take on why the world's highest peaks have long gripped the Western mind.

* ***The Alps*** (Andrew Beattie) A seasoned travel writer explores the early pioneers of mountaineering, conquering Romans and occupying Nazis, who have all left their mark on Europe's defining mountain range.

SKIING ST MORITZ

St Moritz first ski school opened in 1929, and powder remains the big draw. For groomed slopes with big mountain vistas, head to Corviglia (2486m), accessible by funicular from Dorf. From Bad a cable car goes to Signal (shorter queues), giving access to the slopes of Piz Nair. There's varied skiing at Corvatsch (3303m), above nearby Silvaplana, also a kite-boarding mecca, including spectacular glacier descents and the gentle black run Hahnensee. Set against the silhouettes of 4000m peaks, Diavolezza (2978m) is a must-ski for free riders and fans of jaw-dropping descents. Avid cross-country skiers can glide through snow-dusted woodlands and plains on 160km of groomed trails.

With its perfect lake and aloof mountains, the town looks a million dollars. Yet despite the Gucci set propping up the bars and celebs on the pistes (Kate Moss and George Clooney included), this resort isn't all show. The real riches lie outdoors with superb carving on Corviglia, hairy black runs on Diavolezza, and miles of hiking trails.

SHORTCUT

To taste the panoramic rail journey, board the train in Zermatt and rumble past the Matterhorn as the track winds down the valley to Brig, then disembark, re-board and watch the whole scene again as you go back up the Alpine spine.

DETOUR

Don't miss the Goms, a string of bucolic villages of timber chalets and onion-domed churches waiting to be counted off like rosary beads, on either side of the turquoise torrent that is the Rhône. Behind these villages lies the 23km Aletsch Glacier (Aletschgletscher), a long swirl of deeply crevassed ice that slices past thundering falls and jagged spires of rock. The longest glacier in the Alps and a Unesco World Heritage Site, it stretches from Jungfrau in the Bernese Oberland to a plateau above the Rhône.

GUNTER GRAFENHAIN | 4CORNERS IMAGES

OPENING SPREAD The spectacular Matterhorn welcomes you. **ABOVE** Exposing the route in all its glory: the Panorama Wagon on the *Glacier Express*. **BELOW** The *Express* knifing through the snow.

THE PRIDE OF AFRICA

THIS LUXURY BOUTIQUE HOTEL ON RAILS SKIRTS SOME OF AFRICA'S MOST
FABLED LANDSCAPES. IT INCLUDES BUSH WALKS AND GAME DRIVES IN PRIVATE
SOUTH AFRICAN RESERVES, A WINDING DESCENT INTO THE EVOLUTIONARY
RIFT VALLEY, AND TWO DAYS AT THE MAGNIFICENT VICTORIA FALLS.

It's luxury all the way on Rovos Rail's iconic two-week rail journey from
the Atlantic winds of Cape Town through southern and East Africa and
into Dar Es Salaam on the Indian Ocean. From Cape Town the *Pride of
Africa* rolls north to Pretoria, then west into the savannah around Zeerust.
Next you'll rumble north through Botswana into Zimbabwe where you'll
veer west again towards Victoria Falls. You'll pass through Zambia's
capital city, Lusaka, then disembark at Kasama for an excursion to
luscious Chisimba Falls, just south of the Tanzanian border. Crossing the
border just south of Lake Tanganyika, you'll traverse the pass to Milimba,
then Mzenga and Dar Es Salaam's Tazara Station.

This journey covers five nations and over 3600km in two weeks. The
train is just 20 years old, but the natural and human history you'll
confront along the way runs much deeper. It starts with apartheid
echoes on Robben Island and Cape Town's District Six Museums before
rewinding into Kimberly's 19th-century diamond mines and then the
ageless savannah and Kalahari Desert.

In Zimbabwe, Mugabe continues to maintain his stranglehold on a nation
that has huge potential. Zambia is synonymous with British explorer David
Livingstone, who travelled up the Zambezi and 'discovered' Victoria Falls. His
work inspired missionaries to venture north of the Zambezi; close on their
heels came explorers, hunters and prospectors searching for riches. They
found vast copper belts, and in 1924 Northern Rhodesia (present-day Zambia)
was swept under the British flag. Nationalists won independence in 1964.

History gets primordial in Tanzania's Great Rift Valley, where
mountains soar above the deep cut and the Rift Valley lakes are among
the deepest in the world. This is where the earliest known fossils of our
hominid ancestors were found, dating back three million years.

ESSENTIAL EXPERIENCES

❋ **Indulging in what is easily the most
luxurious rail journey in the world.**

❋ Exploring the Table Mountain trails,
vineyards, and the golden beaches of Cape
Town, considered by locals and tourists alike
to be Africa's greatest city.

❋ **Becoming part of the paparazzi and
snapping wildlife photos on game drives
in Madikwe Game Reserve in northern
South Africa.**

❋ Rolling through the parched Kalahari Desert in
Botswana, made famous in the 1981 film *The
Gods Must Be Crazy*.

❋ **Crossing a narrow footbridge into swirling
clouds of mist at Victoria Falls, one of
Africa's most spectacular sights.**

DISTANCE - OVER 3600KM | **COUNTRIES COVERED** - SOUTH AFRICA, BOTSWANA, ZIMBABWE, ZAMBIA, TANZANIA | **IDEAL TIME
COMMITMENT** - 14 DAYS | **BEST TIME OF YEAR** - JUNE TO OCTOBER | **ESSENTIAL TIP** - SEEK OUT ZAMBIA'S SIGNATURE HANDICRAFTS:
BASKETS, MALACHITE JEWELLERY, WOODCARVINGS AND SOAPSTONE SCULPTURES.

CAPE TOWN TIPPLES

The Boland, stretching inland and upwards from Cape Town, isn't South Africa's only wine-growing region, but it's certainly the most famous. Its name means 'Upland', a reference to the dramatic mountain ranges that shoot up to over 1500m, and on whose fertile slopes the vineyards form a patchwork. There are too many good wineries in the area to list all of them, so it's simply best to drive around and stop on a whim. The area's signature gateway is the attractive wine and student town of Stellenbosch, South Africa's second-oldest European settlement, established on the banks of the Eerste River in 1679.

LIFE AS THE OPPOSITION

In 1999 thousands of Zimbabweans attended
a trade-union rally to launch the Movement for
Democratic Change (MDC). Secretary general
Morgan Tsvangirai stated he would lead a social
democratic party fighting for workers. The arrival
of the MDC brought waves of hope for the end
of Robert Mugabe's era. Mugabe responded with
waves of violence and a destructive land reform
program, claiming the next three elections.
But pressure was growing. The economy had
collapsed, and Mugabe couldn't pay his army
or civil service...then came the cholera. In
February 2009, Tsvangirai signed a deal with the
government, a mutual promise to restore the
rule of law and, unfortunately, uphold Mugabe's
tenuous hold on power.

THE JOURNEY TODAY

The train is a chain of 20 rail cars, some built in the 1920s. A maximum of 72 guests enjoy 24-hour service. Everything from plush bathrobes to goggles (for peering out the window into the breeze) is provided. With all five countries en route sporting the Big Five in large numbers, expect to see wildlife.

In Cape Town you'll swoon at the sight of Table Mountain, its summit draped with cascading clouds, its flanks coated with unique flora and vineyards, its base fringed by golden beaches. Accentuating this natural majesty is the Capetonians' imaginative flair. From Bo-Kaap's brightly painted facades to the contemporary Afro-chic decor of the city's guesthouses, restaurants and bars, this is one good-looking metropolis, and you'd be wise to fly in early enough to enjoy it.

After manic Johannesburg and staid Pretoria, you'll stop for two nights at the Madikwe Game Reserve, just long enough to become part of the wildlife paparazzi, watching lions feasting on zebras, cheetahs stalking antelope and herds of elephants bathing. After two days rolling through the Kalahari Desert in Botswana and the cool green climes of Zimbabwe you'll arrive at Victoria Falls. View the Eastern Cataract close up: it's a hair-raising walk across the footbridge through swirling clouds of mist, to the Knife Edge. If the water is low, you'll get magnificent views of the falls and the yawning abyss below. If not, you will be nicely drenched by spray. Take the steep track to the riverbank to see the Boiling Pot – a huge whirlpool. On the Zimbabwean side, the park is open in the evenings around the full moon for viewing the amazing lunar rainbow. This is the highlight of the trip. Of course, that gorgeous descent into the Eastern Rift Valley in Tanzania makes for a fine chaser.

SHORTCUT

You can get a taste of African pride on the three-day, 1600km journey from Pretoria, through Botswana and Zimbabwe to Victoria Falls. There are plenty of opportunities to spot the Big Five as you roll through the Hwange National Park and you can fly out of Zambia from the border town of Livingstone.

DETOUR

Floating off the Tanzania coast is the luscious Spice Island of Zanzibar. Its main attraction is Stone Town, where influences have drifted in from ancient Persia, the old Omani sultanate and India's Goan coast. Here are quaint shops and bazaars sprinkled along winding, cobbled streets, and a lively seaside night market. The interior is quilted with aromatic spice plantations, and it's edged by fine, white-sand beaches, whitewashed coral-rag houses and waving palms.

OPENING SPREAD Descent into the maelstrom: the swirling mist of Victoria Falls. **ABOVE** Spanning generations and continents: a Dutch colonial house at Stellenbosch, Western Cape, South Africa. **LEFT** Cheetahs at the Masai Mara National Reserve, Rift Valley, Kenya.

ARMCHAIR

* **The Africa House** (Christina Lamb) Tells the story of Stewart Gore-Brown and his grand plans for a utopian fiefdom in a remote part of Zambia during the 1920s.

* **Desertion** (Abdulrazak Gurnah) Epic in scope, shortlisted for both the Booker and Commonwealth Prize, and written by a native Zanzibari, it offers a glimpse into the Swahili cultural stew that saturates Zanzibar.

* **The Zanzibar Chest** (Aidan Hartley) A riveting memoir penned by a Kenyan-born war reporter who started as a Dar es Salaam stringer and spent the 1990s covering under-reported wars throughout Africa.

* **Dark Star Safari** (Paul Theroux) A travelogue by a former Peace Corps volunteer in Africa and one of the great travellers.

THE EASTERN & ORIENTAL EXPRESS

THE EASTERN & ORIENTAL EXPRESS WHISKS PASSENGERS ACROSS SINGAPORE, MALAYSIA AND THAILAND IN CLASSIC STYLE, TRAVELLING THROUGH DIVERSE AND EVER-CHANGING LANDSCAPES, FROM LUSH EQUATORIAL RAINFORESTS TO ANCIENT TEMPLES, RUBBER PLANTATIONS AND ISOLATED VILLAGES.

50

The *Eastern & Oriental Express*, the sister train to Europe's storied *Orient Express*, ranks among the world's most scenic rail journeys. It passes through dramatic southeast Asian landscapes, beginning in Bangkok and travelling across the famous Bridge on the River Kwai in western Thailand, before snaking down the coast of Malaysian to Kuala Lumpur, then on to Singapore. Of course, the journey can be done in reverse, and there are also a variety of packaged routes offered by the company that offer excursions and off-train adventures. Sightseeing stops and detours include trips through Thai national parks and villages; the highlands of Thailand and Malaysia; a journey through some of the peninsula highlights of the region, including the spectacular Tham Krasae Viaduct; and a Laotian tour with an atmospheric crossing over the Mekong on the Thai-Lao Friendship Bridge.

The *Eastern & Oriental Express* was the first passenger train to travel direct from Singapore and Kuala Lumpur to Bangkok. Previously, Malaysia and Thailand maintained separate railway systems, and to travel the entire distance passengers needed to change trains at Butterworth (Penang). In 1993 the Express began operations, commencing a service for the entire route. From Bangkok to Singapore, the journey takes four days and three nights, while Singapore to Bangkok is three days and two nights.

The train's fit-out is plush: all wooden marquetry, Eastern designs and Chinese and Thai lacquer, evoking the bygone colonial atmosphere of the region. There are three cabin styles – Pullman Superior, State Cabin and Presidential Suite – and their names say all you need to know about the luxury levels enjoyed during this journey through lush jungle and past a backdrop of bazaars, villages, temples, colonial artefacts and WWII monuments.

ESSENTIAL EXPERIENCES

* **Admiring Thailand's most famous temple, Wat Phra Kaew, and getting lost at Wat Pho.**

* Wandering through the crowded markets of Bangkok's Chinatown.

* **Revelling in the greenery of Kuala Lumpur's Lake Gardens with its showpiece KL Bird Park; appreciating Islamic art at the Islamic Arts Museum Malaysia; and soaking up the atmosphere of the heavenly Thean Hou Temple.**

* Absorbing the cultural complexities of Straits Chinese culture in Singapore at both the Peranakan Museum and the Asian Civilisations Museum, and talking to the animals in the Singapore Zoo and at the Night Safari wildlife park.

DISTANCE - 2030KM | COUNTRIES COVERED - SINGAPORE, MALAYSIA, THAILAND | **IDEAL TIME COMMITMENT** - ONE WEEK
BEST TIME OF YEAR - NOVEMBER TO FEBRUARY, WHEN IT RAINS LEAST AND ISN'T TOO HOT | **ESSENTIAL TIP** - BRING FORMAL CLOTHES – DINNER IS STRICTLY BLACK-TIE.

LORONG BUANGKOK

While in Singapore, try to see Lorong Buangkok's kampung (village), perhaps the mainland's last resistance against rampant development. It's hidden behind a wall of trees and a ragtag network of wooden houses, many with zinc roofs. The few residents live much as many Singaporeans did before development descended. Chickens and dogs roam the grounds, the song of crickets and birds fills the air and there's an overall sense of carefree nostalgia. But get in quick as this small parcel has been slated for 'renewal', too. No one knows how long its present state will last.

■ THE JOURNEY TODAY

At Singapore railway station, you catch your first sight of the E&O pulling in to the platform. It's as if it has arrived through a wormhole from a rapidly fading past when men wore white linen suits and the only chairs around were rattan, preferably placed on a verandah overlooking a jungle, with a gin and tonic somewhere close by. As you sight the green-and-cream carriages, you think of exotic tales of the Far East, of the murder mysteries of Agatha Christie at one extreme and the dying colonialism captured by Somerset Maugham at the other.

You board the train to be greeted by staff dressed in crisp uniforms that match the train's colour scheme. You take an early lunch, and then an hour later, make your way to the observation car where the floors are teak, the walls panelled and the furniture, naturally, is rattan. You're served brandy and a cigar as you sit among the potted plants and gaze at the away-rushing scenery: palm plantations, buffalo, rice fields, endless rivers, sun-dappled skies…

You return to your cabin for a snooze to find freshly pressed robes on the bed and fresh flowers all around. You sleep, then wake for dinner, which is a black-tie affair, and as you take your seat you feel like Ian Fleming. You, as Fleming, glance at your fellow diners: 'That couple over there, the wealthy Russians, her with the pearls and him with the waxed moustache – they are clearly spies. And the American couple – he is carrying some kind of secret device inside that very expensive cigarette case that he keeps flicking open… Now, what would Bond do?' Bond would order another martini, shaken not stirred, and act calm until inspiration strikes. So that's what you do, and as you sip your drink you smile, knowing that you have truly travelled back in time.

■ SHORTCUT

The Singapore to Bangkok route is shorter by one day than the reverse journey. On the first day you cross from Singapore to Malaysia; on the second day you arrive in Penang; and on the third day you travel via the Rivzer Kwai to Bangkok.

■ DETOUR

One of the packaged side-trips the company offers goes to Laos, which does not feature in the regular, classic journey. The train crosses the Mekong River, continuing into the Laotian capital, Vientiane, a delightful, friendly place, with crumbling French mansions, bougainvillea-laden streets and steaming noodle stalls, somewhere between a big town and a small city. The train also stops at Phimai in Thailand, where you'll be able to explore one of northeastern Thailand's finest surviving Khmer temple complexes and the vineyards in the scenic Khao Yai hills.

OPENING SPREAD Throwing shapes: the evocative sight of Tai Chi practitioners at the Chinese Thean Hou Temple, Kuala Lumpur. **ABOVE (L)** Old-school charm aboard the train, and vivacious scenery outside. **ABOVE (R)** All board the E&O.

ARMCHAIR

* ***The Beach*** (2000) This film, based on Alex Garland's novel and directed by Danny Boyle, is about a beach paradise on a secret Thai island.

* ***The Bridge on the River Kwai*** (1957) David Lean's WWII film, starring William Holden and Alec Guinness, is set against the backdrop of the construction of the Burma Railway.

* ***The Man with the Golden Gun*** (1974) James Bond does battle with the titular villain on a secret island off Thailand, and in Bangkok.

* ***A Town Like Alice*** (1956) Based on Nevil Shute's novel about two prisoners of war who fall in love, this was partially filmed in Malaya and Australia.

* ***King Rat*** (1965) Starring George Segal as a prisoner of war near Singapore.

THE BRIDGE ON THE RIVER KWAI

Known as the Death Railway Bridge, this little structure is dwarfed by the war history surrounding it. During Japan's 1942–43 occupation of Thailand, materials were brought from Java by the Imperial Japanese Army to build the bridge. The first version was made of wood, completed in February 1943, and in April that year a second steel bridge was built. In 1945 the Allies bombed it and it was only rebuilt after the war. Trainspotters will note the old WWII locomotives nearby, and during the last week of November and first week of December, there's a nightly sound-and-light show commemorating the Allied attack.

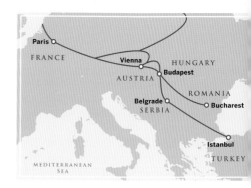

THE ORIENT EXPRESS

THE ORIENT EXPRESS TRIP FROM PARIS TO ISTANBUL NO LONGER EXISTS IN ALL ITS FORMER GLORY, BUT RECREATING THIS EUROPEAN ODYSSEY, WHERE YOUR SENSE OF THE EXOTIC INCREASES WITH EVERY EASTWARD MILE TAKEN, IS TO RECAPTURE THE REAL ROMANCE OF RIDING THE RAILS

54

Is anything in travel more romantic than the *Orient Express*? The promise of being delivered to an exotic land in a style fit for kings, with mahogany panels, white linen, dining cars a-chink with fine china and silver cutlery?

The first *Orient Express* service pulled out of Paris in 1883, bound for Romania. Passengers then sailed across the Danube into Bulgaria, where another train took them to Varna, for a Black Sea ferry to Constantinople. In 1889 the first through-train ran, connecting Paris with Istanbul in 67½ hours.

The most authentic route is Paris to Istanbul, via Vienna, Budapest and Belgrade (or Bucharest). The timetable has changed over years – due to budget cuts and border closures. The 1920s and '30s were the heyday of the *Orient Express*, when the glamour of the service fitted the spirit of the times, and commercial planes had yet to provide a faster alternative. Nobles, diplomats and assorted starlets, cocooned in swaying luxury, whizzed across a war-scarred Europe.

Leaving Paris, the train traversed the battlefields of northern France en route to Strasbourg and the border. German towns dashed by – Stuttgart, Ulm, Munich – before the Alps signalled Austria. Pretty Salzburg led to Vienna, where the Danube was traced via Bratislava to Budapest. From here there were two options: to Bucharest, for the Black Sea boat; or south via Belgrade and Sofia. In Istanbul passengers retired to the Pera Palace, hotel of the Wagons-Lits company, for more soirées and history making: it was in Room 411 that Agatha Christie wrote *Murder on the Orient Express*.

From 1919 the *Simplon Orient Express* plied a more southerly route – from Paris to Istanbul via Lausanne, Milan, Venice, Trieste and Belgrade. This had the advantage of skipping Germany, a nation then viewed with suspicion. But whatever the route, it was the essence of the train that caught the imagination.

ESSENTIAL EXPERIENCES

✳ **Raising a glass at Le Train Bleu, the gilded and gorgeous station cafe at the Gare de Lyon, Paris, where passengers from the original *Orient Express* once dined.**

✳ Hiking amid the vineyards and rustic *heurigen* (wine taverns) on the hills within Vienna's city limits.

✳ **Taking in a show at Budapest's dazzling (and astonishingly cheap) opera house.**

✳ Steaming yourself in one of Budapest's traditional baths – the Gellért for finery, Széchenyi for outdoor fun.

✳ **Gazing over the Danube and Sava Rivers from the fortifications of Kalemegdan Park, Belgrade.**

✳ Catching the ferry over the Bosphorus in Istanbul, for fine views and to link Europe and Asia in a matter of minutes.

DISTANCE - 3180KM | **COUNTRIES COVERED** - FRANCE, GERMANY, AUSTRIA, HUNGARY, SERBIA, BULGARIA, ROMANIA, TURKEY
IDEAL TIME COMMITMENT - ONE MONTH | **BEST TIME OF YEAR** - APRIL TO JUNE | **ESSENTIAL TIP** - PACK EARPLUGS FOR SLEEPING IN SHARED COUCHETTES.

GRAND ARRIVALS

Istanbul's Sirkeci Terminal was opened in November 1890 to receive the elite locos of the *Orient Express*. Designed by a German architect, it's a fine example of Islamic Eclecticism – a blend of the European neoclassical and the Turkish baroque. Its clock tower, rose windows and grand arches remain, though it's a little run-down these days. It's still home to the Orient Express Restaurant, which flourished as a media meeting place in the 1950s and is still popular with tourists today. Sirkeci also hosts whirling dervish performances, in which sufi mystics in voluminous robes spin across the old station.

MOTIVATION FOR MURDER

In February 1929 the westbound *Orient Express* became stuck in a snowdrift at Çerkezköy, 130km from Istanbul. Passengers relied on supplies brought by Turkish villagers as the train sat immobile for five days. Sleeping Car 3309, used today by the Venice Simplon company, was one of the carriages thus stuck.

Crime queen Agatha Christie first travelled on the *Orient Express* in 1928, and in 1931 got delayed on the train herself when flooding stalled it for 24 hours. While waiting, she wrote letters to her husband detailing the occurrence. In 1934, *Murder on the Orient Express* was published, the grim tale of a homicide on the train when it is stopped by a snowstorm.

THE JOURNEY TODAY

It's not there. The *Orient Express*, a service that ran for over 100 years, is nowhere to be seen in your well-thumbed Thomas Cook European Rail Timetable. Of course you can still get from Paris to Istanbul by train, but the direct *Orient Express* service, with its plush Wagons-Lits, ceased running in 1977. The name lived on, applying to increasingly curtailed routes: first it was shortened to Paris–Bucharest, then Paris–Vienna, until finally only the stunted overnight service from Strasbourg to Vienna continued to bear the *Orient Express* tag. In December 2009 this, too, was replaced. An era ended.

If you want a taste of belle époque high life, the Venice Simplon-Orient-Express runs restored original coaches primarily between London and Venice. Cabins are resplendent in polished wood and art deco detailing. Dressing for dinner is positively encouraged. Service is exquisite – stewards in royal-blue gold-trimmed blazers, matching the train livery, attend your every whim as if you were Ms Christie herself.

If that's out of your price range, you can still trace the journey of the original Orient Express. Make your own route from Paris to Istanbul, stopping often – if you can, spare a month to combine great cities and more offbeat sidings. One advantage of the demise of the service is the fun of poring over the multitude of separate trains, and linking them together according to your preferences. Sleeping cars may not be as fancy, but the romance of the rails is still there. And if you want to put on a posh frock to sip a can of lager or munch a bag of peanuts in the snack bar of your modern train, we're not about to stop you.

SHORTCUT

You can ride a succession of trains from Paris to Istanbul without pausing. It takes four nights (three, if you risk a tight connection) via Munich, Budapest and Bucharest; there are sleeper compartments on the overnight legs. To travel so quickly is a shame (and probably more expensive than a three-hour flight), but the scenery provides rewards, especially entering Salzburg and the mountainous stretch after Braşov, Romania.

DETOUR

Don't stop when you hit Istanbul – plunge into Asia proper by continuing on to Iran. Since 2001 the Trans-Asia Express has connected Turkey to Tehran. The journey, a scenic trundle, takes three days and includes two ferry rides: the first, a quick hop over the Bosphorus in Istanbul, to access departure point Haydarpaşa Station, on the Asian side of the city; the second, a six-hour sail across Lake Van. The train enters Iran at Razi, where you'll disembark briefly to complete formalities (be sure to have an Iranian visa).

OPENING SPREAD The finest in Islamic architecture: Mosque domes in Istanbul. **LEFT** Snowy Frankfurt in winter, a picturesque backdrop for the *Orient Express*. **ABOVE (L)** An Austrian chapel dwarfed by the mighty Alps. **ABOVE (R)** Exotic destinations and first-class service – that's the Orient way.

ARMCHAIR

* ***Murder on the Orient Express*** (Agatha Christie) A peerless whodunnit that evokes the spirit of the train – but with a macabre twist; it was made into a film in 1974, and featured an all-star cast.

* ***The Man in Seat 61: A Guide To Taking The Train Through Europe*** (Mark Smith) Helpful book by the founder of the excellent and informative Seat61 website.

* ***The Great Railway Bazaar*** (Paul Theroux) Writer Theroux travels through Asia by train – and gets part way there via the Orient Express.

* ***Stamboul Train*** (Graham Greene) Intrigue, espionage and death on the *Orient Express* in Greene's breakthrough spy thriller.

* ***The Orient Express*** (Anthony Burton) An illustrated history of the service, from 1883 to 1950.

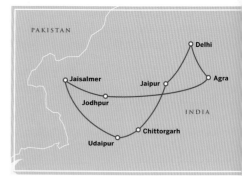

THE PALACE ON WHEELS

EXPERIENCE SEVEN DAYS AS AN INDIAN RAJA ON A TRAIN SO LUXURIOUS IT
HEARKENS BACK TO THE DAYS OF ROYALTY, AS IT RUMBLES FROM INDIA'S LARGEST
CITY, THROUGH THE SPECTACULAR STATE OF RAJASTHAN, AND TERMINATES
A STONE'S THROW FROM THE LOVE MONUMENT THAT IS THE TAJ MAHAL.

58

The Istanbul to Cairo route is a favourite for novice backpackers and
seasoned travellers alike, and the reasons for that are not hard to
divine. Firstly, Istanbul straddles two continents, making it an excellent
entry point into the Middle East. From there, the route snakes its way
down through Turkey, which has an abundance of historical riches
including the Gallipoli peninsula and the poignant Anzac battlefields;
the amazing Istanbul; Ephesus, with its marvellous Roman remains; and
Cappadocia's extraordinary fairy chimneys. The route then enters Syria
and the stimulating bazaar at Aleppo, not to mention the stunning city
of Damascus. Many travellers follow their nose to Jordan, where there is
so much to enjoy: the ruins of Petra, for example, or the chance to float
in the Dead Sea. A detour to Jerusalem is always worthy regardless of
your religious views, while snorkelling in the Red Sea provides more of an
earthly thrill. Crowded Cairo is the end point and a trip to the Pyramids
the icing on the cake.

The route is versatile and exciting and can encompass many different
adventures: diving among spectacular marine scenery, trekking through
waves of sand dunes, spending days adrift on a small Nile felucca
or whiling away nights at old colonial drinking dens and pounding
Mediterranean nightclubs. There are five millennia of history and culture
here, including the pyramids and the rock-cut city of Petra, the desert
oasis ruins of ancient Palmyra and the gigantic columns of the Roman
temple at Baalbek. Every town and city, valley and hillside seems like it's
a living museum: the field that saw Ramses triumph over the Hittites;
the site where Alexander the Great sought the advice of the Oracle; the
location where Cleopatra bathed; the route walked by Christ; the spot
where Napoleon put ashore.

ESSENTIAL EXPERIENCES

* **Exploring the many faces, and enduring
  the many travails, of Delhi, India's capital
  and one of the fastest growing cities in
  the world.**

* Riding an elephant toward the Hindu-meets-
  Mughal masterpiece that is the Amber Fort
  just outside Jaipur.

* **Tiger-spotting at sunrise in Ranthambore
  National Park, one of the largest and most
  diverse national parks in all of India.**

* Cruising around the magnificent Lake Palace
  in Udaipur by boat.

* **Visiting the Taj Mahal, an epic monument
  of love, and long considered one of the
  most beautiful buildings in the world.**

DISTANCE - 1972 KM | COUNTRIES COVERED - INDIA | **IDEAL TIME COMMITMENT** - 8 DAYS | **BEST TIME OF THE YEAR** - NOVEMBER
TO MARCH | **ESSENTIAL TIP** - IT MAY NOT BE ROYAL, BUT IT'S POSSIBLE TO EXPERIENCE INDIA'S RAIL SYSTEM AND SEE ALL OF THESE
AMAZING SITES SANS LUXURY, IF YOU HOP ON SECOND-CLASS TRAINS AND DO YOUR OWN HEAVY LIFTING.

COLOURS THAT SPEAK

The colours of everyday Rajasthani life dazzle against the desert: top-heavy turbans (*safa*, *paag* or *pagri*); fluttering scarlet, yellow and saffron saris; glittering traditional Rajasthani skirts (*lehnga* or *ghaghra*); and headscarves (*odni* or *dupatta*). These are not just decorative, but speak a language of their own, tied up with the strictures of society. Turban colour may signify caste, religion and occasion. Rajputs traditionally wear saffron, signifying chivalry. Brahmins wear pink, Dalits brown and nomads black. Jubilantly multicoloured turbans are for festivals. White, grey, black or blue turbans are worn by Hindus to signify sadness.

■ THE JOURNEY TODAY

The journey begins in Delhi, a sprawling metropolis at turns medieval then opulent then stately. Forever unruly and crowded, certainly aggravating, polluted and hectic, it also has the power to capture your heart. Here are museums and ruins, temples, mosques and some of the subcontinent's finest foods.

Come a few days early, because boarding time is 4pm and by the time you wake up the next morning, you'll be in Jaipur, a city filled with stunning hilltop forts, glorious palaces and bargain-filled bazaars. The amost fascinating site, the Amber Fort, is in the foothills 11km north of town. You can climb up to the fort, once Jaipur's capital, or make like a real raja and hitch a ride with an elephant.

The next morning starts early with a sunrise jungle safari through Ranthambore National Park, the best place to spot wild tigers in Rajasthan. Interspersed among the dense brush are ruined temples and mosques as well as lakes lurking with resident crocs. The day ends with a fabulous sunset tour of the Chittorgarh fort, its crenulated walls looming from a rocky plateau. Inside are arched gateways, peaceful temples, and the exquisite Jaya Stambha, Tower of Victory.

Udaipur, arguably India's most romantic city, is famous for the cupola-crowned City Palace, rising abruptly from the glassy waters of Lake Pichola, which you'll want to explore by boat. That massive sandcastle rising from the sandy plains like a mirage is the breathtaking fort of Jaisalmer, which you'll visit on the fifth day before departing for the Keoladeo National Park, a terrific bird-watching spot.

ARMCHAIR

✳ *Taj: A Story of Mughal India* (Timeri Murari) A novel based on the building of the Taj Mahal, and the love between the queen and the shah that inspired it.

✳ *The Many Lives of a Rajput Queen* (Ramya Sreenivasan) More a piece of scholarship than an easy read, this ambitious, yet still accessible, book offers a glimpse of the life of royal women in northern India between 1500 and 1900.

✳ *The Reluctant Rajput* (Richard Moverley & David Dean) Here's one for the kids. In this illustrated children's book, a bored, young student learns about the Rajput warriors in class, falls asleep and wakes up among them in battle.

From here it is onto Agra. Yes the magical allure of the Taj Mahal is the signature set-piece and, despite the hype, it is every bit as magnificent as you've heard. But the Taj is not a stand-alone attraction. The legacy of the Mughal Empire has left a magnificent fort and a liberal sprinkling of fascinating tombs and mausoleums. There's also fun to be had in the bustling chowks (marketplaces) nearby.

SHORTCUT

It is possible to have a shorter experience of the *Palace on Wheels*. The four-day itinerary begins in Delhi and ends in Udaipur, making all the stops in between. Or, enjoy a blast of Delhi and make the short trek to Agra and the ever-looming Taj.

DETOUR

One of the world's oldest cities is also one of India's most electric. Varanasi is a place to wash away a lifetime of sins, an auspicious place to die and it's where families cremate their loved ones in the holy Ganges. Here, the most intimate rituals of life and death take place in public, and the sights and sounds in and around the tumbledown, riverside ghats, best viewed from a boat ride down river, shape memories of a lifetime.

DAVE BARTRUFF / CORBIS

OPENING SPREAD Sporting colours to delight and amaze: a participant in Jaisalmer's Desert Festival, India. **ABOVE** Enthusiastic car captains greeting lucky passengers to the *Palace on Wheels*. **BELOW** The incomparable Taj Mahal.

TAJ MAHAL

The Taj was built by Shah Jahan, as a memorial for his beloved second wife, Mumtaz Mahal, who died giving birth. Construction of the Taj began that same year and was completed in 1653. Not long after it was finished, the shah was overthrown by his son Aurangzeb and imprisoned in nearby Agra fort, where for the rest of his days he could only stare out the window at his lovesick creation. Following his death in 1666, the shah was buried here alongside his wife. Rabindranath Tagore described it as a 'teardrop on the cheek of eternity'.

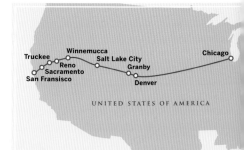

UNITED STATES OF AMERICA

CALIFORNIA ZEPHYR

THE CALIFORNIA ZEPHYR SHOWS HOW THE WEST WAS WON: RIDE THIS
ROUTE, WHICH STRADDLES NORTH AMERICA'S MIGHTIEST MOUNTAIN RANGES,
TO APPRECIATE ENGINEERING MASTERY, NATURAL SPLENDOUR, THE COMPANY
OF NEW FRIENDS AND THE ADVENTUROUS SPIRIT OF PIONEERS PAST.

62

Zephyrus was the ancient Greek god of the west wind, blower of the gentlest spring breezes. Trains on his namesake rail route, which puff across America in the same direction, from Chicago to the Pacific coast, are rather less demure.

The California Zephyr doesn't do gentle. The scenery outside the windows of the 'Silver Lady' is massive and majestic, domineering and elemental. For sections the mountains, soaring up to over 4000m, are tipped with snow, even in summer; raw gorges are gouged by white water; hostile desert extends seemingly forever; and tunnels and switchbacks do battle with the Continental Divide. This is wild country, which man has, just about, sneaked through.

It was in 1869 that Abraham Lincoln's dream was realised: railroaders hammered in the final spike at Promontory, Utah, and the Atlantic and Pacific sides of the United States were finally connected by train. This paved the way for convoys of cowboys, gold prospectors, oilmen and outlaws to expand into the western frontier. A journey that would previously have taken months to complete on horse and foot could now be done, for a few dollars, in just a week.

Today that original line, the Overland Route, transports freight only (unless snowfall forces Zephyr trains to divert onto its historic tracks). But the California Zephyr, which has run under various guises since 1949, follows some of the same line, and showcases similarly impressive feats of engineering along the way: the 10km Moffat Tunnel, which burrows through the Continental Divide to save a 260km detour around it; and the stretch of track atop 2160m Donner Pass, which allowed the first rail passage over the Sierra Nevadas, and just happens to be one of the country's most scenic stretches of track.

Like the breeze, travel west. Starting from Chicago you should still pass the mountains in daylight, even if the train departs late. You'll also be channelling the spirit of those original pioneers and travelling into dazzling desert sunsets.

ESSENTIAL EXPERIENCES

❋ **Hitting the Obama trail on a tour of Chicago's rejuvenated South Side.**

❋ Disembarking at Winter Park for high-altitude pistes and miles of cross-country ski trails.

❋ **Rafting, mountain-biking and hiking around Glenwood Springs, or simply enjoying the views of the Colorado River scouring 20km-long Glenwood Canyon.**

❋ Winning big at the casinos of fluoro-kitsch Reno.

❋ **Finding a prime Sightseer Lounge Car seat to take in the peaks, canyons and cascades of the Sierra Nevada.**

❋ Complementing your train travel with a visit to the California State Railroad Museum in Sacramento.

❋ **Raising your binoculars at Suisun Marsh, a vast brackish wetland teeming with birds.**

❋ Sailing out to Alcatraz Island, the notorious prison stranded in San Francisco Bay.

DISTANCE - 3900KM | COUNTRIES COVERED - USA | IDEAL TIME COMMITMENT - 10 DAYS | BEST TIME OF YEAR - YEAR ROUND
ESSENTIAL TIP - TRAVEL EAST-WEST FOR THE BEST SUNSETS.

THROUGH THE ROCKIES

In 1870 America's railway-building pioneers ploughed south from Denver, their goal being to reach El Paso, Texas. The Denver & Rio Grande Western Railroad (D&RGW) aimed to conquer the Rockies, cutting through the ranges rather than detouring around them. The tracks never made it to Texas, terminating instead at Santa Fe, New Mexico. But the D&RGW was still impressive. Its 3120m Tennessee Pass was the highest mainline track in the USA. The Durango & Silverton Narrow Gauge section, which serviced gold mines in the San Juan Mountains, is now a 72km heritage track plied by steam locos, and one of the best rides in the country.

TRAIN DRIVER FOR THE DAY

The Western Pacific Railroad Museum occupies the former train servicing depot in Portola, California, a small town nestled in the upper reaches of the Feather River Canyon. Amid its vast collection of locos and cabooses, which you're encouraged to climb on and over, are an engine car and four passenger cars from the original California Zephyr train. Better still, from mid-April to mid-November any train buff can play train driver – the museum's Run A Locomotive programme allows you to rent one of a selection of its vintage diesel engines and operate it under the supervision of a private instructor.

■ THE JOURNEY TODAY

You've swapped blackjack tips with a croupier from Reno, and discussed politics with a Sacramento-bound student. Meanwhile, out the window, the most remarkable mountain scenes are streaming by – white-whip tops and river-rumbled gorges. And you haven't even had to move a muscle yet.

The Sightseer Lounge Car is the place to be. In these panoramic carriages, walls have been swapped for windows, offering uninterrupted views of whatever you're passing: the marshy Mississippi, the bright lights of Denver, the drama of the Rocky Mountains. This is also the place to chat, to meet the Americans who've swapped airplanes and automobiles in favour of the train.

They're a growing breed, from a low base. In 1970, usage was so low that the Zephyr ceased operation until 1983. But in 2010 it carried almost 378,000 passengers, a 9% increase on 2009. Air travel is increasingly laden with security rigmarole, and fuel prices are rising; Obama has promised investment in Amtrak, the company running the railways. Put simply, US trains are on the up.

And it's about time too – this is travel at its most civilised. Seats are comfy, even in Coach class. A reasonably priced dining car offers sit-down meals – though if you want to bring your own supplies that's fine. You'll even get commentary, with experts from the California State Railroad Museum pointing out the sights between Sacramento and Reno. Still, it's nice to get off now and then. This iconic journey is steeped in cultural history and landscapes as old as the hills. But with so many stops with so much potential, it's a journey you can mould into your own glimpse of rail-side USA.

■ SHORTCUT

Ridden nonstop, trains on the Zephyr route take 51 hours and 20 minutes to connect Chicago with San Francisco. While getting off en route is more fun, you can still get a taste of America during your 2½ days on board: the panoramic viewing lounges offer tantalising views of the plains and mountains, and the bar and dining cars allow long chats with the locals.

■ DETOUR

Take a different route from Chicago to the Pacific Ocean. Ploughing a more southerly trail than the Zephyr, Amtrak's Southwest Chief (40 hours) heads from Chicago to LA via the red-rock badlands of the American West; stop off at Albuquerque, for forays into New Mexico, and Flagstaff, for access to the Grand Canyon. Alternatively, trains on the Empire Builder route head north from Chicago, meeting the West Coast at Seattle, having trundled for 46 hours via the sweeping plains of North Dakota and Montana's big-sky country.

NATIONAL GEOGRAPHIC SOCIETY | PHOTOLIBRARY

OPENING SPREAD Reno at dusk, and the sign that says it all. **ABOVE (L)** Dinner with all the trimmings onboard the Zephyr. **ABOVE (R)** Cattle grazing below Mount Tom, Sierra Nevada. **LEFT** The unearthly beauty of Mono Lake, Sierra Nevada.

ARMCHAIR

❋ *Stranger on a Train* (Jenny Diski) The British author travels America by rail, documenting the fleeting landscapes and quirky characters she meets, quite reluctantly, en route.

❋ *Nothing Like it in the World: The Men Who Built the Railway That United America* (Stephen Ambrose) The story of the hardy souls who constructed the transcontinental railroad.

❋ *Riding the Rails in the USA* (Martin Sandler) From opening up the Wild West to shifting modern-day commuters, a look at the impact of trains in American life.

❋ *California Zephyr* (Hank Williams) Classic country-music crooner's paean to the eponymous train.

❋ *Denver & Rio Grande* (1952) High-drama Hollywood version of the construction of the railroad over the Rocky Mountains, filmed on location near Durango, southern Colorado.

TOY TRAIN TO DARJEELING

SPREAD OVER A STEEP MOUNTAIN RIDGE, SURROUNDED BY TEA PLANTATIONS, WITH A BACKDROP OF HIMALAYAN PEAKS, THE HILL STATION OF DARJEELING IS SPECTACULAR, AND THE MOST ROMANTIC APPROACH IS ABOARD ONE OF THE MOST FAMOUS NARROW-GAUGE TRAIN LINES IN THE WORLD.

The Darjeeling Himalayan Railway, listed as a Unesco World Heritage Site in 1999, begins its slow, sinuous approach in New Jalpaiguri, a crowded trading hub in the plains, before winding its way on two-foot or 610mm wide tracks through the West Bengal hills to the idyllic hill station of sweet Darjeeling, perched on the doorstep of the Himalayas. Hatched as a concept in 1879, the original stretch from Siliguri to Kurseong was completed on 23 August 1880, while the Darjeeling line didn't open until 4 July 1881.

Over the 130 years it has been in existence, the railway has survived earthquakes, cyclones and seasonal flooding, ferried military personnel to camps around Ghoom and Darjeeling, and fended off increased competition from bus services plying the Hill Cart Road. The tracks are often simply on the road's shoulder, crossing various roads more than 100 times, and skimming the edge of homes and businesses along the way. In size and proximity it resembles a trolley rather than an important overland train, which is why it was nicknamed the 'Toy Train of Darjeeling'. Powered by steam, the locomotives, which haul the Toy Train, were all built before 1925. And the look and feel of the train hasn't changed much since, which is why rail enthusiasts from around the world are among the on-board hordes.

While the trip itself is fanciful, the destination of Darjeeling is sublime. When you aren't gazing at Khangchendzonga (8598m), you can explore colonial-buildings, Buddhist and Hindu temples, and botanical gardens. The steep, narrow streets are crowded with colourful souvenir and handicraft shops, a good steaming brew and excellent Indian and Tibetan fare are never far away, and walkers can enjoy superb treks that trace ancient trade routes.

ESSENTIAL EXPERIENCES

❋ **Boarding the rickety, quaint and classic Toy Train in the busy shopping hub of New Jalpaiguri.**

❋ Watching as the scenery rolls from dry, dusty plains to wooded foothills to mountain communities surrounded by tea plantations and snowy peaks.

❋ **Enjoying the mountain views, clean air and a 2km walk to Eagle's Crag in Kurseong.**

❋ Taking long, luxurious walks through sweet Darjeeling and a trek to Tiger Hill, where you'll find awesome views, just outside of town.

❋ **Visiting tea plantations, trekking and river rafting or otherwise enjoying the mountain environment in and around Darjeeling.**

DISTANCE - 86KM | COUNTRIES COVERED - INDIA | **IDEAL TIME COMMITMENT** - ONE DAY | **BEST TIME OF YEAR** - MARCH TO MAY, OCTOBER TO DECEMBER | **ESSENTIAL TIP**: WHEN BOOKING A 'JOY RIDE', RESERVE SEATS AT LEAST A DAY BEFORE AT DARJEELING STATION.

GOMPAS & PAGODAS

Darjeeling and Ghoom are sprinkled with fascinating Buddhist monasteries. The most scenic is Bhutia Busty Gompa, with Khangchendzonga providing a spectacular backdrop. Originally on Observatory Hill, it was rebuilt in its present location by the Chogyals of Sikkim in the 19th century. It houses a fine gold-accented mural and the original copy of the Tibetan Book of the Dead. Yiga Choling Gompa, the region's most famous monastery, has more wonderful old murals, enshrines a 5m-high statue of the Maitreya Buddha (Future Buddha) and 300 beautifully bound Tibetan texts. It's just west of Ghoom, about a 10-minute walk from Hill Cart Rd.

TIGER HILL

To set your eyes on a spectacular 250km stretch of Himalayan horizon, including Everest (8848m), Lhotse (8501m), Makalu (8475m), Khangchendzonga (8598m), Kabru (6691m) and Janu (7710m), get to Tiger Hill, 11km south of Darjeeling, and above Ghoom. The sunrise over the Himalaya from here can be spectacular if the weather is clear, which is why it has become a major tourist attraction, with convoys of jeeps leaving Darjeeling for Tiger Hill every morning at around 4.30am. Wise ones take the jeep one way to Tiger Hill and then spend their day wandering back to Darjeeling, visiting the gompas (Tibetan Buddhist monasteries) in Ghoom along the way.

THE JOURNEY TODAY

The hardy traveller signs up for the full-day experience and boards the train in New Jalpaiguri in the arid plains. From here you'll chug through Siliguri Town (the original southern terminus of the line) past Siliguri Junction (where you can hop on a broad gauge train to Assam), and into the woods at Sukna. The wooded foothills become even more picturesque above Rangtang Station, where you'll glimpse tea plantations and intact forests, before the panoramic views begin to rattle through the viewfinder above Chunbhati. After passing through Tindharia, the switchback traverse is in full effect as the train grinds slowly past Giddaphar, one of several jagged mountains now looming above.

The thriving hill station of Kurseong offers the first taste of India's mountain people, some of whom fly Tibetan prayer flags as the train passes through maple and chestnut forests on the way to Tung, offering an excellent look at Kurseong Ridge. If your luck holds you'll see the buzz of the Sonada Bazaar and Buddhist pilgrims making offerings at a Tibetan *chorten* (stupa) as you chug through the Senchel Forest Reserve.

Next comes Tiger Hill, with spectacular Himalayan vistas and epic birding before you make the final, often traffic-choked approach, to Darjeeling Pass at Ghoom (2260m), the highest point of the journey. From here the train descends along the Batasia Loop, past a memorial to the Gorkha soldiers, with pretty Darjeeling town appearing below and special views of Khangchendzonga, India's highest peak (and the world's third highest) at 8598m, in the distance. The majestic mountain looms from an icy Himalayan spine that cracks the mind open and invites the kind of dreamy euphoria that only the best journeys can muster as you pull into Darjeeling.

SHORTCUT

You can join the train from any stop to shorten the 7½-hour trip, but consider a two-hour 'joy ride'. Offered only during the high season, trains leave twice daily from Darjeeling Station for a steam-powered return trip to Darjeeling Pass.

DETOUR

Darjeeling is a fine portal to the former kingdom, and current Indian state, Sikkim. Think plunging, lushly forested mountain valleys interspersed with rice terraces and flowering rhododendrons. Tibetan-style Buddhist monasteries (gompas) add splashes of white, gold and vermillion to the green ridges and are approached through avenues of colourful prayer flags. The charming people are among India's most friendly, and the state's main attraction, Khangchendzonga (also called Kanchenjunga), rises like an ice god above all else.

TIM MAKINS | LONELY PLANET IMAGES ©

OPENING SPREAD The Toy Train winding around the Batasia Loop, West Bengal. **ABOVE (L)** Tibetan monks blowing horns to wake up their brethren in Ghoom, outside Darjeeling. **ABOVE (R)** The Toy Train: a joyous experience for all. **LEFT** Traditional work that still endures: picking tea in West Bengal.

ARMCHAIR

❋ ***Darjeeling: A Novel*** (Bharti Kirchner) Set in the mountainous tea plantations of Darjeeling, India and in New York City, this is the story of two sisters, Aloka and Sujata, long separated by their love for Pranab, an idealistic young revolutionary.

❋ ***The Darjeeling Limited*** (2007) Directed by the great Wes Anderson, this dark screwball comedy about three grieving and clinically depressed brothers traveling through India, stars Owen Wilson, Jason Schwartzman, Adrian Brody and a train that bears a striking resemblance to the Toy Train.

❋ ***Jhumroo*** (1961) This screwball Bollywood film deals with love, arranged marriage and class in the hills of northern India. The Toy Train has a cameo.

❋ ***Aradhana*** (1969) This Bollywood classic is a remake of the 1946 Hollywood fave, *To Each His Own*, partly shot on the Toy Train.

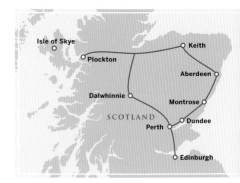

THE ROYAL SCOTSMAN

SCOTLAND IS RENOWNED FOR ITS WILD COUNTRYSIDE: HIGHLAND PEAKS; MYSTERIOUS CASTLES; WINDSWEPT MOORS; AND DEEP LOCHS. THE ROYAL SCOTSMAN LUXURY TRAIN BRINGS PASSENGERS UP CLOSE TO THIS RUGGED LANDSCAPE, AN ENVIRONMENT THAT HAS INSPIRED COUNTLESS LEGENDS.

Luxury trains are all the rage, but the *Royal Scotsman* retains its status as one of the most exclusive of all. It's certainly up there in price, and a maximum of 36 passengers can travel at any time. Now you can begin to sniff the rarefied air that passengers on this train breathe – that's 'rarefied' literally, for Scotland's Highland air is renowned for its purity, and while your air on board the *Royal Scotsman* will invariably be air-conditioned, there is the chance to step outside and explore the countryside on guided tours of distilleries and historical residences or attend events such as the Highland Games. The on-board facilities even include beds and linen decked out in tartan. There's also lovely wood panelling and a magnificent observation car, where you can sip whisky and watch the magic countryside slip slowly by. The train also has packages that encompass a Grand Tour of Great Britain, Scotland and Wales.

The Classic journey does what it says on the tin – it's the default jaunt around the Highlands and what the train is most renowned for. This monumental, four-day, 1100km round trip takes off from Edinburgh to pass through Arbroath, Montrose and Aberdeen before arriving in Keith. The next day, the train visits Inverness and the Glen Ord Distillery for a private tour and tasting. After that, it passes Loch Luichart and the Torridon mountains, climbing to Luib Summit and Achnashellach Forest before descending to Strathcarron and travelling along the edge of Loch Carron. It then stops at Plockton, where passengers have an opportunity to see wild seals from a boat or walk through woodlands. The highlight of the third day is a visit to Ballindalloch Castle, and on the next day, Rothiemurchus Estate, where travellers can fish or shoot clay pigeons.

By now, you surely get the picture: this trip is so Scottish, you could carve it!

ESSENTIAL EXPERIENCES

* **Falling in love with Edinburgh, one of the world's great cities, with its dramatic location and amazing architectural heritage.**
* Visiting Scotland's incredible cathedrals and churches.
* **Exploring the many historic houses dotted around the countryside.**
* Sampling Scotland's finest whiskies aboard the *Royal Scotsman*.
* **Ticking off the numerous castles and castle ruins.**
* Gazing longingly across the seas to Scotland's islands, and maybe even visiting some of them.
* **Visiting the museum of the Argyll & Sutherland Highlanders to learn about the history of one of Scotland's legendary regiments.**
* Having a tartan overdose.
* **Wishing the sound of bagpipes would leave your brain.**

DISTANCE - 1100KM (THE 'CLASSIC' JOURNEY) | **COUNTRIES COVERED** - SCOTLAND | **IDEAL TIME COMMITMENT** - ONE WEEK
BEST TIME OF YEAR - MAY TO SEPTEMBER | **ESSENTIAL TIP** - EDINBURGH IS IMPOSSIBLY CROWDED IN AUGUST DUE TO THE FESTIVAL, SO BOOK ACCOMMODATION WELL AHEAD.

LITERARY EDINBURGH

Edinburgh, the starting point of your *Royal Scotsman* journey, has produced many famous writers including:

✻ **Robert Louis Stevenson (1850–94), who, along with Sir Walter Scott, ranks as Scotland's best-known novelist (Scott himself was the son of an Edinburgh lawyer).**

✻ Sir Arthur Conan Doyle (1859–1930), who based the character of Sherlock Holmes on one of his medicine lecturers at Edinburgh University.

✻ **Norman MacCaig (1910–96), who wrote sharply observed poems such as 'November Night, Edinburgh' that vividly captured the atmosphere of his home city.**

✻ Dame Muriel Spark (1918–2006), whose best-known novel, *The Prime of Miss Jean Brodie*, is a shrewd portrait of 1930s Edinburgh.

✻ **Irvine Welsh (b 1958), whose novels and stories about modern Edinburgh have become famous, particularly *Trainspotting*.**

THE JACOBITE STEAM TRAIN

For a Highlands rail journey that's almost as thrilling, but totally different in most other ways, try the Jacobite steam train, which runs along the scenic West Highland Line between Fort William and Mallaig. Many say it's Scotland's most scenic rail trip, a big claim when stacked up against the *Scotsman*. The 135km round trip starts near Ben Nevis, travels to Britain's most westerly train station, Arisaig, then passes by Loch Morar and River Morar before arriving at Loch Nevis. Along the way, it steams by the beaches that were used as locations in the classic Scots films *Local Hero* and *Highlander*, as well as Glenfinnan Viaduct, which starred in the Harry Potter films.

■ THE JOURNEY TODAY

The time: early afternoon. The place: Edinburgh, one of Europe's most beautiful cities. You've just spent two days exploring its many-splendored delights and every corner revealed sudden and unexpected views: green, sunlit hills, distant rusty-red crags, an electric-blue flash from the far-distant sea, a warm glow from pub doors. But now it's time to board the *Royal Scotsman* for your tour of the Highlands. At the station you show your ticket and are greeted by a piper in full garb – hat, kilt, sporran, bagpipes – who welcomes you on board. You feel a little silly among all this pomp, but special all the same, following him down the red carpet that leads to the blood-red carriage.

On board, you settle into the observation car, nodding hello to the senior citizens, minor celebrities and property magnates already seated. You look at the drinks list and see names that melt your eyes and brain with happiness: Lagavulin, Macallan, Balvenie, Laphroaig, Dewar Rattray. The journey is four days. There are 30 fine whiskies in all. Can you get through them all? Of course you can. Oh yes, and the scenery. After a few hours, Loch Lomond looms into view, with the track descending until the train almost runs right alongside the water's edge. This is the largest lake in Britain. The train stops and everyone gets out to climb the waterfall at Glen Falloch.

It's night time. You retire to your stateroom, a wood-panelled delight that's like a mini-hotel suite. It's very old school and very indulgent. You sleep peacefully. The next day, the train takes off again, passing Britain's highest mountain, Ben Nevis. You admire its cloud-shrouded peak with its sub-Arctic climate, and then tuck into lunch: chicken and langoustine salad with baby squash and queen scallops. You decide you are very happy indeed.

■ SHORTCUT

The *Scotsman's* 'Classic' journey is four nights. Longer options are available, as are shorter ones. The 'Highland' journey is over two nights and packs a lot into this time frame, passing through Dundee, Montrose, Aberdeen, Keith, Inverness, Dalwhinnie and Perth. Activities include clay-pigeon shooting, fly-fishing and a Highland safari, and there are tours of Dalwhinnie Distillery, Rothiemurchus Estate and Culloden Battlefield.

■ DETOUR

As beautiful as Edinburgh is, the surrounding countryside is also worth a look. The old counties around Edinburgh, collectively called 'the Lothians', are filled with attractions including Hopetoun House, one of Scotland's finest stately homes; North Berwick, an attractive Victorian seaside resort with sandy beaches; and the ruins of Linlithgow Palace.

OPENING SPREAD Incredible Edinburgh Castle – the view from Arthur's Seat. **ABOVE** You've never seen so much tartan! Life aboard the *Royal Scotsman*. **LEFT** A classic Highlands scene: Eilean Donan castle in Dornie.

ARMCHAIR

❋ *Culloden* (1964) Peter Watkins' film purports to be a documentary of the 1746 Battle of Culloden, in which the British crushed the Jacobite uprising and, in the narrator's words, 'tore apart forever the clan system of the Scottish Highlands'.

❋ *Highlander* (1986) Russell Mulcahy's preposterous supernatural-warrior film features Christopher Lambert as an immortal Highland champion travelling through the ages from medieval Scotland.

❋ *Braveheart* (1995) Another classic Highlands film, with Mel Gibson swashbuckling his way through Scots scenery as William Wallace.

❋ *Trainspotting* (1996) Danny Boyle's famous film about Edinburgh junkies.

❋ *The Wicker Man* (1973) Very scary, unnerving film starring Christopher Lee, about pagans on a fictional island in the Inner Hebrides. As you look out to those remote Scottish isles from your train window, remember Lee's manic smile...

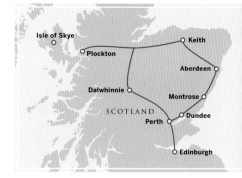

THE BLUE TRAIN OF SOUTH AFRICA

TRAIN JOURNEYS RARELY COME MORE OPULENT THAN THIS AND IF THEY DO, THEY'RE RARELY AS STUNNING. THE BLUE TRAIN PASSES THROUGH SAHARAN PLAINS, OFFERING PRIME VIEWS OF CLASSIC LANDSCAPES AND UNTAMED BEASTIES. IT'S UNIQUE, SPECTACULAR, EXCLUSIVE – AND HIGHLY ADDICTIVE.

74

The *Blue Train* is an evolution of the train route run by Union Limited and Union Express, which operated up until WWII. Originally, this glorious service was designed to enable passengers to travel in comfort to Cape Town, where they would catch the ships to England that were operating at the time. The service returned after the war and in 1998 it was refurbished and relaunched as the *Blue Train*, running between Pretoria and Cape Town twice weekly.

The *Blue Train* traverses a distance of around 1600km and bills itself as the world's most luxurious train service. Indeed, it has strong claims: one butler for every three passengers, with no more than 84 passengers at any one time; an observation car with massive windows covering almost all wall space; two lounge cars; sleeping cabins with all the trimmings including carpet and en suites, opulent linen on the beds, gold fixtures and marbled detailing in the bathrooms; and classy chefs in the dining car. People say that it's like an exclusive hotel on wheels, and that's much of the charm – you can see some amazing, untamed landscapes without getting your fingernails dirty or your hair mussed, and you get pampered all the while by your own personal third-of-a-butler. Others say that it's like having your own personalised nature film unspooling before you, which is also pretty apt, for this is virtual tourism, in a certain sense, albeit with more thrills.

But all that's the icing on the cake, because it's the landscape the train passes through that really blows people away, such as incredible waterfalls and the amazing Kimberley diamond mine, all to the accompaniment of wild ostriches and other beasties running beside your carriage.

ESSENTIAL EXPERIENCES

✳ **Hobnobbing with celebrities and the mega-rich – including 'kings and queens', according to Blue Train publicity.**

✳ Being so pampered by butlers, fine food and wine that the real world will seem decidedly 'unreal' when it's all over.

✳ **Sitting in the observation car at night and watching the stars in the sky over the veldt – almost like travelling through space.**

✳ Snapping more types of terrain with your zoom lens than your poor, overloaded camera knows what to do with.

✳ **Pulling in at the end of your journey and seeing the extraordinary 1086m flat-topped Table Mountain swing into view.**

DISTANCE - 1600KM | **COUNTRIES COVERED** - SOUTH AFRICA | **IDEAL TIME COMMITMENT** - TWO DAYS | **BEST TIME OF YEAR** - ANYTIME, ALTHOUGH JUNE TO SEPTEMBER IS BEST FOR SEEING WILDLIFE THROUGH WINDOWS | **ESSENTIAL TIP** - DON'T PICK THE WEEK YOU GO TO GIVE UP ALCOHOL.

THE BIG HOLE

If you're on the southbound route, you'll be shepherded into Kimberley to see the Big Hole. Diamonds were first discovered in the Kimberley area in 1866 and five years later South Africa's great diamond rush began with the biggest of big bangs. The Big Hole mine was the focal point of this rush – at 215m deep, the world's largest hand-dug hole. A town called New Rush was formed just north of the Big Hole and renamed Kimberley in 1873. By 1872 there were around 50,000 miners in the area, and when mining ended in 1914, the final yield was 2722kg of diamonds and 22.5 million tons of excavated earth.

■ THE JOURNEY TODAY

You've been on the train for 20 hours, with another seven to go, and you're showing no signs of cabin fever at all. On the contrary, you wish the journey could go on forever. The ever-unfolding landscape is like your own private movie, a safari on wheels. Amid the plush surrounds of the lounge carriage, you feel like an extra in an Agatha Christie murder mystery. The waiter brings you another bottle of desirable South African wine, and you don't mind in the slightest that it's only 11am – a ride on the Blue Train is no time to become teetotal.

It's not just you – everyone on board is buzzing with excitement. Some are rich, some have saved their pennies to be here and some are on honeymoon, but no matter how they came, all feel as though they're part of something special. You head for the wood-panelled observation car – its walls are virtually all window, so you can see everything – and recline into the enormous leather couch. You're the only one there, except for the smiling barman. The old-school lamps

and well-stocked bar make you feel even more out of time – in a good way. You sip some more of that wine.

And then you're in a trance, just sitting there, watching the endless African veldt roll effortlessly past your window. A pack of wild baboons bounces up and down, seemingly for your own private amusement. There's amazing colourful fauna, the craggiest of mountains... on and on until you reach the end.

■ SHORTCUT

You can't condense the Blue Train experience. It only has one stop, at Matjiesfontein on the northbound route and Kimberley on the southbound, and that's only for an hour and

ARMCHAIR

❋ **Boyhood: A Memoir** (JM Coetzee) The *Blue Train* passes through the bleak desert lands of the Karoo, which is a setting in this memoir by the renowned South African author. The sparse landscape is home to plenty of wildlife.

❋ **Danke Auntie** (Zakes Mda) This play, in which a group of poor black children scrabble for scraps of food thrown from the train by rich passengers, casts a different perspective on the *Blue Train*. Mda is also an acclaimed novelist whose most recent

book, *The Whale Caller* (2005), takes a sceptical look at the optimism surrounding the new South Africa.

❋ **Wah-Wah** (2005) For a more light-hearted view of the country, Richard E Grant's film recounts his childhood in the country's pre-independence English community.

BLUE TRAIN CUISINE

In a recent interview, *Blue Train* chef Allen Pfister expounded upon what he thinks makes the on-board menu so special. The ideal, he says, is to impart the flavour of South Africa with a modern turn, recognisable but with an unexpected twist, such as Karoo lamb with waterblommetjies, a South African aquatic plant with white, scented flowers. Otherwise he likes to cook 'anything Thai', indeed anything from Southeast Asia, because he feels the combination of vibrant flavours adds to the overall sensory experience of the train journey.

a half. Otherwise, it's 27 hours of nonstop bliss back on board.

▨ DETOUR

Other than the standard route, the train can be chartered for packaged excursions; you'll need 20 guests or more to take advantage of this. Options include the Kimberley Excursion to the famous old diamond mines; the Outdshoorn Excursion to the Cango Caves; and the Matjiesfontein Excursion to Matjiesfontein, a colonial town dating from the Boer War, which, with its double-decker bus and well-preserved period architecture and lamp posts, is a pretty weird experience, like some kind of stage set that you've accidently walked into. But then again, the entire *Blue Train* experience can seem like that.

DALLAS AND JOHN HEATON | PHOTOLIBRARY

OPENING SPREAD Has there ever been a more aptly named tourist attraction? Welcome to the Big Hole, Kimberley. **ABOVE** The Blue Train on its approach to Matjiesfontein. **BELOW** The end of the journey and the view that awaits you: Table Bay and Table Mountain.

THE COPPER CANYON RAILWAY

THIS IS ONE OF THE MOST DRAMATIC TRAIN RIDES OF ALL: 655KM OF RAILS RIGHT UP, OVER AND THROUGH NORTHWEST MEXICO'S STUNNING COPPER CANYON (BARRANCA DEL COBRE), 20 SPECTACULAR CANYONS, THAT IS FOUR TIMES LARGER THAN ARIZONA'S GRAND CANYON AND, IN PARTS, DEEPER.

78

The name 'Copper Canyon' was applied by the Spanish, who mistook the greenish-glow of lichen in the area for copper. As a physical location, it refers to the incredible Barranca de Urique, the canyon's deepest point at 1879m (although an altitude of only 500m). That's not the only amazing detail. The Barranca de Urique has a subtropical climate with peaks 2300m above sea level and an ecosystem of conifers and evergreens. The region is also home to the Rarámuri, among Mexico's largest indigenous groups.

Imagine a big knife – a knife used by the gods. Now, imagine that gods have cars, and that one of them decides to scrape their big knife across a car the size of North Carolina. Finally, envisage the owner – some other god – coming home to find the damage: in scale, that scraped scar would be something along the lines of Copper Canyon's amazing chasms. OK, forget the metaphors, maybe you really do need to see it for yourself. Luckily, you can travel right through some of the steepest areas on the Ferrocarril Chihuahua al Pacífico – the fabled Copper Canyon Railway. It boasts 36 bridges and 87 tunnels and traverses 655km between Los Mochis at its western terminus and Chihuahua in the Midwest. It was opened in 1961, after taking many decades to build, and is the major link between Chihuahua and the coast, used heavily by passengers and for shipping freight. Two passenger trains ply the route: *clase económica* (economy class), and *primera express* (first class), which makes fewer stops and has a restaurant, bar and reclining seats. Alternatively, there is a privately operated rail car with an open-deck area.

Either way, the beauty of the landscape – sweeping mountain vistas, sheer canyon walls, sparkling lakes, fields of flowers, waterfalls and high desert plains (mostly free of human development) – will make any encounter truly priceless.

ESSENTIAL EXPERIENCES

❋ **Thrilling to each hairpin bend, deep tunnel and high bridge along the way.**

❋ Admiring the colonial ambience and Spanish architecture at the charming town El Fuerte, which many use as either an end or start point for the journey.

❋ **Being unable to believe your eyes as you photograph endless dreamlike vistas, desert sunsets and mystical cerulean skies.**

❋ Sucking in the brisk canyon air, as big an adrenaline hit as you're likely to find.

❋ **Getting to the end, only to ride all the way back and do it all again.**

DISTANCE - 655KM | COUNTRIES COVERED - MEXICO | **IDEAL TIME COMMITMENT** - FIVE DAYS | **BEST TIME OF YEAR** - LATE SEPTEMBER AND OCTOBER | **ESSENTIAL TIP** - MAKE OVERNIGHT STOPS TO GET UP CLOSE TO THE CANYONS.

THE RARÁMURI

Around 50,000 indigenous Rarámuri live in the Sierra Tarahumara's numerous canyons, including the Barranca del Cobre. You'll see mostly women dressed in colourful skirts and blouses, peddling beautiful handwoven baskets and carrying infants on their backs. 'Rarámuri' means 'those who run fast'. Their traditional hunting method is to chase and exhaust deer, driving them over cliffs to be impaled on wooden sticks placed at the bottom. Today, the Rarámuri run marathon footraces of at least 160km through the rough canyons, all the while kicking a small wooden ball ahead of them, and compete in ultra-distance races throughout the world.

■ THE JOURNEY TODAY

You arrive at the optimum time, when temperatures are not as hot at the bottom of the canyon or too cold at the top. You did your research – best to come just after the summer rains, late September and October, when vegetation is still green. You are on the train, heading inland to the east. You sit on the carriage's right side because that's where the best views were. Every so often you rise from your seat just to hang out in the vestibules between cars, where you enjoy the simple pleasure of the open windows and the cool, fresh mountain air whipping your face. Here, too, is your chance for unobstructed photos of the mighty landscape passing before your eyes. You thought the trip was all hype between Los Mochis and El Fuerte, when you passed through flat, gray farmland. 'That's it?' you thought, but you were impatient, and you knew it. Things got interesting quickly as the train clawed its way through fog-shrouded hills speckled with dark cacti pillars and you went snap-happy with your camera.

About three hours after leaving Los Mochis, you pass over the long Río Fuerte bridge and through the first of 87 tunnels. Along the way, you cut through small canyons and through three ascending loops at Témoris. 'That's La Pera,' you inform a fellow passenger, 'for its shape, like a pear.' The train hugs the sides of dramatic cliffs as it climbs higher and higher through the mountains of the Sierra Tarahumara. Finally, at Divisadero, you catch your first and only glimpse of the actual Barranca del Cobre. Everyone on board seems to exhale at the same time. Then that sound is replaced by the faintly surreal sound of a hundred camera shutters firing at once, like a flock of chirping mechanical birds.

ARMCHAIR

❋ **Where the Air Is Clear** (Carlos Fuentes) The first novel of Fuentes, one of the best-known Mexican writers, written in 1958 and one of his most highly regarded.

❋ **Pedro Páramo** (Juan Rulfo) This 1955 short novel has been described as 'Wuthering Heights set in Mexico and written by Kafka'.

❋ **The Labyrinth of Solitude** (Octavio Paz) First published in 1950, this collection of essays is a probing analysis of the Mexican character.

❋ **Light Feet: A Rarámuri Tale** (2008) Short film focusing on a Rarámuri boy who travels to the city after a parent dies.

❋ **Amores Perros** (2000) Directed by Alejandro González and set in contemporary Mexico City, this raw, graphic film boasts three plots connected by one traffic accident.

❋ **Y Tu Mamá También** (2001) Alfonso Cuarón's tale of two privileged teenagers from Mexico City is the biggest grossing Mexican film ever.

THE SCHEDULE

The timetable is really very important on this trip. Well, not really. Both the *primera express* and *clase económica* trains run daily, but they tend to run late, although you will hear folk go on about 'normal' times as if they were the official word. You should listen to them: they're locals and they have the knowledge that can help you. Though the train can run on time, it has also been known to show up two hours earlier or later, so when all else fails, check with your hotel, at train stations or with conductors.

And then the train moves again, circling back over itself in a complete loop inside the canyon at El Lazo before steaming into Creel and Chihuahua.

■ SHORTCUT

The best way to experience the Barranca del Cobre region is to make a few stops along the way. Each stop will give you 24 hours before the train comes again: ample opportunity to get closer to those wonderful canyons. However, many people simply ride the train all the way through and then stop overnight before returning.

■ DETOUR

Cerocahui, a hub for local travellers, is a place where tourists are rarely found. Yet disembark here and you'll be rewarded by the sight of a tiny pueblo amid a verdant valley. Alongside Urique is where you'll first glimpse the Rarámuri, as well as Cerocahui's pretty yellow-domed church, San Francisco Javier de Cerocahui, dating from 1680. Today, the town is an *ejido* (communal landholding) devoted to forestry. There are a few good places to stay, a peaceful atmosphere and, best of all, proximity to the surrounding countryside, excellent for bird watching, hiking and horse riding.

GERALD FRENCH | CORBIS

OPENING SPREAD A Rarámuri woman and child vending their wares. **ABOVE** Up and over the Santa Barbara Bridge, crossing Rio Mina Plata. **BELOW** Chihuahua – and a vista without compare.

THE TRANS-SIBERIAN RAILWAY

A JOURNEY ON THE TRANS-SIBERIAN RAILWAY IS AMONG THE ULTIMATE TRAVEL EXPERIENCES: MOSCOW'S RED SQUARE, BEIJING'S FORBIDDEN CITY, THE GREAT WALL, ICY LAKE BAIKAL, MONGOLIA'S STEPPES. AND THEN THERE'S THE ON-BOARD EXPERIENCE, SWAPPING STORIES AND SLINGING BACK VODKA.

82

In the second half of the 19th century, the more advanced industrial states began to conquer the continents: Africa, Asia and the Americas. Interiors were explored, material riches plundered and 'uncivilised' natives tamed and exploited. Railways became a symbol of this conquest, their scope and scale signifying enormous power. More kilometres of track, bigger locomotives, more opulent stations, it all expressed the sheer excess of imperial pomp. Of course, Russia was not immune to the process, sallying forth into the immense Siberian hinterland and distant Pacific coastline. At stake was the undeveloped and undiscovered natural wealth of Inner Eurasia, seemingly out of reach due to the sheer physical scale of these far-flung eastern territories. Thus the solution: construction of the world's longest railroad, the vast Trans-Siberian.

The classic Trans-Siberian service runs from Moscow's Yaroslavl Station to Vladivostok. That's a span of 9288km, seven time zones and a third of the globe, and it's memorable every step of the way. The railway skirts Lake Baikal, resplendent in the middle of the Siberian taiga, while the Trans-Mongolian tributary continues past classic Russian vistas – gingerbread houses and evocative forest views – before submitting to the sublime Mongolian steppes. Both the Trans-Mongolian and Trans-Manchurian lines chart a course for Beijing and the crème de la crème of sights: the mighty Great Wall of China.

The Trans-Siberian has an average speed of around 60km/h – the epitome of 'slow travel'. The carriages are not especially glamorous, either: think faded and functional. On the other hand, they're never dull, whether you experience the Trans-Siberian route nonstop, savouring the slowly evolving landscapes through your window, or take the time to explore the numerous fascinating stops along the way.

ESSENTIAL EXPERIENCES

✳ **Sailing down canals and admiring the facades of glorious palaces and mansions in St Petersburg.**

✳ Taking in Moscow – Red Square, Lenin's corpse, the nightlife and contemporary art.

✳ **Cruising along the Volga from Nizhny Novgorod.**

✳ **Admiring the grand old buildings in Tomsk, Siberia's prettiest city.**

✳ Taking a train ride right alongside Lake Baikal on the Circumbaikal Railway.

✳ **Arriving at the Mongolian capital, Ulaanbaatar, a cosmopolitan city with impressive restaurants, Buddhist monasteries and very attractive countryside.**

✳ Climbing the Great Wall, entering the Forbidden City and enjoying the many delights of Beijing.

DISTANCE - 9288KM | **COUNTRIES COVERED** - RUSSIA, MONGOLIA, CHINA | **IDEAL TIME COMMITMENT** - ONE WEEK TO TWO MONTHS | **BEST TIME OF YEAR** - OCTOBER TO APRIL | **ESSENTIAL TIP** - DO THOROUGH RESEARCH BEFORE BOOKING. AVOIDING CROWDS IS ONE THING, BUT DETERMINING THE BEST WEATHER ACROSS MULTIPLE TIME ZONES IS ANOTHER.

TRANS-SIB CUISINE

Russia's wonderful culinary history has been bolstered by many influences from the Baltic to the Far East. However, as with any cold-climate country, fatty dishes predominate so don't plan on starting your new-fangled diet here. Appetisers are a feature and soups such as borscht, made with beetroot, and chicken noodle can be a meal in themselves, served with bread and sour cream. China has a bewildering array of regional delicacies. The most common method of cooking in Beijing is deep-fried in peanut oil. Meanwhile, Mongolia offers up nomadic-inspired dishes – a hearty, somewhat bland selection of meat and dairy dishes.

THE BAM

Few Trans-Siberian travellers know about the Baikal-Amur Mainline (Baikalo-Amurskaya Magistral; BAM). This railway is an altogether different experience to the Trans-Sib – most towns along the way were used for construction workers and feature that classic '70s functionalist look, yet the incredible remote, wild scenery is awe-inspiring. It's also a world-class engineering feat: the BAM travels almost half Russia's length, beginning at Tayshet, curling around Lake Baikal and cutting through endless taiga, around snow-covered mountains and through numerous tunnels on its way east to Sovetskaya Gavan on the Tatar Strait.

ARMCHAIR

* **The Great Railway Bazaar, Riding the Iron Rooster and Ghost Train to the Eastern Star** (Paul Theroux) All three books have sections in which Theroux boards the Trans-Siberian, with predictably moody results.

* **Horror Express** (1973) Cult film starring Peter Cushing, Christopher Lee and Telly Savalas, about an alien-inhabited prehistoric fossil that turns Trans-Sib passengers into zombies.

* **Trans-Siberian** (2008) Brad Anderson film starring Woody Harrelson and Emily Mortimer as a couple entangled in a messy drug transaction between Beijing and Moscow.

* **The Big Red Train Ride** (Eric Newby) Hilarious, classic account of hopping on and off the train between Moscow and Nakhodka.

* **Journey Into the Mind's Eye** (Lesley Blanch) A semiautobiographical tale about the author's romantic obsession with the Trans-Sib.

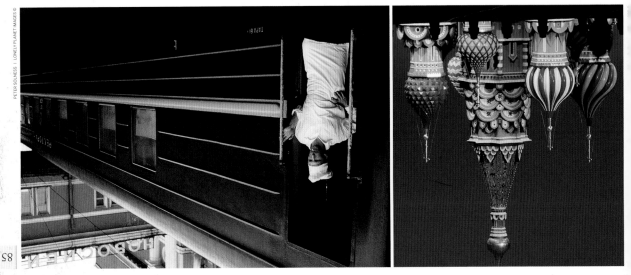

OPENING SPREAD Snow and rails: that's what the Trans-Siberian experience is all about. **ABOVE (L)** The classic onion domes of St Basil's Cathedral, Red Square, Moscow. **ABOVE (R)** A Trans-Sib chef takes a break. **LEFT** An attendant turns on the charm.

PETER SOLNESS | LONELY PLANET IMAGES ©

THE JOURNEY TODAY

Moscow to Beijing nonstop sounds like a sea voyage on land. Sleeping and reading for a week while the ultimate backdrop rolls by your window. You could hone your card skills and chess tactics with a fellow passenger, maybe even fall in love. But despite the pros, instead you resolve to hop on and off at will, aiming to explore each country you pass through. There'll be time to get to know your passengers in between stops… right? Right. You've decided.

The first stop is Irkutsk, with its fancifully rebuilt churches, majestic 19th-century architecture and imaginative eateries. From there, Lake Baikal, the 'Pearl of Siberia' – the world's deepest lake – is but a short trip away. Then, back on the train, after a few more days shunting across the Eurasian landmass, the Mongolian capital, Ulaanbaatar, awaits you.

The approach into Ulaanbaatar feels otherworldly. Horsemen gallop alongside your carriage and the rolling green hills are covered in pine trees. And then you see the city itself: an enormous, sprawling, bizarre cocktail of crumbling Soviet-built apartment blocks, belching smokestacks and derelict suburbs. Despite appearances, it's just what you need after so much time away from city life, and you eagerly settle in for a new night's sampling the chaotic capital, with its frenzied street life abuzz with friendly locals. You reboard the Trans-Sib and become enchanted anew by the long, arching ride through the Siberian wilderness and Gobi Desert. Finally, Beijing is the promised land for the next stage of your adventure: the Great Wall and all its associated delights.

SHORTCUT

There are a few shorter options, although 'short' is a relative concept. The highly popular route between Moscow and Beijing goes via the Mongolian capital of Ulaanbaatar, a 7865km journey through three very different countries and cultures. Allow a week to make detours and fully explore attractions such as Lake Baikal and the three capitals: Moscow, Ulaanbaatar and Beijing. Trains run once a week and take almost seven days to complete the journey.

DETOUR

If you are a connoisseur of the offbeat, you will invariably find yourself gravitating towards the Baikal-Amur Mainline (Baikalo Amurskaya Magistral, or BAM), an alternative Trans-Siberian route through some of the most remote, rugged and beautiful parts of Siberia. From Krasnoyarsk to Vladivostok, it covers 5500km and takes at least six days without overnight stops. If you begin in Moscow, your journey will last an extra 4098km and another four days on the train.

NEW ZEALAND'S TRANZCOASTAL

ALTHOUGH NOT AS FAMED AS THE TRANS-SIBERIAN OR THE ROYAL SCOTSMAN, THE TRANZCOASTAL IS UNIQUE, PASSING THROUGH SCENERY THAT'S STUNNING. TRAVELLING BETWEEN CHRISTCHURCH AND PICTON, THE TRAIN IS SANDWICHED BETWEEN THE KAIKOURA RANGES AND THE PACIFIC OCEAN.

The *TranzCoastal* passes through 22 tunnels and over 175 bridges, and provides almost as many scenic delights. The route has been operating since 1945, when it was first known as the Picton Express and then the Coastal Pacific. In 2000 it was rebranded as the *TranzCoastal*. The journey takes almost five hours and covers 347km, a popular favourite for travellers who want to get the best out of New Zealand.

The train winds around the South Island's panoramic coast, where there are numerous opportunities to see penguins, seals and schools of dolphins frolicking in the Pacific, as well as that inimitable Kiwi scenery: farm, winery and horticultural land on the one side, low sea mist and rocky headlands on the other. Another popular feature of the train is the open-air viewing carriage, touted by the company as a golden chance to fill your lungs with clean New Zealand air. The train stops at Kaikoura, a picture-perfect peninsula town backed by the snowcapped peaks of the Seaward Kaikoura Range. Here, many passengers break the journey for a spot of whale watching or swimming with dolphins. Indeed, there are few places in the world with such awesome mountains so close to the sea and such a proliferation of wildlife so close at hand. Whales, dolphins, NZ fur seals, penguins, shearwaters, petrels and wandering albatross all stop by or make this area their home, ensuring Kaikoura is an opportunity too good to resist.

The *TranzCoastal* journey ends at Christchurch, one of New Zealand's most relaxed cities. It's a place that combines an easy-going provincial charm with the emerging energy and verve of a metropolis, where modern bars and restaurants complement English-style architecture and the locals know how lucky they are to blend all the attractions of a city with the relaxed ambience of a small town. It's the perfect end to a rail journey that has a similarly relaxed feel.

ESSENTIAL EXPERIENCES

✳ **Exploring Christchurch's history any way you can: tram, river punt or on foot.**

✳ Visiting the diverse areas within easy reach of Christchurch, everything from the chance to view humpback whales to the spectacular mountains that appeared in the *Lord of the Rings* films.

✳ **Marvelling at the views of the Mackenzie Country from atop Mt John.**

✳ Hiking in the shadow of New Zealand's highest peak in the wonderful Aoraki/Mt Cook National Park.

✳ **Getting up close to Kaikoura's magical wildlife.**

✳ Exploring the Marlborough Wine Region and sampling the tipples on offer.

✳ **Travelling from New Zealand's Far North to its Deep South.**

✳ Exploring the full gamut of experiences – everything from bustling cities to lonely beaches.

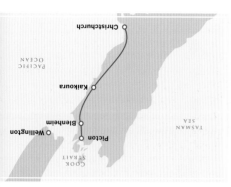

Christchurch · PACIFIC OCEAN · Kaikoura · Blenheim · Wellington · Picton · TASMAN SEA · COOK STRAIT

98

KAIKOURA PENINSULA WALKWAY

If you're in or passing through Kaikoura, the Kaikoura Peninsula Walkway is a must-do. This looping walk begins in the town and takes three to four hours to complete, heading out to Point Kean, along the cliffs to South Bay, then back to town over the isthmus. Along the way there is ample opportunity to spot fur seals and red-billed seagull and shearwater (also known as mutton bird) colonies. There are also plenty of lookouts and interesting interpretive panels.

THE JOURNEY TODAY

Your mind is racing as you ride the ferry from Wellington, on New Zealand's North Island, to Picton on the South Island. This three-hour, 92km trip across the Cook Strait is the ideal preliminary to your TranzCoastal adventure. The boat reaches Picton, clustered around a deep gulch at the head of Queen Charlotte Sound. It's a small town but has an inviting atmosphere. At the start of summer, it's positively hyperactive, absorbing eight fully-laden ferry arrivals per day from the north.

You board the TranzCoastal. The windows are panoramic and the photo opportunities are endless, with varied, always-changing scenery: beautiful rivers, lush farmland, ocean views, vineyards, high mountains. You even see seals sunning themselves on the rocks by the beach as waves crash and break against the shore and snowcaps melt on mountaintops. You drink some fine New Zealand wine and think about previous train trips you've done: the Blue Train, the Trans-Siberian Express, the Royal Scotsman, all amazing of course, especially the Trans-Sib, which no rail journey can really match for knock-you-dead attractions or sheer monumental, physical scale. And yet you keep thinking of the one you're on now, and you form a conclusion about it. As the vista outside the windows unfolds, it takes its time to work itself on you, and then when the journey's over, it hits you with its almost indefinable beauty. Finally, you decide that taking the TranzCoastal after the 'big ticket' rail journeys is like listening to ambient music after banging your head to heavy metal: an altogether different, possibly deeper experience.

■ SHORTCUT

As the trip is only five hours, it's worth riding it all the way. However, you could overnight at Kaikoura, the midway point, returning by train the next day if so desired. Other options include one-way tickets from Blenheim to Christchurch; Kaikoura to Christchurch; Picton to Kaikoura; and Blenheim to Kaikoura.

■ DETOUR

When the train pulls in at Kaikoura, stop over for a few nights to explore this wonderful region. Marine animals are abundant here due to ocean-current and continental-shelf conditions, and the town is a tourist mecca, with quality accommodation and many other enticements including eye-popping wildlife tours. Don't miss the chance to see whales (sperm, pilot, killer, humpback and southern right), dolphins (Hector's, bottlenose and dusky) and New Zealand fur seals up close.

88

OPENING SPREAD How's the serenity? Sunrise on the Kaikoura peninsula. **ABOVE** Sweet, charming Castlepoint Lighthouse, Wellington.

MASSIMO RIPANI | SIME | 4CORNERS IMAGES

ARMCHAIR

❋ **The Bone People** (Keri Hulme) A new era of New Zealand fiction began in 1985 when this haunting book won the Booker Prize. In 2007, Lloyd Jones's *Mister Pip* almost won the Booker again for New Zealand.

❋ **Heavenly Creatures** (1994) Directed by Peter Jackson, who, of course, delivered the Lord of the Rings trilogy to the world. Other well-known Kiwi films include Campion's *The Piano* (1993), Brad McGann's *In My Father's Den* (2004) and James Napier-Robertson's *I'm Not Harry Jenson* (2009).

❋ **Once Were Warriors** (1994) Lee Tamahori's harrowing film depicts the difficult transition of Maori pride into the modern world.

❋ **An Angel at My Table** (1990) New Zealander Janet Frame's life on display in Jane Campion's film of her autobiography.

EXPLORERS & CONQUERORS

GREAT JOURNEYS

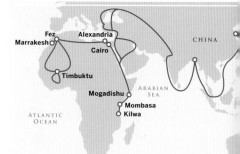

IBN BATTUTA IN AFRICA

FOLLOW IN THE FOOTSTEPS OF ONE OF THE WORLD'S GREAT NOMADS,
EXPERIENCE THE EVOCATIVE BUZZ OF MOROCCO'S GREAT CITIES, EXPLORE
DYNAMIC NORTH AFRICA, THEN JOURNEY DOWN THE SWEET AND SPICY
SWAHILI COAST ALL THE WAY TO ZANZIBAR.

90

To call Abu Abdullah Muhammad Ibn Battuta the Islamic Marco Polo would be insulting...to Battuta. Over 30 years, starting when he was 21 in 1325, he took a circuitous route from his native Morocco to Mecca, on to present day Tunisia and Egypt, across the Red Sea to the Middle East and across the Arabian peninsula by caravan. In 1326 he travelled through Iraq and Persia before doubling back into Arabia and down into Somalia on the Gulf of Aden.

By the time he reached Mogadishu in 1331, the city was at its most prosperous and packed with wealthy merchants who exported high-quality Somali fabric to Arabia. Battuta boarded a dhow and sailed to Mombasa, then a small settlement that would become an important port a century later, and continued south along the coast to the island town of Kilwa, in present day Tanzania. When Battuta visited, it was a vital transit centre in the gold trade, and in his epic travelogue, *Rihla*, he describes it as, 'one of the most beautiful and well-constructed towns in the world'.

When the monsoon season rolled in he sailed back to Arabia and travelled to Mecca again before venturing into the Byzantine Empire for the first time. He lingered in Constantinople (today's Istanbul) before moving through Central Asia into Afghanistan, India, and onto China and Southeast Asia. In 1346 he journeyed back to Morocco, Syria, Palestine and Arabia and was a witness as Black Death tore through the region. After travelling much of the world, he finally explored his home nation of Morocco in 1350, before joining a camel caravan into Mali and the soon-to-be-great city of Timbuktu. He stayed there for eight months before returning to Morocco in 1354, amidst a caravan transporting 600 female slaves from sub-Saharan Africa. After dictating his famous and much debated tome, he died a Moroccan judge in 1369.

ESSENTIAL EXPERIENCES

* **Having a Casablanca moment in Morocco's enchanting coastal city of Tangier, where there are just enough oddball expatriates and corrupt officials to give you Bogart flashbacks.**

* Bartering with the silversmiths and snake charmers in the backstreets of Marrakesh, where you can sharpen your bargaining chops.

* **Sailing the Swahili coast aboard an authentic hand-hewn dhow with Swahili Rastas, who happen to be adept at lobster diving.**

* Venturing into the vast Sahara Desert by camel, decked out in a long Berber-style tunic.

* **Rubbing shoulders with the poets, novelists and intellectuals in Alexandria, Egypt's second city.**

DISTANCE - 7886KM | **COUNTRIES COVERED** - MOROCCO, EGYPT, KENYA, TANZANIA, MALI | **IDEAL TIME COMMITMENT** - THREE WEEKS | **BEST TIME OF YEAR** - DECEMBER TO APRIL | **ESSENTIAL TIP** - BOOK FLIGHTS FROM EGYPT TO KENYA AND KENYA TO MALI OR MOROCCO TO DO IT IN ONE SHOT.

RIHLA

After Battuta returned to Morocco in 1354, and at the behest of the sultan, he dictated an account of his long voyage to Ibn Juzayy, a scholar he'd met in Granada. The Arabic title of his book translates as *A Gift to Those Who Contemplate the Wonders of Cities and the Marvels of Travelling'*, but it's most often referred to as the Rihla, or 'The Journey'. Scholars suggest there is no evidence that Battuta took any road notes, which means he relied on an imperfect memory and when describing the Middle East, Ibn Juzayy plainly plagiarised passages written by a 12th-century traveler, Ibn Jubayr, and a 13th-century nomad.

THE SWAHILI DHOWS

Hand built from wood and the first watercraft
outfitted with the lateen sail, which eventually
enabled Europeans to navigate the Atlantic and
land in America, the dhow remains the preferred
mode of transport in the Swahili archipelago. Arab,
Persian and Indian traders sailed to Africa's east
coast as early as the 2nd century and international
commerce accelerated after Islam took hold in
the 14th century. Over time, cultures and customs
fused and Swahili life – with its Arabian-tinged
architecture and Indian-accented cuisine –
bloomed. Modern dhows still ferry people and
cargo between the Kenyan and Tanzanian islands,
and several fly the Rastafarian flag.

■ THE JOURNEY TODAY

There's a lot of ground to cover here, and it should be navigated as three separate itineraries. The North Africa branch begins in Tangier, Battuta's birthplace. Head south to ancient Fès, before journeying onto Marrakesh, where you'll be waylaid by snake charmers, out-of-control donkey carts, trendy poufs and ancient Berber balms. It's possible to travel overland through Algeria and Tunisia to Egypt, but consider flying to Cairo or Alexandria. The domain of Alexander the Great and Cleopatra is now an edgy, modern town with legions of young artists and writers haunting midnight cafes, which may explain its recent role in the country's political upheaval.

Your coastal ramble begins on the Kenyan island of Lamu, the most authentic Swahili island on the Indian Ocean. Lamu Town is a carless Unesco treasure trove with labyrinthine alleys, ancient and tall Swahili buildings made from coral, and clamorous ports stacked with wooden dhows. On the windward side of the island, the village of Shela rises from, and disappears into, silky white dunes.

Further south, sprawling Mombasa is essentially a string of beach towns with a faded and frayed ancient core. In Tanzania, Kilwa's ports are now in ruins, but they are Unesco sites and still worth a visit, and Zanzibar is sublime. Its interior is suffused with spice cultivation, its beaches are powdery white and kissed by turquoise bays, and the Stone Town night market has old school Swahili grace. The music of Bamako, the dusty, brainy streets of Timbuktu and the salt market on the Niger River in Mopti are all good reasons to follow Battuta to Mali, where you can taste caravan life in the Sahara. But when it's time to go back to Morocco, you might consider flying.

■ SHORTCUT

Narrow down Battuta's path to a single bite by staying in his native Morocco and visiting its three fine cities. Alternatively, head to the island of Lamu and ply the waters from sweet Lamu to luscious Zanzibar aboard a dhow.

■ DETOUR

Battuta spent time in old Constantinople, but you can retrace the steps of Byzantine emperors in Istanbul where you'll marvel at the magnificent mosques built by Ottoman sultans on the city's seven hills and wander the cobbled streets of ancient Jewish, Greek and Armenian neighbourhoods. Centuries of urban sprawl unfurl before you on ferries up the Bosphorus or Golden Horn and you can quickly cross between religiously conservative suburbs in Asia to hedonistic hot spots along the European shore.

93

OPENING SPREAD Ready for business: a water seller in Rabat, Morocco. **ABOVE** All aboard: a Tuareg camel train crosses the Sahara. **LEFT** Back to basics: traditional dhows near Zanzibar.

ARMCHAIR

❋ *The Travels of Ibn Battuta: in the Near East, Asia and Africa, 1325–1354* (Ibn Battuta) The man's own account of his world travels translated by Samuel Lee in the 1820s. The prose is dated, but the story can still stir the soul.

❋ *Traveling Man* (James Rumford) Rumford distills the essence and poetry of Battuta's journey for young readers. It's perfect for eight- to 12-year-olds.

❋ *The Adventures of Ibn Battuta* (Ross E Dunn) A much more accessible read, this biography follows Battuta along his entire route into China and India as well as Africa and the Middle East, and was the first Battuta book to gain a wide Western audience.

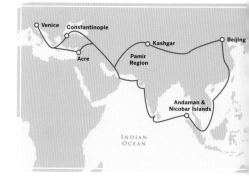

MARCO POLO'S EXPLORATION ROUTE

In the 13th century, Marco Polo sailed along Greece's west coast to Turkey, then through the Middle East and Central Asia to China, clocking over 39,000km. Or did he? Some sceptics dispute the extent of Marco's journey, inadvertently cementing his fame even further.

94

In the mid-13th century, Venice was a major power in the Mediterranean, always on the lookout for fresh commercial ventures. This inspired Venetian brothers Nicolo and Maffeo Polo to sail with a cargo of precious stones from Constantinople to the Crimea. They ended up in Karakoram (now in Mongolia), the seat of Kublai Khan, who made them ambassadors to the pope on the condition that the pope send 100 of his best priests to argue the merits of their faith. If they won Kublai over, he promised to convert his whole empire to Christianity. When they returned home, no one believed a word of their exploits.

Marco wasn't born when father Nicolo and uncle Maffeo set out on their journey; when they returned, he was a teenager. Soon after, the Polos returned to Kublai's court, taking Marco, aged 20, with them. They headed for Balkh and the Hindu Kush, Badakhshan and the Pamirs, past Kashgar, Yarkand and the southern route around the Taklamakan Desert, reaching China via Dunhuang and the Gansu Corridor. Kublai found Marco exceptionally intelligent and made him a trusted adviser, charged with the task of bringing news of Kublai's far-flung empire, little of which the khan had ever seen. After 16 years, the Polos were allowed home, taking the sea route from the east coast of China around India and up the Gulf, arriving back in Venice in 1295. History repeated itself: no one recognised the Polos or believed their story.

Years later, during a war with Genoa, Marco was captured. In prison, he dictated the story of his travels, the basis for arguably the first and most popular and widely read travel story ever. Even now, many still doubt poor Marco, pointing to the fact that Chinese imperial records make no mention of him. On his deathbed, Marco refused to recant, parrying the doubters for one final time with the comeback: 'I have not told the half of what I saw.'

ESSENTIAL EXPERIENCES

Visiting Venice, Marco's home town.

✱ Arriving at Acre, the wonderfully preserved city of stone that hasn't changed much since Marco passed through.

✱ **Discovering that the Andaman and Nicobar Islands, rather than being home to cannibals with dog's heads, as Marco reported, are in fact a tropical paradise.**

✱ Visiting the famed Marco Polo Bridge in Beijing. Dating from 1189 and praised by the great traveller himself, it has 485 carved stone lions, each different from the other.

✱ **Trying to find the 'dogs as big as donkeys' that Marco claimed he saw in Tibet.**

DISTANCE - 39,000KM | **COUNTRIES COVERED** - ITALY, GREECE, TURKEY, ISRAEL, IRAN, INDIA, CHINA | **IDEAL TIME COMMITMENT** - 16 TO 24 YEARS | **BEST TIME OF YEAR** - ANY TIME YOU FEEL THE MARCO SPIRIT COURSING THROUGH YOUR VEINS. **ESSENTIAL TIP** - WHEN YOU ARRIVE HOME, STICK TO YOUR STORY, NO MATTER WHAT.A

MARCO TRIVIA

The sheer scale of Marco's journey can be measured by the number of far-flung countries where he left his mark:

✳ Marco was credited with igniting Europe's feverish hunt for a quick sea passage to the aromatic Spice Islands for the precious namesake.

✳ Sumatra in Indonesia was once known as Samudra (Ocean) – Marco corrupted the name to 'Sumatra' in his 1292 report on the area.

✳ It's said that Marco was born on Lorcula Island in Croatia in 1254, where the house that was believed to have been his is open to the public today.

HANGZHOU

Hangzhou, the capital of Zhejiang, is one of China's most famous tourist sites. Located at the southern end of the Grand Canal and surrounded by fertile farmlands, it's been a significant cultural centre for hundreds of years. Today, the main reason for visiting is the storied West Lake, an oasis of beauty. Praised by emperors and revered by poets, the lake has figured large in the Chinese imagination. For Polo buffs, the other reason to visit is to experience a city Marco described as one of the most splendid in the world (realistically, though, Hangzhou has become a generic modern-Chinese city).

THE JOURNEY TODAY

Tajikistan is an anomaly, a Persian-speaking outpost in a predominantly Turkic region in ex-Soviet Central Asia. It's also the land that Marco Polo passed through on his way to China, and where today the rare, curly-horned Marco Polo sheep graze. You contemplate its fragile patchwork of mountain valleys, clans, languages and identities, and how the fierce civil war in the 1990s took tens of thousands of lives. Guarded optimism has returned to the people, who are looking to the future, but you are firmly looking to the past, wondering what Marco saw when he came to the Pamir region – the 'Roof of the World'.

Marco was struck by the Pamirs and its otherworldly qualities, describing the region as 'so lofty and cold that you can not even see any birds flying. And I must notice also that because of this great cold, fire does not burn so bright, nor give out so much heat as usual'. It's this stark natural location that makes it Tajikistan's most beautiful sight, with stupendous high-altitude scenery, warm mountain hospitality and the Pamir Highway, a monumental road trip.

You take a minibus to the Tajik half of the atmospheric, remote Wakhan Valley. As you travel further into the valley, you experience a giddy rush from the knowledge that Marco travelled through here in 1274. Perhaps what Marco meant with his famous final comment, you ponder, is that mere words are woefully inadequate in a place of such astounding wonderment as this.

There are many side valleys along the route that reveal stunning views of the 7000m peaks of the Hindu Kush (Killer of Hindus). With a name like that, you realise you're in a place where the weight of history is thick and heavy.

SHORTCUT

Venice, Marco's home town, is a good shortcut for those wanting to quickly absorb that Marco Polo feeling. At Palazzo Ducale, the grand Sala delle Mappe contains maps from 1762 that depict the Republic's territories and Marco's voyages. In Cannaregio, at No 5845 in Corte Seconda del Milion, you can admire what is supposed to be the Polo family house, although others say his house disappeared to make way for the Teatro Malibran.

DETOUR

Any of the countries Marco visited could provide satisfying itineraries. As he went to so many places over three continents, it's really just a matter of choosing your poison – whichever culture, continent or country takes your fancy – opening up a guidebook and planning your trip. Try the Pamir region in Tajikistan, which enchanted Marco so much and which today is still known as the 'Roof of the World': magical, beguiling and spectacular. It will get your Polo juices oozing in no time at all.

OPENING SPREAD Marco sailed through the Indonesian Archipelago on the way to Sri Lanka and India. **ABOVE** Market women in Little Andaman, a far cry from Marco's tall tales of strange hybrid creatures in these parts. **LEFT** Practice makes perfect: Tai Chi devotees in Hangzhou, one of Marco's favourite cities.

ARMCHAIR

* ***Marco Polo*** (1938) Starring Gary Cooper as Marco, this is a typically risible Hollywood attempt to bring ancient history to the screen. For her role, Lana Turner, playing an 'oriental', was forced to shave her eyebrows off and replace them with black, slanting fakes.

* ***Marco Polo*** (1964) The cult British TV series *Doctor Who* tackled the Marco Polo legend, with the good doctor traveling back through time to thwart an assassination attempt on the Kublai Khan.

* ***Casanova*** (1927) Alexandre Volkoff's silent film re-creates 18-century Venice. Other films set in Marco's home town include Orson Welles' *Othello* (1952), Luchino Visconti's *Death in Venice* (1971), Nicolas Roeg's *Don't Look Now* (1973) and Paul Schrader's *The Comfort of Strangers* (1990).

* ***The Travels of Marco Polo*** (Marco Polo) Thrill to Marco's original adventures spread across two volumes.

BURKE & WILLS

TRACK THROUGH THE AUSTRALIAN DESERT AND TROPICS ON THE ILL-FATED TRAIL OF THE COUNTRY'S MOST FAMOUS EXPLORERS. THE LAND IS RIFE WITH REMINDERS OF THE FIRST EXPEDITION TO CROSS THE CONTINENT, EVEN THOUGH IT DIDN'T RETURN.

98

In a nation that celebrates a wartime defeat as one of its major holidays, and then names a swimming pool after a drowned prime minister, it's unsurprising that the ill-fated Robert O'Hara Burke and William Wills should have become national heroes and icons.

In August 1860, with much fanfare, Burke, with Wills as his second-in-charge, led an expedition out from Melbourne, intent on being the first to cross the Australian continent. Chosen by a committee of the Royal Society of Victoria, Burke was neither an explorer nor a surveyor, had no scientific training, had never led an expedition of any kind and was considered to be, if anything, a very poor bushman. He also ignored the advice from earlier explorers to enlist the help of Aboriginal guides.

At Cooper Creek they set up a depot and Burke, Wills and two others left for the Gulf of Carpentaria, setting out at the height of summer to walk 1100km through central Australia to the sea. It says something of their fortitude and sheer guts that, on 11 February 1861, they made it, reaching the mangroves that barred their view of the gulf. Camp 119 was their northernmost camp and can be visited today.

Turning their backs on the sea, the rush back south became a life-and-death stagger. When they arrived back at the Cooper Creek depot, they were astonished to find that their men had retreated to Menindee just hours before. The famous Dig Tree, on which the departing men had carved the message 'DIG 3FT N.W. APR. 21 1861', still stands on the banks of Cooper Creek. The buried supplies weren't enough to revive the explorers, and Burke and Wills wasted away, dying on the banks of this desert oasis. They were survived by rescued expedition member John King, and a legend as large as the Australian outback itself.

ESSENTIAL EXPERIENCES

✳ **Digging the carved message in the Dig Tree – no Burke and Wills pilgrimage is complete without a visit here.**

✳ Paying homage at the separate Burke and Wills Memorials along the banks of Cooper Creek, in the Innamincka Regional Reserve, marking the spots where the pair died.

✳ **Celebrating the survivors at the memorials to John King and Alfred Howitt, the leader of the search party, also in the Innamincka Regional Reserve.**

✳ Seeking out the blazed trees at Camp 119 – 15 trees were blazed with the letter 'B'; some are still alive and are marked with metal discs.

DISTANCE - 3300KM | **COUNTRIES COVERED** - AUSTRALIA | **IDEAL TIME COMMITMENT** - ONE TO TWO MONTHS | **BEST TIME OF YEAR** - MAY TO SEPTEMBER | **ESSENTIAL TIP** - HONE YOUR 4WD SKILLS BEFORE TACKLING THE CENTRAL DESERTS.

ROBERT O'HARA BURKE

History has laid so much of the blame for the expedition's tragic end on the head, and the inexperience, of its leader, Robert O'Hara Burke. Born in 1820 in the town of St Clerans in Ireland (a plaque marks his childhood home in Dominick St) he joined the Irish Constabulatory before migrating to Australia in 1853. Here, he worked as a policeman, rising to police inspector and police superintendent, throughout the state of Victoria. Somehow it was a background that endeared him to the Royal Society of Victoria, which selected him to lead the Victorian Exploring Expedition. The rest, as they say, is history.

▨ THE JOURNEY TODAY

There are memories of, and memorials to, Burke and Wills along the length of their expedition. Conversely, you began your journey at their graves, in Melbourne's General Cemetery, just metres from the spot where they started their expedition in Royal Park and so far from where it ended. And you will end at Camp 119, where they made their final camp before slogging off into the impenetrable mangroves and mud, assuming (correctly) that the salty taste of the water meant they'd reached the sea. But it's around the South Australian desert town of Innamincka that you'll spend most of your time.

Near to here, just across the border in Queensland, Burke and Wills established their depot before setting off north for the Gulf of Carpentaria. Few travellers make it here – it's 1600km from Sydney, after all – but the Dig Tree on the banks of Cooper Creek at Nappa Merrie is part of the national psyche and perhaps the most important reminder of early European exploration in Australia. The blaze on the coolabah tree is faded, though it still bears an aura of history, but it's the irony of the location that most strikes you: this muddy Cooper Creek and its environs supported generations of Aboriginal people and yet Burke and Wills starved to death. This desert heat that could cook a rock does, however, give you some idea of the potential for hardship.

Back closer to Innamincka, the expedition's death throes are visible. East of town, nearing Cullyamurra Waterhole, is the stone cairn marking the spot where Burke's body was found. On the other side of town, by Tilcha Waterhole, is a similar monument to Wills. There's a happier end to the day, because a short distance from the Wills Memorial is the

ARMCHAIR

* ***The Dig Tree*** (Sarah Murgatroyd) The classic Burke and Wills history, with the author retracing the pair's steps across Australia.

* ***Burke's Soldier*** (Alan Atwood) Enjoyable fictional account of the expedition, told from the perspective of its surviving member, John King.

* **Cooper's Creek** (Alan Moorhead) The early (1963) definitive account of the expedition.

* ***Correspondence of WJ Wills*** (William Wills) Letters from before and during the expedition from Wills, kept at the State Library of Victoria.

* ***Burke & Wills*** (1985) This movie, starring Jack Thompson, recounts the story of the expedition.

marker indicating the place where John King was found alive by a search party. That seems worth celebrating back at the bar in Innamincka.

SHORTCUT

You needn't leave the cities to get some taste of Australia's Burke and Wills passion. At the National Museum in Canberra, the Burke and Wills Collection includes a leather water bottle belonging to Burke, and a breastplate given to the Yandruwandha people of Cooper Creek for the assistance they gave to the expedition. In Melbourne you can visit their large grave in the General Cemetery in inner-suburban Parkville. Burke's Bible and camel saddlebags are in a museum in Beechworth in country Victoria.

DETOUR

If you're adhering to Burke and Wills' route, you'll find yourself in Menindee at some point. Here, Burke and Wills stayed at the Maidens Hotel, which still has guest rooms. From the small town you can venture out to experience a couple of other bits of classic Australiana: the inland, oh-so-ocker city of Broken Hill; and nearby Silverton, an old silver-mining town made famous as a setting for the *Mad Max* films.

HERVE HUGHES | CORBIS

OPENING SPREAD A harsh Aussie landscape, yet suprisingly diverse: dead trees, pelicans and wetlands at the Coongie Lakes, Innamincka Regional Reserve. **ABOVE** The Simpson Desert's track. **BELOW** Life on Mars? No – eroded peaks in the Simpson Desert.

COOPER CREEK

No single place is as central to the Burke and Wills story as Cooper Creek, the site of their depot, the Dig Tree and the pair's eventual deaths. Though it was named a 'creek' in 1845 by explorer Charles Sturt, it is Australia's fifth-largest river, flowing more than 1100km from central Queensland to Lake Eyre. One of its most enticing sights is Cullyamurra Waterhole, 13km east of Innamincka, stretching upriver for more than 6km and reputed to be the deepest waterhole in central Australia – it has been measured at 28m and has never been known to dry up, which is a great rarity in these parts. Near its end there are Aboriginal rock engravings.

FERDINAND MAGELLAN

BRAVE THE HIGH SEAS OR JUST WITNESS THE KEY MOMENTS IN THE WORLD'S FIRST CIRCUMNAVIGATION, AN EXPEDITION THAT TOOK THE PORTUGUESE EXPLORER ACROSS WILD LANDS AND EVEN WILDER SEAS.

102

On 10 August 1519, Ferdinand Magellan and a fleet of five ships and more than 230 crewmen set sail from Seville, heading down the Río Guadalquivir and out into the Atlantic Ocean. Their mission – and Magellan's private passion – was to sail west, round Cape Horn at the southern tip of South America and set out across the Pacific to the Spice Islands (the modern-day Maluku Islands of Indonesia), famed for their spice production.

After a year of leapfrogging down the South American coast, he found the waterway that now bears his name, the Strait of Magellan, cutting through southernmost South America and out into a new ocean, the largest in the world, which he named the Pacific. An island-hopping journey – French Polynesia, Marianas, Guam – took the expedition across the Pacific and near to its goal as it sailed into the Philippines in March 1521.

A few weeks later, Magellan made the fatal mistake of underestimating the fighting spirit of Chief Lapu-Lapu on the island of Mactan. As the standard-bearer for Spain, Magellan had managed to curry the favour of all the most powerful chiefs of the region, with the single exception of Lapu-Lapu. So with 60 of his best soldiers, Magellan sailed to the island to teach him a lesson in gunboat diplomacy. Lapu-Lapu and his men defended their island with unimagined ferocity, and Magellan was soon back on his boat, fatally wounded by a spear to his head and a poisoned arrow to his leg. He died on 27 April.

The expedition continued on without its leader, reaching the Spice Islands and rounding the Cape of Good Hope at the African tip. Only one ship, the *Victoria*, made it back to Spain, arriving three years after it departed. Just 18 members of the original crew survived the voyage, but the world's first circumnavigation was complete.

ESSENTIAL EXPERIENCES

✻ **Visiting Sanlúcar de Barrameda, at the mouth of the Río Guadalquivir, where Magellan sailed out into the sea.**

✻ Rubbing the toe of one of the indigenous figures at the base of the Magellan statue in Punta Arenas, an act said to guarantee good luck and a future return to the region.

✻ **Docking at Umatac in Guam, the site of Magellan's landing, to visit the Magellan Monument.**

✻ Paying homage to the Magellan Cross in Cebu City.

✻ **Mourning the death of an explorer at the Mactan Shrine, the site of Magellan's slaying.**

DISTANCE - APPROXIMATELY 30,000KM │ **COUNTRIES COVERED** - SPAIN, BRAZIL, ARGENTINA, CHILE, FRENCH POLYNESIA, GUAM, PHILIPPINES, INDONESIA │ **IDEAL TIME COMMITMENT** - SIX MONTHS TO ONE YEAR │ **BEST TIME OF YEAR** - DEPENDENT ON SEA CONDITIONS   **ESSENTIAL TIP** - STICK TO MAGELLAN'S LANDINGS UNLESS YOU'RE A TRUE SALTY DOG.

FERDINAND MAGELLAN

Born in northern Portugal in 1480, and orphaned at the age of 10, Ferdinand Magellan first took to the seas at 25, travelling to Portuguese India, where he spent eight years. It was the Spice Islands, however, that obsessed him, and when permission to lead an expedition to the islands, sailing around the tip of South America, was refused by King Manuel I, he took his plans across the border into Spain. The Spanish king was more taken by the idea, and in 1519 he set out on an expedition that would become the first to circumnavigate the world, though Magellan himself was killed in the Philippines during the voyage.

THE JOURNEY TODAY

You could chase Ferdinand Magellan across the globe, but the most tangible reminders are in the Philippines, Magellan's last, fatal stop. You begin on the island of Samar, boarding a public bangka (outrigger canoe) in Guiuan for the two-hour sail across to tiny Homonhon Island, the first island in the Philippines that Magellan set foot on. There's little here to see – Magellan's footprints blew away centuries ago – but you have the sense now that you're on his trail.

Cebu was his next goal, and it is yours also. It's unrecognisable from the island of 600 years ago – it's now the most densely populated island in the country – but it's clear that he was here...and welcome. In a stone rotunda opposite the city hall in Cebu City is the so-called Magellan's Cross, a crucifix that apparently contains a few splinters from a cross Magellan planted on the shores of Cebu in 1521. Even if you doubt its authenticity, it is something tangible, and you're in the minority of doubters, for this is one of the island's most revered and sacred objects. Looking up inside the rotunda, there is a painted scene showing Magellan erecting the cross (actually, the locals are doing all the work – Magellan's just standing around with his mates).

Journey's end (and hopefully it ends better for you than it did for Ferdinand) isn't far away. Just a taxi ride from the city is Mactan Island, the improbable site of one of the defining moments in the Philippines' history. Now home to an oil depot and a string of ritzy beach resorts, the island was also the death of Magellan – literally. His death is commemorated at the Mactan Shrine, where a stone plinth bears the date that Magellan was felled, though you're more taken by the statue next to it, of a ripped and pumped Lapu-Lapu, Magellan's slayer, looking a bit like a fantasy action figure – history, as ever, being written by the victors.

SHORTCUT

For a glimpse of Magellan's lingering influence, head for Punta Arenas in Chile. This Patagonian city sits on the Strait of Magellan and at its heart, in Plaza Muñoz Gamero, is a large statue of Magellan, his chin raised heroically to the sky. You can take a kayaking trip into Magellan's namesake waterway, or a tour to Monumento Natural Los Pingüinos, home to Magellanic penguins – named after guess who?

DETOUR

Magellan began his grand journey in Seville, just as Christopher Columbus did 21 years before him. To pay homage to the earlier explorer, visit Seville's cathedral. Inside the cathedral's southern door stands Columbus' elaborate tomb, dating from 1902. The contents of the tomb are the subject of debate, with some arguing that the explorer is (mainly) buried in the Dominican Republic.

104

NICO STENGERT | PHOTOLIBRARY

OPENING SPREAD Troubled waters in the Strait of Magellan, named after the hero of our story. **ABOVE (L)** One of the 'lucky' indigenous figures at the base of the Magellan statue in Punta Arenas. **ABOVE (R)** An aerial view of the Cape of Good Hope. **RIGHT** A colourful performer in the Spice Islands.

ARMCHAIR

* ***Over the Edge of the World: Magellan's Terrifying Circumnavigation of the Globe*** (Laurence Bergreen) Read the full story of Magellan's circumnavigation.

* ***The First Voyage Around the World (1519–1522): An Account of Magellan's Expedition*** (Antonio Pigafetta) A first-hand account of the expedition from one of the 18 original crewmen who survived it.

* ***Magellan*** (Tim Joyner) Detailed biography of the explorer, going beyond his famous journey.

* ***In Pursuit of Longitude: Magellan and the Antimeridian*** (André Rossfelder) Focuses on the more prosaic fact of Magellan's journey: that he didn't set out to circumnavigate the globe, just to show that the Spice Islands were in Spain's political sphere.

MALUKU

Magellan had his eye on Maluku and so now does a growing trickle of visitors. These petite little morsels of paradise are a dream-come-true for seekers of superb snorkelling and picture-perfect white-sand beaches. Protected from mass tourism by distance and a (now outdated) reputation for civil unrest, its dreamy desert islands remain remarkably hospitable and inexpensive. Known as the original 'Spice Islands', they beckoned Indian, Chinese, Arab and, later, European adventurers who all came here in search of cloves and nutmeg. It marked the beginning of European colonialism. The Portuguese arrived in 1510, sparking interest in the islands from a bloke named Ferdinand Magellan.

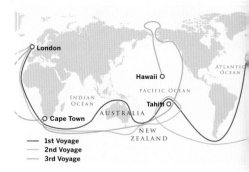

CAPTAIN COOK IN THE PACIFIC

CAPTAIN COOK'S PACIFIC SOJOURN WAS ONE HELL OF A TRIP. HE LEFT HIS MARK EVERYWHERE, AS NUMEROUS STATUES AND PLAQUES COMMEMORATING HIM TESTIFY. IN THREE VOYAGES TO THE SOUTH SEAS, HE DISCOVERED JUST ABOUT EVERYTHING THERE WAS TO DISCOVER IN THIS VAST REGION.

106

Captain James Cook (1728–79) explored more of the earth's surface than anyone in history, a legacy that is impossible to ignore when travelling in the Pacific. In a converted coal ship, the *Endeavour*, Cook sailed to Tahiti and then became the first European to land at New Zealand and the east coast of Australia. Though the ship almost sank after striking the Great Barrier Reef, with almost half of the crew dying from disease and accidents, the *Endeavour* managed to return home in 1771 with amazing accounts of exotic curiosities.

Emboldened, Cook made a return voyage from 1772 to 1775, becoming the first navigator to reach the Antarctic Circle and putting paid to the ancient myth that a vast, habitable continent surrounded the South Pole. Cook also crossed the Pacific from Easter Island to Melanesia, charting dozens of islands along the way.

On his final voyage from 1776 to 1779, he was determined to find a Northwest Passage between the Atlantic and Pacific, becoming the first European to visit Hawaii before sailing along North America's west coast from Oregon to Alaska. Forced back by Arctic pack ice, he returned to Hawaii where islanders initially greeted him as a Polynesian god before killing him. In a single decade of discovery, Cook had filled in the map of the Pacific, and as one French navigator lamented, 'left his successors with little to do but admire his exploits'.

Today, most visitors to the Pacific avoid the wet season, when rain is dumped in either isolated showers or seasonal deluges. As the region is in the tropics, the temperature doesn't vary much – it's always hot – but during the wet season, heat, humidity and persistent rain can combine to make things uncomfortable. It's also the time when most cyclones hit and when some places may be impossible to reach. On the other hand, most of the rain falls at night, and this is the time when other tourists will not accompany you.

ESSENTIAL EXPERIENCES

✳ **Marvelling at Mt Yasur in Vanuatu, one of the world's most accessible volcanoes.**

✳ Surfing in the Solomons and at surfing's birthplace in Tahiti.

✳ **Visiting laid-back Fiji and any of its 300 exotic islands.**

✳ Getting down at an island night in Rarotonga, spectacular shows that combine traditional dance and music with a lavish buffet of local food.

✳ **Wondering at the evocative volcanic setting of Easter Islands' Rano Raraku, birthplace of the mysterious moai statues.**

✳ Swimming in the Cook Islands' stunning Anatakitaki Cave.

DISTANCE - AROUND 12,000KM | **COUNTRIES COVERED** - TAHITI, NEW ZEALAND, AUSTRALIA, FIJI, THE COOK ISLANDS, TONGA, EASTER ISLAND, NORFOLK ISLAND, NEW CALEDONIA, VANUATU, HAWAII | **IDEAL TIME COMMITMENT** - TWO MONTHS | **BEST TIME OF YEAR** - ANYTIME BUT THE WET SEASON | **ESSENTIAL TIP** - BRING EVERYTHING YOU NEED, AS YOU MAY NOT BE ABLE TO BUY IT IN THE PACIFIC.

THE SCIENCE OF CAPTAIN COOK

In his three great expeditions between 1769 and 1779, Captain Cook filled the map of the Pacific so comprehensively that future expeditions could do little more than join the dots. His missions were charged with ambitious tasks. One, for the Royal Society, was to observe the transit of Venus as it passed across the sun from three very distant places with the hope that the distance from the earth to the sun could be calculated. Tahiti was one of the three measuring points (the others were in Norway and Canada). The instruments of the day were insufficiently accurate to achieve Cook's first objective, although his expeditions did yield impressive scientific work.

PACIFIC TATTOOS

The journals of Captain Cook are full of references to the tatau (tattoos) of Pacific islanders; both sexes were tattooed from the age of 14 to mark puberty and their arrival into adulthood, and later to signify tribal status. The apotheosis of the art was on the flesh of Marquesan warriors who sported a full-body 'armour' of toughened tattoos, even on their eyelids and tongues. In Tahiti, Samoa and Tonga, elaborate tattoos were worn on the buttocks and hips, and in Melanesia body scarring was a popular alternative. Today, Samoan tattooists remain strongly traditional and Tahitian tattoos are a powerful link to pre-colonial cultures. Full arm and leg designs and even full-body patterns have become popular, particularly among Tahiti's traditional dancers.

■ THE JOURNEY TODAY

You land in Rarotonga, in the Cook Islands, named after the man himself. You've heard that there are 15 tiny specks of land that make up the Cooks, scattered over 2 million sq km of empty sea. You yourself feel like a speck in the middle of the Pacific, making you very aware of the monumental scale of Cook's journey. Rarotonga is a South Seas paradise: coconut trees, cerulean lagoons, sweeping arcs of powder-white sand. But you also find funky cafes, swish restaurants and cool bars. Cook was definitely onto something, you think, as you head to one of those bars to down another island cocktail. There you meet a friendly local, who suggests that you really need to visit an outer island. You accept, thinking that for all Rarotonga's charms, you need to get as close as possible to the authentic culture that Cook would have witnessed.

You book a flight to the rocky, reef-fringed island of 'Atiu, where Cook arrived in 1777. Once, 'Atiu was legendary for its ferocious, ruthless warriors. Today it's far more sedate, a haven for naturalists and bird-lovers. A few hours after you land, another local befriends you and treats you to a traditional 'Atiuan *tumunu* (bush-beer drinking session). After that, you're exhausted and ready for sleep.

The next day, you bump into your friend in the street, and he offers to be your guide to Marae Orongo, near Oravaru Beach. This, he explains, was once the most sacred *marae* (ceremonial place) on the island and many locals won't go near it. 'But I will show you,' he explains. You follow him down the track, and can't help thinking that your trip to the islands, which was only meant to be a few days, could easily extend to several weeks.

■ SHORTCUT

To cover Cook's tracks would be a monumental task. Try a mini-itinerary, although 'mini' in the case of the Pacific should be taken with a pinch of salt. One to two months should be enough to hop around in style. Begin in Fiji, Vanuatu and New Caledonia, then explore Polynesia in Tahiti and French Polynesia and Rarotonga in the Cook Islands for a total distance of around 12,000km.

■ DETOUR

Because the Pacific is so vast, it's remarkably easy to get 'off the beaten track'. Try Pitcairn Island, one of the world's most isolated places, and infamous for both the *Bounty* mutiny and the 2004 sex-abuse trials. Another option is Tokelau, although it's difficult just getting there: there are no planes, only a boat every couple of weeks. In the Solomons, Rennell Island is a World Heritage Site that few travellers visit. Tuvalu is also a little-visited destination. Locals make up for its isolation, with around 4500 Tuvaluans packed onto tiny Fongafale Islet, the main island.

OPENING SPREAD The imposing sight of an active volcano on Vanautu. **ABOVE** Lovely Bora Bora, Tahiti. **LEFT** One of the Pacific's greatest enigmas: the stately stone heads on Easter Island.

ARMCHAIR

* *Blue Latitudes: Boldly Going Where Captain Cook has Gone Before* (Tony Horwitz) A frustrating, funny and insightful look at Cook's voyages.

* *The Happy Isles of Oceania – Paddling the Pacific* (Paul Theroux) Details the author's kayaking trip through the Pacific Islands.

* *Mutiny on the Bounty* (1962) Starring Marlon Brando in this version, and more recently, Anthony Hopkins and Mel Gibson.

* *The Thin Red Line* (1998) Terrence Malick highlights the beautiful singing of the Solomon Islanders and Guadalcanal's stunning scenery.

* *Rapa Nui* (1994) Kevin Costner's film gives the feel of Easter Island's remote charm.

* *His Best Pacific Writings* (Robert Louis Stevenson) Essential reading for travelling to Samoa, French Polynesia, Kiribati and the Marshall Islands.

AMELIA EARHART: THE FINAL FLIGHT

AMELIA EARHART: AUTHOR, WOMEN'S-RIGHTS ADVOCATE, CELEBRITY, FASHION ICON, AVIATION PIONEER. TRACE HER FINAL JOURNEY, WHEN SHE ONLY HAD TO CROSS THE PACIFIC TO COMPLETE A QUEST TO BE THE FIRST WOMAN TO FLY AROUND THE GLOBE – ONLY TO DISAPPEAR WITHOUT TRACE.

110

In 1932, Amelia Earhart, aged 34, became the first woman to fly solo nonstop across the Atlantic. Five years later, she set out to be the first woman to fly around the world, this time along with a navigator, Fred Noonan. On 21 May 1937, she took off from Oakland, California on the first leg of a journey that would take her from the US to New Guinea via South America, Africa, India and Southeast Asia, and across the Pacific.

Simply listing her stops on this monumental 35,000km-journey is enough to impart the scope and achievement of the journey: Burbank, California; Tucson, Arizona; New Orleans, Louisiana; Miami, Florida; San Juan, Puerto Rico; Cumana, Venezuela; Paramaribo, Suriname; Fortaleza, Brazil; Natal, Brazil; St Louis, Senegal; Dakar, Senegal; Gao, Mali; N'Djamena, Chad; Al-Fashir, Sudan; Khartoum, Sudan; Massawa, Ethiopia; Assab, Ethiopia; Karachi, Pakistan; Calcutta, India; Sittwe, Burma; Rangoon, Burma; Bangkok, Thailand; Singapore; Bandung, Indonesia; Surabaya, Indonesia; Hupang, Indonesia; Darwin, Australia; and Lae, New Guinea.

On 2 July 1937, she left Lae bound for Howland Island, the last leg of her journey. She never made it, the plane vanishing completely without trace. This disappearing act has spawned many theories as to what happened. Was she shot down from the sky by the Japanese, held prisoner on Saipan and executed as a spy? Was Noonan a raging alcoholic who fatally compromised the mission with his erratic behaviour? Of course, there's the obligatory UFO theory, *de rigueur* for disappeared pilots. So this one goes: Earhart was in the employ of US intelligence. This led her to make contact with an alien ship, which either malfunctioned on contact or deliberately blew her out of the sky, depending upon which conspiracy theorist you believe.

ESSENTIAL EXPERIENCES

✻ **Making a pilgrimage to the Amelia Earhart Birthplace Museum in Atchison, Kansas.**

✻ Photographing the Amelia statue at Burbank Airport, where she took off to begin her journey.

✻ **Photographing Amelia's original home in Toluca Lake, California, which has been carefully preserved and maintained by the current owners (Amelia planned her fatal trip in the courtyard here).**

✻ Visiting Trepassey in Newfoundland, Canada, the launching place of Amelia's first-woman-across-the-Atlantic flight in 1928.

✻ **Travelling to Lae, the launching place for the beginning of the end.**

DISTANCE - 35,000KM | **COUNTRIES COVERED** - USA, PUERTO RICO, VENEZUELA, SURINAME, BRAZIL, SENEGAL, MALI, CHAD, SUDAN, ETHIOPIA, PAKISTAN, INDIA, BURMA, THAILAND, SINGAPORE, INDONESIA, AUSTRALIA, NEW GUINEA | **IDEAL TIME COMMITMENT** - THREE MONTHS | **BEST TIME OF YEAR** - ANY TIME YOU FEEL A BOUT OF HEROISM COMING ON | **ESSENTIAL TIP** - DON'T CRASH.

It was first thought that the mystery of Earhart and Noonan had been solved in 1941, when British soldiers discovered two sets of bones and shoes on remote Nikumaroro. However, a British doctor declared that the bones were of two European men and the matter was put to rest. Then in 1998 the doctor's notes were re-examined by modern specialists, who concluded that he must have got it wrong. According to them, one set of bones belonged clearly to a Caucasian female, 170cm tall – which just happened to be Earhart's vital statistics. Typically, the bones have long since vanished, allowing the mystery to remain.

'AMELIA – IS THAT YOU?' PART 2

In 2010, it was announced that more bone fragments had been found, on another deserted Pacific island located along the course of Earhart's final flight. Found nearby was old make-up, glass bottles and shells that had been prised apart. Scientists at the University of Oklahoma are trying to extract DNA from the bones to test the theory that Earhart and Noonan died as castaways. For now, the scientists are advising restraint – the bones may very well be a turtle's, as a turtle shell was also found nearby. Yet, even that fact opens a can of worms, because the shell was hollowed out. Did our castaways use it to collect rainwater?

■ THE JOURNEY TODAY

As you settle into the padded seat of your Lockheed Electra 10E, the sun rises beneath you, a truly wondrous sight. The Electra has custom-fitted gas tanks, larger than normal capacity, so you feel safe and secure as you slice through the air, knowing you have enough fuel to make the 4113km journey to Howland Island. You caught dysentery in Bandung, but it appears to have eased now – hopefully, you think, for your navigator's sake sitting behind you.

You quickly leaf through your log, noting all the stages of the journey and how happy you have felt. But you know you can't take too many things for granted, because the journey from Lae to Howland is the longest stretch you've done across water. At that point, your navigator tells you how utterly thankful he is that you had the foresight to strip all nonessential items from the plane so that more fuel could be taken on. You understand that Howland is but a tiny speck in the Pacific, very easy to miss, and so you are further reassured by the US Coast Guard, which sent ships to the island with instructions to burn all their lights at once for you to use as landing beacons.

After a while, you see something ominous: storms ahead. 'I thought they said the forecast was favourable!' cries the navigator, and you bite your lip with worry. 'We've come this far,' you reply. 'Nothing to fear.' Inside, though, you are scared because although you're near Howland you can't see the ships. You radio to the lead ship: 'Where are you? We can't see you.'

You check the fuel: it's low. 'Please reply,' you continue. 'We're at 1000ft.' And then the sky cracks.

■ SHORTCUT

For the potted history, visit one or more of the various Earhart landmarks scattered across the US, detailed in Essential Experiences (see boxed text, p110). But there is no easy or 'short way' into the mystery of everyone's favourite aviator: almost 75 years later, people still can't agree on how she disappeared or even what her true purpose was.

■ DETOUR

Visit the Amelia Earhart Birthplace Museum in Atchison, Kansas. The building is the home where Amelia was born, and contains the original rooms and interiors; family portraits on the walls; furniture that she owned, such as her desk and books; replicas of the Lockheed Electra 10E that flew her to her death; and photographs, interactive displays, maps and numerous curios. What it doesn't have is the answer to the mystery.

113

OPENING SPREAD For Amelia, a long way from home – a Lae highlander wearing a birds-of-paradise head dress. **ABOVE** A crowd at Burry Port in Wales watches as Amelia leaves, having arrived there as the first woman to cross the Atlantic. **LEFT** The magnificent beach at Fortaleza, Brazil.

ARMCHAIR

✳ **Flight For Freedom** (1943) This film popularised the theory that Earhart was working for US intelligence.

✳ **The Search for Amelia Earhart** (Fred Goener) This 1966 book worked on the assumption that the Japanese had captured her.

✳ **Close Encounters of the Third Kind** (1977) In Steven Spielberg's film, Earhart can be seen walking out of the alien mother ship along with other abductees.

✳ **'The 37s'** (1995) This episode of Star Trek Voyager played up the UFO angle, suggesting Earhart and Noonan had been abducted.

✳ **Amelia** (2009) The obligatory swanky Hollywood biopic starring Hilary Swank as the titular aviatrix.

VASCO DA GAMA DISCOVERS THE SEA ROUTE TO INDIA

PORTUGUESE EXPLORER VASCO DA GAMA COVERED AMAZING GROUND. IN THE 15TH CENTURY, HE DISCOVERED AN OCEAN PASSAGE FROM PORTUGAL TO THE EASTERN LANDS, THOUGHT IMPOSSIBLE. HE ARRIVED IN INDIA A YEAR LATER – A TRIP THAT, FOR ITS TIME, WAS AS MOMENTOUS AS MEN ON THE MOON.

114

Vasco da Gama's enduring fame resides in the fact that in 1497 he opened up a sea route previously thought impossible. From Lisbon he sailed to India via Africa, smashing the widespread belief that the Indian Ocean was not connected to any other ocean. But more than discovering a new route, his mission led to Portugal dominating the spice trade in the east and establishing the tiny nation as a global superpower.

Vasco's party rounded the Cape of Good Hope in Africa, sailed up the coast of East Africa and landed in Calicut, India, in 1498. A year later, they arrived back in Portugal with most of the crew dead from the hardships and travails of setting up trade posts in India and East Africa. In 1502, Vasco sailed again to India, this time with 20 ships to fight against Arab traders who were not willing to side with him, and to establish military dominance in Calicut and Goa. When he returned to Portugal with even more treasure and overseas power, he was feted by the king and was well on the way to becoming a legendary figure in his homeland. In 1524 he was named Viceroy of India, the country in which he eventually met his end, dying of malaria.

The irony of Vasco's hero worship is that he was actually a barbarous and heartless man, intent on crushing with the utmost savagery anyone who got in his way. Stories of his murderous ways are there if you look for them, and none are more horrific than the poor Brahmin spy who, upon being captured, had his lips and ears cut off and dog ears sewn on to his head before being sent back to his people, his hideous new appearance a warning to everyone not to mess with the great and good Vasco da Gama. Thus was the violent cruelty upon which the Age of Exploration was founded.

Remember that the next time you stay in one of the many 'Vasco da Gama Hotels' or eat in the numerous 'Vasco da Gama' restaurants dotted around the world.

ESSENTIAL EXPERIENCES

❋ **Sniffing out Vasco's trail in beautiful, relaxed Lisbon.**

❋ Looking for the florid Vasco da Gama clock in Durban, Natal, a Victorian monument presented by the Portuguese government in 1897.

❋ **Admiring the atmospheric, time-ravaged Tongoni ruins in northeastern Tanzania, an inadvertent port of call for Vasco when his ship ran aground there.**

❋ Visiting Malpe in southern India for St Mary's Island, where Vasco apparently landed in 1498.

❋ **Travelling to Inhambane, one of Mozambique's most charming towns, described by Vasco in a rare fit of goodwill as 'land of the good people'.**

DISTANCE - 9000KM | **COUNTRIES COVERED** - PORTUGAL, SOUTH AFRICA, TANZANIA, KENYA, INDIA | **IDEAL TIME COMMITMENT** - TWO YEARS | **BEST TIME OF YEAR** - WHENEVER VASCO'S SPIRIT COURSES THROUGHOUT YOUR VEINS | **ESSENTIAL TIP** - BE NICE TO EVERYONE.

PADRÃO DOS DESCOBRIMENTOS

Lisbon's massive Padrão dos Descobrimentos stands by the Tagus River. It's 52m high and carved in stone in the shape of the prow of a Portuguese caravel. The monument is a tribute to the Portuguese Age of Exploration, that golden time during the 15th and 16th centuries when Portuguese explorers boldly sallied forth and forged new trading routes to far-flung destinations all across the globe. Carved into the tip of the prow are the likenesses of 30 of Portugal's heroes of the age, including Vasco, of course, Ferdinand Magellan and King Manuel I.

■ THE JOURNEY TODAY

Lisbon, Portugal. The steep hillsides overlooking the Rio Tejo, regal monasteries, Gothic cathedrals, charming museums. And the delightful, narrow lanes of its backstreets, where you find yourself lost in thought, following one nook after another, thinking all the while about Vasco da Gama and his legacy. How did such an unassuming place come to dominate the East? In the 15th and 16th centuries, Lisbon was booming, unassailable, the opulent centre of a vast empire after Vasco's famous discovery of the sea route to India. His presence is all around, and yet you are still no closer to discovering the real connection between Lisbon and world domination.

You visit the National Museum of Ancient Art, which features religious treasures encrusted with gems, including the Monstrance of Belém, a reliquary made with gold brought back by Vasco on his second voyage. Your next stop is the National Pantheon, where you find marble cenotaphs commemorating historic and literary figures, with Vasco present and correct. You walk to the rooftop for some fresh air, and you are struck by the fabulous Alfama, Lisbon's oldest district, the river and of course the mighty Vasco da Gama Bridge, 17km long and 30m wide. The bridge vanishes into the distance, much like Vasco. Monuments and memorials are well and good, but they don't tell the real story – just what do people think of Vasco today? But then you just give up and go with the flow, letting Lisbon embrace you. You savour the warmly lit 1930s-era cafes, where you linger with espresso and fresh pastries, before walking along the seaside and embracing the city's youthful spirit that's all around. And yet underneath it all, despite this invigorating spirit-of-the-moment, Vasco remains on your mind.

ARMCHAIR

✳ *A Journal of the First Voyage of Vasco da Gama, 1497–1499* (Vasco da Gama) Vasco's journals have been produced in many editions – try this one, reissued in 2010.

✳ *Vasco da Gama: Renaissance Crusader* (Glenn J Ames), *The Three Voyages of Vasco da Gama* (Gaspar Corrêa) and *The Career and Legend of Vasco da Gama* (Sanjay Subrahmanyam) These are some of the numerous biographies and historical accounts.

✳ *Os Lusíadas* (Luís Vaz de Camões) Portugal's most outstanding literary figure enjoyed little fame or fortune in his lifetime. Only after his death was his genius recognised, thanks largely to this epic poem, written in 1572, telling of da Gama's 1497 Indian sea voyage.

■ SHORTCUT

Lisbon will definitely give you the flavour of Vasco da Gama's journey. Aside from those already mentioned, other Vasco attractions include the neighbourhood of Belém, from where Vasco set sail for India. His discovery of the sea route to India inspired the glorious Mosteiro dos Jerónimos, a Unesco World Heritage Site with exuberant architecture that broadcasts Vasco's triumphant journey. Vasco is interred in the lower chancel, just to the left of the entrance, in a place of honour opposite venerated 16th-century poet Luís de Camões.

■ DETOUR

If you are really intent on tracing Vasco's journey from Portugal to India via Africa, try to fit in a detour to the KwaZulu-Natal province of South Africa, originally named 'Natal' by Vasco for the natal day of Jesus, after he sighted the coastline in 1497. It's a contradictory, enthralling place: rough and ready, smart and sophisticated, rural and rustic, with relaxed beaches, laid-back adventuring, amazing wildlife, big-city attractions and teeming African life.

EMILIO COLAVEZZI | PHOTOLIBRARY

OPENING SPREAD An intrepid Vasco fan climbs the Padrão dos Descobrimentos, Lisbon. **ABOVE** The Vasco da Gamas sepulchre in the Monastery of the Hieronymites, Belém. **BELOW** On the beach front, Inhambane, Mozambique.

LUÍS VAZ DE CAMÕES

Luís Vaz de Camões (1524–80) is regarded as Portugal's greatest poet. In 1553, he was banished to Goa after fighting a Lisbon magistrate. There, he enlisted with the army and fought with distinction before falling foul of authorities again when he criticised Goa's Portuguese administration. This time he was exiled to the Spice Islands of Indonesia, returning to Goa in 1562 where he wrote his most famous work, Os Lusíadas, an epic poem glorifying Vasco's adventures. Classical in style and imperialist in sentiment, the poem has become an emblem of Portuguese nationalism.

ALEXANDER THE GREAT: FROM GREECE TO EGYPT

THRILL TO THE INCREDIBLE WAR MARCH OF THE MACEDONIAN WARRIOR-KING. THE CULTURAL IMPACT OF ALEXANDER'S JOURNEY LINGERS ON EVERYWHERE ACROSS THE ROUTE TODAY, ALLOWING FOR A THRILLING EXPERIENCE, WHETHER YOU'RE A TRAVELLER, ADVENTURER OR CASUAL READER.

118

Alexander the Great (356–323 BC) was what we might now think of today as an alpha male – in total overdrive. As expert at making poetry as he was war, he was always destined for everlasting fame. How could it be anything different given his father's overarching shadow? Indeed, Dad – none other than King Philip II of Macedonia – was believed by many to be a descendant of the god Hercules. If that wasn't enough, Mum was Princess Olympias of Epirus, who counted the legendary Achilles among her ancestors. Now you can see why celebrity status was assured, although the precocious young Alexander sometimes claimed Zeus was his real father. How's that for gratitude?

When he was 12, Alexander was already conquering things, namely Bucephalus, a wild horse that even Macedonia's most accomplished horsemen refused to ride. At 13, Aristotle was his personal tutor. Truly, there were no limits: Alexander could play the lyre with aplomb and also learned Homer's The Iliad by heart; and he was sensitive, too, deeply admiring Persian ruler Cyrus the Great for the respect he granted to the cultures he sacked. Thus primed, Alexander rode out of Macedonia in 334 BC to begin his decade-long campaign of conquest. His first great victory was against the Persians at Issus (now southeast Turkey). Then he swept south, conquering Phoenician seaports before pushing into Egypt where he founded Alexandria, the Mediterranean city that still bears his name.

In 331 BC the Alexandrian army triumphantly entered Cyrenaica. In Siwa, the Oracle of Ammon told Alexander that he would conquer the world, and lo and behold he believed her. Crossing the Tigris and the Euphrates, he defeated another Persian army before driving his troops up into Central Asia and northern India. When fatigue and disease put a halt to it all, they turned around. Alexander fell ill along the way, with some convinced he was poisoned. He died in Babylon, aged just 33. No one knows the whereabouts of his body and tomb.

ESSENTIAL EXPERIENCES

❋ **Imagining you are Alexander as you stride from Pella to begin your journey (and take on the world).**

❋ Using the journey as chance to take a detour and explore the best that Greece, Turkey and Egypt have to offer.

❋ **Enjoying the marvellously preserved wonders of antiquity at Ephesus.**

❋ Spending quality time in Alexandria, the Pearl of the Mediterranean: breakfasting in lovely cafes and exploring the Roman amphitheatre, Pompey's Pillar and the Catacombs of Kom ash-Shuqqafa, before swimming at Mamoura and dining in style in a sumptuous seaside restaurant.

DISTANCE - APPROXIMATELY 2000KM | **COUNTRIES COVERED** - GREECE, TURKEY, EGYPT, IRAN | **IDEAL TIME COMMITMENT** - TWO WEEKS TO ONE MONTH | **BEST TIME OF YEAR** - GREECE: EASTER TO MID-JUNE; TURKEY: LATE APRIL TO MAY AND LATE SEPTEMBER TO OCTOBER; EGYPT: OCTOBER TO MAY | **ESSENTIAL TIP** - DON'T GET NAKED IN PUBLIC, AS ALEXANDER OFTEN LIKED TO DO.

THE DELPHIC ORACLE

The Delphic Oracle was Greece's most powerful, and she sat on a tripod at the entrance to a chasm that emitted intoxicating vapours. Apparently, the earliest oracles were young women who regularly ran off with their advice-seeking pilgrims, leaving the post temporarily vacant. Problem solved: it became customary for the seer to be at least 50 years of age. When she was consulted for divine advice, the priestess inhaled the fumes and entered a trance. Her answers were translated into verse by a priest. As the answers were suitably ambiguous and cryptic, they allowed for multiple interpretations.

ALEXANDER MEETS THE ORACLE

No one took the oracles lightly: wars were fought and marriages sealed or smashed according to their visions. Alexander was no exception, and when he visited the oracle at Delphi, he wanted to be told what he wanted to hear: that he would conquer the world. But the oracle was unable to tell him this outright, instead suggesting that he return later for a more definitive answer. Consumed with anger, he dragged her by the hair out of her chamber until she wailed, 'Let go of me; you're unbeatable'. Dropping her, he simply replied: 'I have my answer.'

■ THE JOURNEY TODAY

You are in Greek Macedonia, Pella to be exact – ancient Macedonian capital and Alexander's birthplace. You admire the ruins of Alexander's home base, fascinated by the mosaics of the palace that are still intact. You think about Alexander's magic horse, Bucephalus, before deciding driving is the better option. You make it to nearby Vergina, where the stunning gold-studded tomb of Alexander's father, King Phillip II, is laid out before you. Versed in Alexandrian lore, instinct tells you that you must visit next the ruins at Delphi, where Alexander, also acting on instinct, sought the advice of the Oracle of Delphi, who told him he was indeed 'unbeatable'. 'Unbeatable' is precisely how you feel.

Imbued with Alexandrian spirit, you cross continents, driving into the Middle East and Turkey. Alexander ran riot across Turkey and a few of his best-known haunts include Troy, with its famous ruins. It was here where our hero customarily anointed himself in oil and raced naked around the tombs of Achilles and Patroclus in homage. You think of doing the same but decide against it for fear of being arrested for exposing yourself. You want to be free to enjoy the many more highlights in store, such as Ephesus, the best-preserved classical city in the eastern Mediterranean, where Alexander offered to pay for the construction of a new temple (later one of the Seven Wonders of the World), and the ruined but still massive city of Termessos, where the Termessians successfully fought off Alexander in 333 BC.

After visiting them, you're onto the final stretch: Egypt, which Alexander invaded in 331 BC. You visit the ruins of Memphis, south of Cairo, where Alexander was crowned pharaoh, before travelling to the settlement at Siwa Oasis where the oracle confirmed Alexander's divinity. Alexandria is your final stop, the city founded by your hero.

■ SHORTCUT

Greece, Egypt and Turkey – all make a singularly great Alexandrian experience in their own right. A variety of professional tours allow you to undertake detailed, dedicated Alexander tours in each. Experts in various aspects of ancient history run some of these.

■ DETOUR

Thessaloniki in northern Greece, named after Alexander's sister, is a pleasant surprise to many travellers, who discover it to be a sophisticated city with fine Roman and Byzantine architecture and a throbbing nightlife. If you're in the country in mid-April, you can trace a small section of Alexander's journey in a rather novel fashion: by following the annual Alexander the Great Marathon, from Pella to Thessaloniki.

121

OPENING SPREAD Spanning centuries, the ruins of the old town of Shali, Siwa Oasis. **ABOVE (L)** The fabulous Library of Celsus, part of the ruins of Ephesus. **ABOVE (R)** Egypt's oldest pyramid, Memphis. **LEFT** Not conquering the world, but still having fun: kids at the Fort of Qaitbay, Alexandria.

DEA / W BUSS | GETTY IMAGES

ARMCHAIR

✳ *Alexander the Great* (1956) Alexander's story has been filmed many times; in this version Richard Burton had a stab at the role.

✳ *Alexander* (2004) Colin Farrell stars in Oliver Stone's typically bombastic, polarising production.

✳ *The Alexander Trilogy* (Mary Renault) This trio of novels – *Fire from Heaven* (1969), *The Persian Boy* (1972) and *Funeral Games* (1981) – details Alexander's life in every conceivable detail.

✳ *The Man Who Would be King* (Rudyard Kipling) This rousing short story (1888) and John Huston's film adaptation (1975), starring Michael Caine and Sean Connery, tell the story of two British ex-soldiers in Kafiristan in the Himalayas, where Alexander had passed through, vowing to return. The natives are convinced one of these scoundrels is Alexander reincarnated, with tragic results.

THE VIKINGS: SCANDINAVIA TO THE MEDITERRANEAN

NO HISTORICAL RACE SEIZES THE IMAGINATION QUITE LIKE THE VIKINGS. THE UNSTOPPABLE SCOURGE OF THE ANCIENT WORLD, THEY BROUGHT EUROPE TO ITS KNEES BEFORE TURNING THEIR ATTENTION TO FOREIGN CLIMES. TRACE THEIR JOURNEY FROM NORTHERN SCANDINAVIA TO THE MEDITERRANEAN.

Different Viking groups came from the lands we now know as Denmark, Norway and Sweden, and it was scarcity that initially drove their desire for conquest and expansion. In Norway in the 8th century, an expanding population was beginning to exhaust agricultural land. Settlers began to travel to the British Isles, returning to Norway with goods and descriptions of poorly defended coastlines. In Sweden, along with the prospects of military adventure and foreign trade abroad, population pressures were also to blame for a sudden exodus. Thus the seed was sown: the Vikings planned to conquer the world.

The first Viking raid was in 793: St Cuthbert's monastery on Lindisfarne island. After, in their formidable longships, they spread across Britain, Ireland and Europe. Each group established a unique sphere of influence. The Swedes colonised the Baltic countries, launching deep into Russia. The Norwegians' domain included Scotland, Ireland and the Shetland, Orkney and Hebrides island groups, and they colonised Iceland and Greenland. Danish Vikings raided the coasts of Western Europe and northeastern England. The Norsemen attacked in massive fleets. They terrorised, murdered, enslaved, assimilated and displaced local populations, and no coastal region was safe from their perilous intent, including the coasts of Britain and Ireland; France, where Normandy was named for the Norsemen; Russia, as far east as the river Volga; the Mediterranean, including Moorish Spain; and the Middle East, where they even reached Baghdad. The Vikings also crossed the Atlantic to settle the Faroes, Iceland and Greenland during the 9th and 10th centuries, ensuring their dominion was complete. Back home, Viking raids improved standards of living. Emigration freed up farmland and birthed a new merchant class. Captured slaves provided farm labour and Scandinavia was transformed from an obscure European backwater to an all-powerful empire.

ESSENTIAL EXPERIENCES

* **Exploring the arresting museums, galleries and well-restored castle of Kolding in Denmark.**

* Admiring the fine architecture and haunting Viking ruins at Aalborg in Denmark.

* **Sampling Norway's extreme Arctic north, a frozen, awe-inspiring wilderness, and the solitude of island life.**

* Giving in to the delights of the Norwegian capital, Oslo.

* **Driving to Ringebu, and one of Norway's prettiest stave churches.**

* Revelling in Stockholm, Sweden, where mandatory attractions include the Royal Palace, Gamla Stan and Skansen.

* **Visiting the spectacular cathedral and palace at Uppsala in Sweden.**

* Exploring Sweden's Bohuslan Coast.

DISTANCE: APPROXIMATELY 2700KM **COUNTRIES COVERED** - NORWAY, SWEDEN, DENMARK, ICELAND, ENGLAND, FRANCE, SPAIN **IDEAL TIME COMMITMENT** - TWO TO THREE MONTHS **BEST TIME OF YEAR** - JUNE TO AUGUST **ESSENTIAL TIP** - REMEMBER: PILLAGING IS NOW ILLEGAL IN EUROPE.

VIKING CUISINE REIGNS SUPREME

When Norwegians celebrate, food is central to the occasion, and traces of Viking traditions remain. At Christmas, alongside dishes such as *rømmegrøt* (a delicious sour-cream porridge) and *lutefisk* (a glutinous dish of dried cod or stockfish treated in lye solution), you'll find pork roast, a dish stemming from the Viking tradition of sacrificing pigs at yuletide. Norway's ever-popular Christmas drink is *gløgg* – cinnamon, raisins, almonds, ginger, cloves, cardamom and other spices blended with juice, sometimes fermented – although many also knock back *julaøl* (holiday beer), which in the Viking days was associated with pagan sacrifices. Like lutefisk, not all foreigners fully appreciate julaøl so approach with caution.

■ THE JOURNEY TODAY

You are a king, a god, a modern-day VIKING! You're on your way to the Promised Lands and nothing can stand in your way. You're standing on the Normandy coast and gazing out to the Dover Strait. In Norway, you visited the splendid Viking Ship Museum in Oslo, with its twin jewels: the sleek, dark hulls of the Viking ships Oseberg and Gokstad. In Sweden, you journeyed to Foteviken for one of the most authentic experiences of all: the Viking Reserve, a reconstruction of a late–Viking Age village. You marvelled at the houses with reed or turf roofs built on the coast, near the site of the Battle of Foteviken (1134). You savoured the shield-lined great hall, the reconstructed warship and the lethal, working war catapult. You thrilled to the re-enactment of the 1134 battle. You even felt deep pangs of envy at this 'living' village, populated by people who do as the Vikings did, following the old Norse traditions, laws and religions. You're seeing things like the Norsemen, which is why you are already thinking of leaving Normandy, your mind set on the Spanish Mediterranean coast and Seville, just inland. Of course, you'll be taking the train there, but in your mind's eye, you're actually in a Viking longship. You're thinking, as the Vikings must have done when they raided Seville in 844, about how you can satisfy your unquenchable thirst for new lands, new experiences.

■ SHORTCUT

For an abridged taste of the Viking experience, Denmark's impressive ruins provide key insights into this fascinating history. Allow one to two weeks to loop around the country, visiting sites such as Aalborg, a re-invented industrial city with haunting Viking ruins; Roskilde, at the edge of a fjord, where you can get up close to Viking ships at the hands-on museum dedicated to Viking shipbuilding; and Trelleborg, where there's a Viking fortress to fire the imagination.

■ DETOUR

England, particularly York, is a fascinating stop on the Viking route towards the Mediterranean. When the Vikings conquered northern Britain in the 9th century, they divided the territory that is now Yorkshire into thridings (thirds), with Jorvik – or York – as the capital. Contrary to popular misconception, the Vikings were not just bloodthirsty marauders. At Jorvik, their capital for the next 100 years, they focused less on pillaging and more on turning the city into a major trading port. Discover more at York's annual Jorvik Viking Festival and at Jorvik, a reconstruction of the Viking settlement unearthed at York during excavations in the late 1970s.

CINTRACT ROMAIN | PHOTOLIBRARY

OPENING SPREAD Winter in a Norwegian fishing village, hardy weather for even the toughest Viking. **ABOVE (L)** An example of Norway's famous wooden churches. **ABOVE (R)** This Viking church in Greenland may be in ruins, but the Viking legend today still stands tall and strong.

ARMCHAIR

❋ **A History of the Vikings** (Gwyn Jones) A critically acclaimed work featuring comprehensive details of the Viking era.

❋ **The Prose Edda: Norse Mythology** (Snorre Sturluson) The ancient Norse sagas are the ultimate in Viking literature.

❋ **Skimmer** (Shimmering; 1996) Göran Tunström's film is set in Iceland during Viking times.

❋ **Asterix and the Vikings** (2006) Features the beloved cartoon character training a young Gaul to take on the Vikings.

❋ **Erik the Viking** (1989) Terry Jones' gentle comedy tells the story of Erik, on a mission to Valhalla to ask a favour of the gods.

❋ **The Vikings** (1958) Hollywood has churned out some terrible interpretations, but this one, starring Kirk Douglas and Tony Curtis, is probably the best.

RIVERS & SEAS

--- ❧ ---

GREAT JOURNEYS

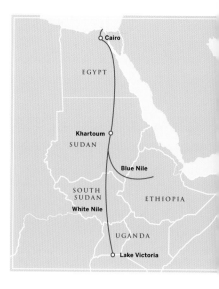

THE NILE

SAILING BOAT OR TIME MACHINE? THE WORLD'S LONGEST RIVER FEELS LIKE IT'S THE OLDEST, AND TO BOARD A VESSEL ON THE NILE IS TO PEEL BACK MILLENNIA AND SLOW DOWN TO RIVER SPEED AS ANCIENT TEMPLES, OXCARTS AND PALM TREES – UNALTERED SINCE PHARAOHS RULED THE ROOST – PASS BY.

126

The Nile is more than the lifeblood of Egypt. It is Egypt. Without its generous overspill, this parched nation could not exist, and though accounting for just 4% of Egypt's surface area, the Nile Valley is home to 95% of its population.

It was also, until the relatively recent advent of roads, the quickest way to move goods and tidings about the country. Thus most of Egypt's key buildings – from the Pyramids to the temple of Karnak – line the Nile, while the river itself has always been awash with vessels, from traditional papyrus skiffs to lateen-sailed cargo ships; an ancient barque, part of Pharaoh Khufu's funerary cache, is on display at Giza. In the Middle Ages it was thought around 36,000 boats plied the river.

Of course, the Nile is not all about Egypt. This is the world's longest river: its most extreme tentacle, the White Nile, reaches 6680km from its Mediterranean mouth into the African interior – the exact location is up for debate but it's roughly around Lake Victoria. The Blue Nile splits off at Khartoum, its headwaters 1450km away in Ethiopia. But it's with Egypt that the Nile is synonymous and where its waters have most infiltrated the national psyche. It is believed to divide the land of the living (east) from the land of the dead (west), water-reliant creatures abound in Egyptology (crocodiles, ibis, hippos, frogs) and Egyptian sun god Ra travels by boat.

The tourists of the early 19th century favoured *dahabiyyas* (houseboats) for their Grand Tours. These elegant sailed barges offered chandeliers and afternoon tea to the privileged. The advent of regular steamers in the 1850s – and a certain Thomas Cook in 1869 – opened up river tourism to the masses. Now boats on the Nile are more likely carrying camera-flashing punters than cargoes of cotton. But a Nile sail today still feels like a step back in time, to when nothing was more important than the Nile itself.

ESSENTIAL EXPERIENCES

❋ **Docking at Luxor for Ancient Egypt's finest: the colossal columns of Karnak, Luxor Temple (best seen lit up after dark) and the Valley of the Kings.**

❋ Quaffing cocktails on the verandah of Aswan's grand Old Cataract Hotel.

❋ **Entering the tombs of Ramses II at Abu Simbel, relocated in the 1960s to avoid being subsumed by Lake Nasser.**

❋ Watching the waters of the Blue Nile and the White Nile combine at Khartoum, Sudan.

❋ **Seeing the 'smoking water' of 45m-high Tis Issat (Blue Nile Falls) in Ethiopia.**

❋ Rafting the White Nile's white water near Jinja, Uganda, near the river's source at Lake Victoria.

DISTANCE - 6680KM | **COUNTRIES COVERED** - EGYPT, SUDAN, UGANDA, TANZANIA, ETHIOPIA | **IDEAL TIME COMMITMENT** - THREE WEEKS | **BEST TIME OF YEAR** - MARCH TO APRIL, SEPTEMBER TO NOVEMBER | **ESSENTIAL TIP** - DON'T DRINK THE TAP WATER.

DOING THE DELTA

Most travellers look south from Cairo, but the Delta region – lush, green, incredibly fecund – is where the Nile is most productive. Dip into the region on a river bus from Cairo to the barrages near Qanater: the 16km journey north takes 90 minutes one way, and is best done on a Friday night when it turns into something of a locals' disco. In the Delta proper, travel by bus. Head to the archaeological site of Tanis, spot spoonbills and flamingos on Lake Manzala, and visit the graceful 18th- and 19th-century mansions of Rosetta. Every October, Tanta's Sufi moulid (religious festival) draws million-strong crowds.

THE JOURNEY TODAY

Your eyelids sense the change first: the world is becoming a little less dark. It's still chilly laying exposed to the elements, and your back is moaning after a night spent on deck, but as you flick your eyes open you can't help but smile. The sun is rising on another beautiful Nile-cruising day, a languorous drift past mud-brick houses, tilling farmers, and a world-beating temple or two.

Feluccas look so romantic wafting their way downstream, tacking with the breeze, being outpaced by ox carts on the banks. Sleeping on one, however, is a different story – no rooms, no roof, no toilet, no frills. But now, with the sky peach-pink over the desert and no one else around, it seems well worthwhile.

A Nile cruise, whether by budget felucca, mod-con cruiser or glamorous houseboat, is central to understanding Egypt. And a sail on the section from Aswan to Luxor is the easiest, and best, introduction to life on the world's longest river, passing eternal desert scenes as well as superstars in stone: the temple of Kom Ombo, well-preserved Edfu, Karnak's mighty Hypostyle Hall.

Indeed, the Egyptian government no longer allows tourists to sail further north than Abydos. In the south you can continue from Aswan by ferry across Lake Nasser into Sudan; once docked you'll transfer to train or bus. From Khartoum, it's a juddery drive into Ethiopia, where you can trace the Blue Nile to Lake Tana. Alternatively, fly down to Kampala to ride the wild White Nile in Uganda.

Sadly, there's no easy way to string together a long, continuous river run. No matter, though. The bits of accessible Nile offer much, from leafy islands (Egypt's Temple of Isis on Agilkia Island) to noisy churn (Rusomo Falls, a distant headwater between Tanzania and Rwanda). And if, one day, boats do sail from source to sea, the timeless Nile will still be there.

SHORTCUT

Take the overnight sleeper train from Cairo to Aswan, and sail the temple-laden stretch from Aswan to Luxor – a journey of around three to six days. Sailing northwards is quicker as you're going with the current – especially important if travelling by wind-powered felucca.

DETOUR

The Blue Nile, source of most of the river's water, springs to life in Lake Tana, Ethiopia. The outlet is a 30-minute speedboat trip from Bahir Dar, but linger on Tana, a 3500-sq-km lake (the country's biggest) dotted with islands and overflown by pelicans. Hire a boat to visit the wealth of centuries-old monasteries lurking on the lake's isles and peninsulas: 17th-century Kebran Gabriel and Ura Kidane Meret, with its paintings, crosses and crowns, are among the best.

OPENING SPREAD There's no finer sight than the Nile at sunset, on display here at Aswan, Egypt. **ABOVE (L)** Aswan's sumptuous Old Cataract Hotel. **ABOVE (R)** The mighty Blue Nile falls: 400m wide, 50m deep and every inch spectacular. **LEFT** The Great Temple of Ramses II, Abu Simbel.

ARMCHAIR

* ***Death on the Nile*** (Agatha Christie) Murderous tale from the Queen of Crime, set on a Nile steamer; it was made into a film in 1978.

* ***A Thousand Miles Up The Nile*** (Amelia Edwards) Tales of riverbank life from the novelist's 1870s sail south from Cairo in a dahabiyya.

* ***The Blue Nile & The White Nile*** (Alan Moorehead) Two-volume tour de force, examining the history and conquest of the Nile region, and the search for the river's source.

* ***In an Antique Land*** (Amitav Ghosh) Entertaining and unpatronising account of a sojourn in a Nile Delta village.

* ***Old Serpent Nile*** (Stanley Stewart) Stewart follows the river, from Delta to Uganda's mountains.

NORTHWEST PASSAGE

Sail through the most legendary shipping route on Earth, following in the wake of a host of Victorian-era explorers seeking the ocean's holy grail: safe boat passage across the frozen top of North America to the riches of Asia.

130

For centuries it was the great marine dream: to find an open passage through the Arctic, creating a sea lane for traders between Europe and Asia to reduce the sailing time between the two continents. A course was sought through the tangle of ice-bound islands and straits across the top of Canada, the so-called Northwest Passage. The search began as far back as the late 15th century, but it was ramped up in the 18th and 19th centuries. James Cook sought it in vain in 1776, sailing with the likes of George Vancouver and William Bligh.

Through the first half of the 19th century, various expeditions chipped away at the route, slowly getting further and further, including the fabulous failure of the Franklin expedition (see the boxed text on p131). The tales of ineptitude and possible cannibalism from this expedition have made it one of the most famous adventure stories in history, up there with Robert Scott's Antarctic expedition.

In 1903, Norwegian explorer Roald Amundsen, who later became the first person to reach the South Pole, set out through the Northwest Passage. Taking a smaller ship and crew, Amundsen spent two winters on King William Island before finally becoming the first person to navigate through the passage in 1906.

Such were its difficulties, though, it had already been abandoned as a feasible trading route, and superseded by the Panama Canal, which began construction while Amundsen was in the ice.

In recent years the Northwest Passage has returned to the forefront of shipping minds. Melting polar ice has opened up the Arctic waters, and the European Space Agency noted that in 2007 the passage had been fully clear of ice, and, for the first time since records began in 1978, fully navigable. The following year the first commercial ship sailed through the Northwest Passage.

ESSENTIAL EXPERIENCES

✳ **Wandering through the Northwest Passage Park and Interpretive Centre at Gjoa Haven, where you'll find traces of Amundsen's expedition as well as the graves of several of Franklin's crew members.**

✳ Stopping in at Beechey Island, a national historic site east of Cornwallis Island, where the Franklin expedition wintered in 1845–46 before vanishing forever – traces of the men and their unsuccessful rescuers remain.

✳ **Viewing the remains of Roald Amundsen's schooner Maud in the harbour of Cambridge Bay, where Northwest Passage explorers often took shelter.**

✳ Contemplating the northern hardships as you visit Marble Island and its graveyard for James Knight and his crew, who sought the Northwest Passage in the 18th century.

DISTANCE - APPROXIMATELY 3000 NAUTICAL MILES | **COUNTRIES COVERED** - CANADA, GREENLAND, UNITED STATES | **IDEAL TIME COMMITMENT** - TWO TO THREE WEEKS | **BEST TIME OF YEAR** - JULY AND AUGUST | **ESSENTIAL TIP** - PACK WARM; EVEN IN AUGUST THE AVERAGE TEMPERATURE IN CAMBRIDGE BAY IS AROUND 9°C.

THE FRANKLIN EXPEDITION

The most celebrated of all Northwest Passage
journeys – even if only for the mystery
surrounding it – was the British expedition led
by Sir John Franklin. The two-ship expedition
sailed into the Passage in 1845, seeking to find
a way through the last few hundred kilometres
of unnavigated waters. The expedition, and
its entire crew of 129 men, never returned and
disappeared without trace. The ships, HMS
Erebus and HMS *Terror*, were eventually found to
have been trapped in ice off King William Island,
but the reasons for some of their deaths – lead
poisoning, cannibalism – remains debated.

POLAR BEARS

In the Canadian province of Nunavut, which incorporates the bulk of the islands through the Northwest Passage, polar bears aren't just found on the license plates. The region is home to almost half the world's population of *nanuq* (the Inuit name for polar bears). Worldwide there are estimated to be around 20,000 polar bears, but it's a population now threatened by global warming and melting sea ice - it's on sea ice that the bears hunt and breed. Unlike grizzly and black bears, polar bears actively prey on people, so inquire about bear sightings before you go trudging about, or go with a shotgun-toting guide.

■ THE JOURNEY TODAY

Though at least one cruise liner has navigated the entire Northwest Passage, it's more likely that any trip here will only sample a snippet of the famed shipping route. At least for now...

Your 21st-century journey through a 19th-century obsession begins in Greenland, weaving through the fjords that fray its west coast. Through Baffin Bay you enter Parry Channel, the closest thing this region has to a direct line of passage, and quickly you have cause to be grateful that it's an ice-strengthened vessel. Within hours there's a thump; you have smacked into your first iceberg. Welcome to the Arctic.

The world here is reduced to a jumble of islands: snapped, fractured, raw, rugged chunks of land brutalised by the harsh conditions. And yet so very beautiful.

Through the Franklin Strait – its name alone replete with tragic Northwest Passage history – and a jigsaw of fragmented ice, the ship docks at Gjoa Haven, the only settlement on King William Island, all but resting against the mainland coast of Canada. As evidenced by the name – Amundsen's ship was named the Gjoa – it was here that Roald Amundsen wintered in 1904 and 1905 before finally punching a way through the Passage in 1906.

You are now nearing the cruise's end at Cambridge Bay, across on Victoria Island, Canada's second-largest, but there's still excitement ahead. The following dawn you head out from the ship in Zodiacs, skimming close to the island shores, when you sight movement on a ridge. You slow, watching as the two figures descend to the ice ledge ahead of you. These waters and islands may still shelter the undisturbed ghosts of past explorers and sailors, but this polar bear and her cub are far more real.

■ SHORTCUT

You can skip the ship travel, and the seasickness, by flying direct into the Northwest Passage, though you'll be limited to single stops. First Air flies into several small island communities, including Gjoa Haven, Cambridge Bay and Resolute Bay (on Cornwallis Island), giving you the briefest of aerial and ground glimpses.

■ DETOUR

If you've made it to Resolute Bay, and have a fortune to squander, keep heading north to Ellesmere Island and remoter-than-remote Quttinirpaaq National Park, Canada's second-largest national park. Park highlights include Cape Columbia, North America's northernmost point; and Mt Barbeau, which at 2616m is the highest peak in eastern North America.

133

OPENING SPREAD The falls and hanging lake of Kynoch Inlet, British Columbia, Canada. ABOVE The uniquely beautiful charms of Red Island, Greenland. LEFT 'All this fur and we still can't get warm.' A polar bear family in the Arctic.

ARMCHAIR

❋ *Arctic Labyrinth: The Quest for the Northwest Passage* (Glyn Williams) Charts the history of the quest to find a route through the Northwest Passage.

❋ *The Man Who Ate His Boots: The Tragic History of the Search for the Northwest Passage* (Anthony Brandt) Another tale of the quest to punch through the Passage, focusing on the personalities and hardships of those who attempted it.

❋ *Frozen in Time: The Fate of the Franklin Expedition* (Owen Beattie & John Geiger) The definitive account of the most famous – and ill-fated – British expedition through the Passage.

❋ *My Life as an Explorer* (Roald Amundsen) Autobiography of the Norwegian explorer who first navigated the Passage, and was also the first person to reach the South Pole.

NORWAY'S FJORDS

SCOURED AND GOUGED BY ANCIENT GLACIERS, NORWAY'S FJORDS ARE A VERITABLE WONDERLAND. THESE DEEP, SEA-DROWNED VALLEYS, SCISSORED BY IMPOSSIBLY RUGGED TERRAIN, WERE RECENTLY VOTED BY NATIONAL GEOGRAPHIC TRAVELER MAGAZINE AS THE WORLD'S BEST TRAVEL DESTINATION.

134

No superlative can do justice to this spectacular region, which assaults your retinas with otherworldly scenery. Hardangerfjord and Geirangerfjord feature steep, crystalline rock walls dropping with awe-inspiring force right down into the sea. Sognefjorden, the world's longest fjord at 203km, is also Norway's deepest at 1308m. It cuts a huge gash right across western Norway and its sheer walls can rise more than 1000m above the water. Undeniably, Sognefjorden's main waterway is impressive, but by cruising into its narrower stems you'll see lovely views of abrupt cliff faces and idyllic, cascading waterfalls. Along its gentler shoreline, Sognefjorden also supports farms, orchards and villages.

It's entirely possible to see the fjords by train, bus and car, and Western Norway has designated National Tourist Routes that give drivers (and buses) access to major sights. For example, the Snøvegen (Snow Road) climbs from sea level, twisting precipitously to the high plateau separating Aurland and Lærdalsøyri (Lærdal). You can only do it in the summer as snowbanks line the road and tarns are still deep-frozen even in late June, but the magnificent observation point is worth it, projecting out over the fjord way down below.

But really, a ferry is the only way to experience the fjords. These hardy vessels don't just lop off huge detours, they're also a fabulous aspect of the journey in their own right, giving you the chance to get as close as can be to these amazing, otherwise inaccessible panoramas and coastlines. For more than a century, the legendary Hurtigruten ferry route has linked the numerous coastal villages and towns, and all year long, 11 modern ferries head north from Bergen, reaching Kirkenes before returning. A popular option is the 11-day round-trip that stops at 34 ports, presenting numerous opportunities for side trips, where you'll see not only fabulous fjords but also islands bathed in the midnight sun, as well as medieval monasteries and art nouveau towns.

ESSENTIAL EXPERIENCES

✳ **Staring gob-smacked at the imposing cliffs of Geirangerfjord.**

✳ Taking the thrilling Flåmsbana railway trip between Hardangervidda and Flåm.

✳ **Appreciating art nouveau architecture in charming Ålesund.**

✳ Nodding your head like a good beatnik at the Molde Jazz Festival.

✳ **Hiking the coastlines to get as close as possible to an almighty fjord.**

✳ Sampling local delicacies such as the brown, slightly sweet cheese found in Undredal, made from boiled and concentrated whey, or a bowl of *rømmegrøt*, a rich sour-cream porridge.

✳ **Thrilling to the delights of Bergen, a beautiful, charming city, with a World Heritage–listed neighbourhood, Bryggen, and buzzing harbour, ringed by seven hills and seven fjords.**

DISTANCE - AROUND 2600KM | COUNTRIES COVERED - NORWAY | IDEAL TIME COMMITMENT - TWO WEEKS | BEST TIME OF YEAR - MAY TO SEPTEMBER | ESSENTIAL TIP - BRING STURDY HIKING BOOTS AND EXCELLENT BINOCULARS – YOU WON'T REGRET IT.

STAVE CHURCHES

Dotted around the region, these typically Norwegian buildings are essentially wooden structures with roof-bearing posts (staves) sunk deep into the earth. Twenty-eight survive mostly from the 12th and 13th centuries, albeit modified over the centuries. Interior walls are often elaborately designed, including traditional rose paintings – for a modern example, visit Stordal's flamboyant church. Complex rooflines are frequently embellished with scalloped wooden shingles and Viking Age dragon-head finials, much like Thai monasteries. Wooden carvings on support posts, door frames and outer walls (especially at Urnes) represent tendrils of stems, vines and leaves. They're frequently entwined with serpents, dragons and other fantasy creatures.

▨ THE JOURNEY TODAY

Let the atmosphere enfold you: steep mountains all around and a palpable sense of drama, wonderment and excitement. You admire mighty Jostedalsbreen, the many-tongued ice-cap that is mainland Europe's largest, a highly unusual, dynamic system. For so long, the ice-cap slowly advanced while most glaciers elsewhere were retreating – global warming, said the scientists. Now Jostedalsbreen has succumbed. Of course, it's not going away anytime soon, but it feels as though it's a living system, as if you can hear it breathe... But no, not really: that noise is just the groaning of the ice.

At another point, at blue, creaking Bøyabreen, you can't believe your eyes as you witness a rare moment: glacial calving as a massive chunk tumbles into the meltwater lagoon beneath the glacier tongue. At Briksdalsbreen, you're out on the ice with a qualified guide, for Briksdalsbreen is cracking and fissuring and you must tread with care. You breath in the air – it feels pure, untainted. The landscape is surreal, like a white planet that is decidedly not Earth.

Your guide drives you further along, to within 300m of the Supphellebreen glacier, where you walk right up to touch the ice. Your guide tells you that ice blocks from here were used as podiums at the 1994 Winter Olympics in Lillehammer. And then he asks where you would like to go to next.

You have no idea. The network is so vast you could spend months exploring individual fjords, each with its own bounteous character, and never grow tired of the experience. You think of the water's edge and the narrow trails hundreds of metres above the shoreline. You marvel at your memory of the pure drama that courses through these remarkable monuments of ice and rock.

'Anywhere,' you reply.

ARMCHAIR

❈ *Norwegian folk tales and legends* feature the fjords in all their glory. Trolls supposedly thrive in this type of landscape; there are many nooks for them to hide from direct sunlight, which turns them to stone.

❈ **Isles of the North: A Voyage to the Lands of the Norse** (Ian Mitchell) Recounts the author's journey into the fjords by boat.

❈ **The dead Norwegian parrot** 'pining for the fjords' in the TV series *Monty Python's Flying Circus* forever fixed an image (of sorts) of the landscape in the English-speaking world.

❈ *Ein Mann, ein Fjord!* (A Man, a Fjord!; 2009) A German made-for-TV comedy film about a man who wins a Norwegian fjord in a competition.

THE SOGNEFJELLET CIRCUIT

This is a stunning circular driving route that runs beside one of Norway's most picturesque fjords. It also follows a goodly portion of the superb Sognefjellet National Tourist Route, meandering along a lonely single-lane road that takes you up and across the heights before dropping in on a scarifying descent back to fjord level. The trip can't be done on public transport, but by car it's a day-long journey. If cycling, make sure your fitness levels are very much up to scratch and give yourself a few days.

▨ SHORTCUT

Try the one-hour scenic ferry trip between Geiranger and Hellesylt along the 20km-long, emerald-green Geirangerfjord, a World Heritage site. This is as much a micro-cruise as a means of transport, well worth taking if you have no special reason to be at the other end. Scattered cliffside farms, mostly long abandoned, still cling along the towering walls of twisting Geirangerfjord, while waterfalls including the Seven Sisters, the Suitor and the Bridal Veil sluice and tumble.

▨ DETOUR

The fjords represent an awful lot of fresh air and wide-open spaces, and it's possible that you may be craving small-town sophistication afterwards. If that's the case, why not drop into the charming coastal settlement of Ålesund? It's as lovely as Bergen, which is arguably Norway's most beautiful city, but on a smaller scale, meaning it's far less touristy. After a devastating fire in 23 January 1904, Ålesund was rebuilt in record time, designed in the characteristic art nouveau (Jugendstil) style of the time, while combining traditional local motifs and ornamentation such as buildings graced with turrets, spires and gargoyles.

JEAN-PIERRE LESCOURRET | LONELY PLANET IMAGES ©

OPENING SPREAD Up close with the glacier face, Jostedalsbreen National Park. **ABOVE** A classic view: the waterfront at Bergen. **BELOW** On the Sognefjellet Circuit, experiencing all the best Norway has to offer.

DOWN THE MISSISSIPPI TO NEW ORLEANS

THE MISSISSIPPI: AMERICA'S MOST IMPORTANT RIVER. IT GAVE BIRTH TO THE BLUES, HUCKLEBERRY FINN, BUDWEISER AND MUCH MORE. IT WITNESSED THE CIVIL WAR AND THE END OF SLAVERY. FOLLOW IT ALL THE WAY DOWN TO NEW ORLEANS AND BID IT FAREWELL AS IT LEAVES, SEEPING OUT INTO THE GULF OF MEXICO.

138

The USA is indeed a country renowned for classic road trips. Yet even among that plethora of riches, one of the most iconic is travelling down the Great River Road to follow the Mississippi down to New Orleans, Louisiana. Established in the late 1930s, the Great River Road is a 1200km journey from the Mississippi's headwaters in the northern lakes of Minnesota, floating downstream all the way to where the river empties into the Gulf of Mexico near New Orleans. You'll be awed by the sweeping scenery as you meander alongside North America's second-longest river, from the rolling plains of Iowa down past the cotton fields of the Mississippi Delta. And you'll never be more than 160km from a riverboat casino.

The Mississippi River defines New Orleans, not just geographically but emotionally, culturally, probably even metaphysically. New Orleans' location commands the entrance to the river, with the most important trade, conquest and exploration of the continent tied to the Mississippi and her variegated moods. Through New Orleans, the river's depth averages around 60m. It runs some 3800km from Minnesota to the Gulf of Mexico, with a drainage basin that extends from the Rockies to the Alleghenies, covering an astonishing 40% of continental USA. It drains more water than the Nile and only the Amazon and the Congo carry a greater volume of water to the sea.

Fittingly, the river's name is a corruption of the old Ojibwe word misi-ziibi, meaning 'great river'. It's a trip redolent with good ol' American history, glam and colour, so make like the narrator in Gary US Bonds' famous 1960 tune, 'New Orleans': 'Well, come on ev'rybody / Take a trip with me / Well, down the Mississippi / Down to New Orleans / You know that ev'ry Southern Belle / Is a Mississippi Queen / Down the Mississippi / Down in New Orleans'.

ESSENTIAL EXPERIENCES

❋ **Visiting the Mark Twain Boyhood Home & Museum in Hannibal to bone up on your Huck Finn knowledge, and finding the places he transposed into his famous novel.**

❋ Exploring Memphis' Slave Haven Underground Railroad Museum to learn about the transportation of slaves down the river to freedom.

❋ **Making a pilgrimage to Elvis Presley's Graceland in Memphis, and getting a dose of the blues in Clarksdale.**

❋ Enjoying the French Market on the river banks in New Orleans.

❋ **Savouring river cuisine: slow-burning tamales and melt-off-the-bone ribs in Clarksdale; chilli tamales and steaks in Greenville; and the full gamut of Cajun and Creole cuisine in New Orleans.**

DISTANCE - APPROXIMATELY 1240KM | **COUNTRIES COVERED** - USA | **IDEAL TIME COMMITMENT** - FOUR TO SIX DAYS
BEST TIME OF YEAR - SEPTEMBER TO JUNE. | **ESSENTIAL TIP** - AVOID MARDI GRAS IF STAYING IN NEW ORLEANS.

CAJUN OR CREOLE?

Many words have been written about the Cajun and Creole cuisine of Southern Louisiana. You could spend weeks searching the alleys of New Orleans for the best samples, but even a few days will give you a taste for the marvellous cooking to be found. It's generally agreed that Cajun food is more rustic while Creole food is more refined, but the differences blur into one meta-cuisine more often than not. Try boiled crawfish (crayfish) in crawfish étouffée, a classic Cajun dish of seafood in a spicy reddish sauce served over rice.

THE JOURNEY TODAY

You're on Highway 61, the top is down, the wind is in your hair and you're following the Big Muddy. When you reach Gateway Arch in St Louis it blows your mind. At 192m it is a massive statement against the clear blue sky. On a tour through the Anheuser-Busch Brewery's Victorian-era building, the guide tells you that beer was once made from Mississippi water and stored in barrels in dugouts on the riverbanks. Quaffing the two free Buds given away at the end, you're reminded of the joke about how American beer is like making love in a canoe...

Now you're back in the car and on the trail of Elvis. You pull out of St Louis, following the I-55S to Memphis, another classic Mississippi town. Graceland is there of course, as is Sun Studio and Stax Records. It's Music City, man. You steep yourself in modern lore at the Smithsonian's Memphis Rock 'n' Soul Museum, which devotes itself to the history of blues music in the Mississippi Delta – the blues, of course, being the fuel that propelled Elvis's legendary Sun Studio sessions. Now it's time for a trip to the Mississippi River Museum, part of Mud Island River Park, itself linked to Memphis by monorail. Satiated with the rich history of the river, you slink back to the Peabody Hotel, where you're staying, to ponder the strange ritual there: every morning and afternoon at 11am and 5pm, a flock of ducks is marched from the penthouse to the marble lobby fountain. Weird, sure, but all part of the way they do things differently along the Mississippi.

And if it was good enough for Elvis, who was known to be delighted by the Peabody ducks, then it's good enough for you.

SHORTCUT

Why not just stay in New Orleans? You'll never get bored and it's Mississippi Central. The best the city has to offer is contained within its neighbourhoods. Unlike countless US metropolises, you can practically cover the entire city by residential roads without ever using the highway.

DETOUR

Clarksdale is the home of genuine Delta blues. Here you'll find the Crossroads, the intersection of Highway 61 and Highway 49, where Robert Johnson sold his soul to the devil to become the very first guitar hero. Clarksdale's Delta Blues Museum has a top collection of blues memorabilia including exhibits honouring Muddy Waters, BB King, John Lee Hooker, Big Mama Thornton and WC Handy. As befitting such a town, Clarksdale has live music at least four nights a week.

OPENING SPREAD Doing the Mississippi, big-boat style – on the steamer *Natchez*. **ABOVE (L)** Elvis gets it on, Beale St, Memphis. **ABOVE (R)** Bridge on the Mississippi River: the Hernando Desoto Bridge, that is, Memphis. **RIGHT** Magnificent Lake Martin at sunset, Lafayette, Louisiana.

ARMCHAIR

❋ **As I Lay Dying** (William Faulkner) The Mississippi is a feature of Faulkner's brilliant and slightly off-kilter novels about the South. This 1930 stream-of-consciousness novel is set in Yoknapatawpha County, Mississippi, a fictionalised version of his home county of Lafayette.

❋ **The Adventures of Huckleberry Finn** (Mark Twain) Synonymous with the river, Twain worked as a riverboat pilot, which informed this, the very first 'Great American Novel'.

❋ **O Brother, Where Art Thou?** (2000) The Coen Brothers are attracted to the river, and their version of Homer's The Odyssey uses the Mississippi to striking effect, notably in the scene where the trio of misfits are seduced by the mythical sirens.

❋ **The Ladykillers** (2004) In their remake of the Ealing comedy about a planned casino heist, the Coens again transfer the action, this time from Britain to a fictional Mississippi river town.

MARK TWAIN

Mark Twain (1835–1910) grew up by the river in Hannibal, Missouri, during the time of slavery. Hannibal's characters, scenery and politics would later inform Twain's fictional town of St Petersburg, home to the character Tom Sawyer and his best friend, the mischievous Huckleberry Finn. In addition to being a writer, Twain was a commercial steamboat pilot on the Mississippi, ensuring an intimate knowledge of the backdrop of towns, islands, nooks and crannies and sandbars that made Huck's escape with Jim, the runaway slave, so realistic.

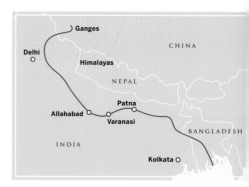

THE RIVER GANGES

GLACIAL TEARDROPS GATHER INTO STREAMS, CASCADING INTO NAVIGABLE WHITE WATER AND EVENTUALLY SMOOTHING INTO A SERENE MOCHA RIVER THAT CLEANSES SINS, TRANSPORTS SOULS AND IRRIGATES PRODUCTIVE FARMLAND. IT IS THE MOTHER GANGA, INDIA'S MOST SACRED RIVER.

142

Few journeys through the subcontinent offer the variety of terrain, culture, spiritual devotion and urban chaos as a long and slow wander tracing the Ganges from source to sea. It begins amidst a moonscape, high in the Himalayas with keyhole vistas of gleaming glacial peaks knifing into blue skies beyond Gangotri Temple, built in the 18th century by Gorkha commander Amar Singh Thapa. Nearby is the rock on which Shiva is said to have received the Ganges in his matted dreadlocks. From here the flow gathers and forms the Bhagirathi River, one of the Ganges' two major tributaries, which rushes down to Dev Prayag where it joins forces with the Alaknanda River and is renamed as the Ganges. The first of three major towns, all of them meccas for seekers, is Rishikesh, where first Ram Dass, then the Beatles reportedly ditched the LSD for Om-time at the ashram of Maharishi Mahesh Yogi, which has led to a flood of yoga centres and a sort of East-meets-West spiritual crossroads.

Next comes the more authentic city of Haridwar, where the Ganges sheds the Himalayan influence and steamy, urban chaos takes over. Pilgrims arrive in droves to bathe in the fast flowing Ganges at sunrise, pay their respects and rest their heads at impressive temples and ashrams – some the size of small villages. The scene becomes even more electric in Varanasi, one of India's most sacred, and the world's oldest, cities. It's a place to wash away a lifetime of sins, an auspicious place to die and where families cremate their loved ones in the holy Ganges.

Brahma, the Hindu god of creation, is said to have landed on Earth in nearby Allahabad, a centre for Hindu mythology. Follow the river long enough, by bus, boat or train and you will eventually reach Kolkata, India's third largest city, and the mouth of the Ganges, where Ganga filters through a vast delta and empties into the Bay of Bengal.

ESSENTIAL EXPERIENCES

❋ **Trekking from Gangotri Temple to Gaumukh, the terminus for the hulking Gangotri Glacier, the source of the Ganges.**

❋ Meditating the ashrams of yoga-mecca Rishikesh, where the Fab Four got their Eastern fix in the 1960s.

❋ **Snapping photos and absorb the devotional spirit of India in the overlooked city of Haridwar.**

❋ Exploring the tumbledown ghats on foot or by boat in Varanasi, as the pilgrims bath in the holy river.

❋ **Joining throngs of Hindu pilgrims as they converge on the beach at Ganga Sagar, at the river mouth, during the Gangasagar Mela festival each January.**

DISTANCE - 2506KM | COUNTRIES COVERED - INDIA, BANGLADESH | **IDEAL TIME COMMITMENT** - THREE WEEKS | **BEST TIME OF YEAR** - MAY TO NOVEMBER | **ESSENTIAL TIP** - GANGOTRI TEMPLE AND GLACIER ARE INACCESSIBLE FROM NOVEMBER TO APRIL.

VARANASI'S GHATS

Spiritually enlightening and fantastically photogenic, Varanasi is at its brilliant best by the ghats, the long stretch of steps leading down to the water on the western bank of the Ganges. Most are used for bathing but there are also several 'burning ghats' where bodies are cremated in public, lit by coals first sparked 3500 years ago. You'll often see funeral processions threading their way through the backstreets to Manikarnika Ghat. The best time to visit any of the ghats is at dawn when the river is bathed in a mellow light as pilgrims come to perform *puja* (literally 'respect'; offering or prayers) to the rising sun, or at sunset, when the *ganga aarti* (river worship ceremony) takes place.

THE MAHARISHI & THE BEATLES

In February 1968, Rishikesh hit world headlines when the Beatles and their partners stayed at Maharishi Mahesh Yogi's ashram. Ringo and his wife didn't dig the vegetarian food and missed their kids, so they left after a couple of weeks, but the others stayed on for over a month and wrote songs destined for the White Album. The original ashram is now abandoned, but over forty years on, foreign seekers still swarm Rishikesh seeking spiritual enlightenment from teachers and healers in their tranquil ashrams along the River Ganges.

■ THE JOURNEY TODAY

To do this trip right, be prepared for a tremendous climatic range, from the thin air and freezing winds of the Himalayas, to the humid, oxygen-rich climes of the mouth of the Ganges. Start by visiting Gangotri Temple, where you can join a trek to the source of the river at Gaumukh, the terminus for Gangotri Glacier, which spans 27 cu km and towers from 4120m to 7000m. The trek takes about three days, covering 48km of trails blessed with postcard vistas throughout. Most stay in the centre of Uttarkashi on either end of the treks.

The most romantic way to enter Maharishi country is to run Class III to IV white-water from just below Dev Prayag to Rishikesh, which has become a Westernised yoga mecca. Here you can learn tabla, join countless yoga and meditation classes, enjoy quiet walks to waterfalls and lazy afternoons on riverside beaches. In Haridwar, it changes, becomes more urbanised, yet somehow even more sacred. Every evening the river comes alive with flames as floating offerings are released into the fast flow.

No trip to India is complete without an overnight train journey. Take yours between Haridwar and Allahabad before heading to Varanasi, where it's common to hire a boat at sunrise or sunset and float down the holy river. Take the train again, between Varanasi and Patna, before either persevering overland through Bangladesh, where it is renamed again as the Hooghly, or flying to Kolkata, where you can hop on a boat travelling through the sultry mangrove delta to Kachuberiya, perched at the end of the mainland in the Ganges delta, before heading to Ganga Sagar, at the mouth of the Ganges, to watch the brown river tumble into blue sea. Thousands of Hindu pilgrims converge here during the Gangasagar Mela in mid-January.

■ SHORTCUT

Taste the natural and the gritty by starting in Rishikesh, heading upstream for a half-day white-water trip before exploring the waterfalls and beaches. Then go downstream to Haridwar to mingle with pilgrims and travel to epic Varanasi via the overnight train to mellow Allahabad.

■ DETOUR

Consider visiting the Corbett Tiger Reserve in Uttarakhand. India's first national park (founded in 1936) is named after the legendary tiger hunter, Jim Corbett, who wrote *The Man-Eaters of Kumaon*. Tiger sightings are a matter of chance, but few will leave disappointed as the 1318-sq-km park has a variety of wildlife, including elephants, sloth bears, langur monkeys, red-faced.

145

OPENING SPREAD The ghats at Varanasi, truly a sight to behold. **ABOVE (L)** A woman makes an offering to the Mother Ganga. **ABOVE (R)** Dawn on the Ganges at vibrant Varanasi **LEFT** Pilgrims bathing at ghat steps, paying their respects to the river.

ARMCHAIR

✳ ***Along the Ganges*** (Ilija Trojanow) Contrasting the ancient and modern aspects of India can lead to travel writing clichés, but Trojanow avoids the pitfalls with his elegant travelogue, which Condé Nast Traveller ranked one of the 100 best travel books of all time.

✳ ***To the Mouths of the Ganges*** (Frederic C Thomas) Written by an aid worker who spent years overseas with the Peace Corps, US AID and the UN, this book touches on the great poverty, environmental degradation and hope for the future in the Ganges delta.

✳ ***Baraka*** (1992) One of the greatest documentary films of all-time shrinks the world with a captivating display of beauty, wonder and chaos. The scenes along the Ganges in Varanasi are nothing short of extraordinary. A must-see for all nomads.

THE AMAZON RIVER

THE AMAZON: PHYSICALLY, IT'S IMMENSE AND MYTHICALLY IT'S THE VERY SAME. A RIVERINE AMAZON JOURNEY NEVER FAILS TO EVOKE OVERLAPPING IMAGERY: EXOTIC, DENSE RAIN FOREST; INDIGENOUS TRIBES; ABUNDANT WILDLIFE; ENVELOPING MYSTERY; SOMETIMES EVEN MENACE.

146

In 1541, a Spanish expedition ran short of supplies while exploring east of the Andes. To look for more, a detachment floated down the Rio Napo to its confluence with the Amazon and then to the mouth of the Amazon. Placed under attack by Indians, the Spanish were shocked that some of the Indian warriors were female. To them, it seemed the warriors were like the Amazons of Greek mythology, an observation that gave the world's greatest river its name (Rio Amazonas in Spanish).

Fittingly, for a river named from mythology, its physical characteristics are truly awe-inspiring. The Amazon is over 6200km long, containing a fifth of the world's fresh water. At its greatest, it is 40km across, dumping 300 million litres of fresh water into the ocean per second, more than the next eight largest rivers in the world combined. If you count its numerous tributaries, the Amazon crosses seven countries, from its inconspicuous source in the Peruvian highlands to its mouth near Belém in Brazil.

Yet often travellers' expectations outweigh the reality. Many arrive for an Amazon cruise expecting to hop off onto the riverbanks for casual, Discovery Channel–like encounters with jaguars, anaconda and spear-toting Indians. They then need to adjust their attitude fast, for the Amazon's quintessential experiences are more sublime than that. The river is massive and unrelenting, as much a life form as the plants and animals that depend on it for their survival. Wildlife is hard to spot amid this intricate, organic superstructure, but is all the more special when it makes itself known. The rainforest, of course, is awesome in both scope and atmosphere. Indigenous tribes are very withdrawn, but the Caboclo (mixed Indian and European) populating the riverbanks buck the trend to some extent.

Truly, within its infinite folds, the Amazon contains wonders galore.

ESSENTIAL EXPERIENCES

✳ **Canoeing through a flooded forest.**

✳ Dozing in a hammock on a slow boat to nowhere.

✳ **Listening to the song of a thousand birds and the eerie cry of howler monkeys.**

✳ Imagining you're Aguirre battling the river, and then being thankful you're not.

✳ **Learning to tolerate the insistent rhythm of forró music, played incessantly on the riverboats.**

✳ Stopping at a riverside town and hiking through the lush rainforest.

✳ **Bringing a rod and fishing from the boat when you grow weary of the bland food on board.**

DISTANCE - 1300KM | **COUNTRIES COVERED** - BRAZIL | **IDEAL TIME COMMITMENT** - ONE WEEK | **BEST TIME OF YEAR** - MAY TO SEPTEMBER | **ESSENTIAL TIP** - DON'T BOOK AN OVERPRICED, STUFFY RIVERBOAT CABIN. SLEEP IN YOUR HAMMOCK INSTEAD.

SURFING THE RIVER

Every month or so, a certain alignment of the sun and moon ensures tides are at their strongest. In the Amazon, this means powerful waves can form at the mouth of certain rivers and barrel upstream with tremendous force. This phenomenon, which occurs when the tide briefly overpowers the river's force, is called a 'tidal bore', but in Brazil they know it as the pororoca, meaning 'mighty noise.' Indeed, waves can reach 4m high and speeds of 30km per hour, and can rip fully-grown trees right off the bank. All of which pleases extreme surfers (and kayakers) in search of the archetypal 'endless wave'. For more, catch the National Pororoca Surfing Championship held at São Domingos do Capim, 120km east of Belém, usually in March.

THE FLOW

The Amazon has not always flowed west to east. About 150 million years ago, when South America and Africa went their separate ways, it flowed east to west. Then, 15 to 20 million years ago, the Andes shot up and blocked the water's exit. At the same time, a smaller ridge of land, now called the Purus Arch, rose like a spine in the middle of the continent. East of the Purus Arch, the river started draining into the Atlantic Ocean, but west of there, the water was trapped and a huge inland sea formed. Eventually the water poured over the Arch, gouging a deep channel near present-day Parintins, and the Amazon returned to being a river, but now flowing west to east. Confirming the theory, biologists showed that Amazonian stingrays are more closely related to Pacific species than Atlantic ones.

◼ THE JOURNEY TODAY

As you string up your hammock on the *gaiola* (riverboat) you boarded back in Belém, at the mouth of the great river, you watch the rainforest and local life glide effortlessly by. You marvel at the activity on the Amazon's edges, crowded with jungle and settlements. Most major towns along the Amazon have a port and an airstrip – but no roads in or out – so travel is limited to plane or boat. In effect, the Amazon is a road – popular, crowded and functional – but what a road!

The boat stops in Monte Alegre and everyone gets off to see the ancient rock paintings there, the Amazon's oldest-known human creations. Across river, there's beautiful, unspoilt countryside near Alenquer, but you'll save that for another time. Another traveller tells you she is going to hike to the virgin rainforest at Floresta Nacional do Tapajós, while another thinks of heading to the fabulous lagoon with white-sand beaches at Alter do Chão, but you're already thinking of life back on the boat. Because you're hooked.

So you're back on board, and the gaiola is suddenly insanely crowded with new passengers, plus there's a fierce Amazonian rainstorm on the way. It hits and due to the boat's open sides, you and everyone else get thoroughly soaked. Someone tells you that gaiola means 'bird cage' and suddenly it all makes sense. You chalk it up to experience, like everything else on board, until finally the storm dies down and you're back on deck.

You climb into your hammock, just near the railing, enjoying the sounds of boat life, and once again lose yourself in the sight of the world's greatest rainforest seductively passing by.

◼ SHORTCUT

The beauty of an Amazon trip is that it can be as long or as short as you make it. Most people do the journey between Brazilian cities Belém and Manaus in four to six days, although the cruise can be extended easily to six weeks, including stopovers, detours and multiple countries.

◼ DETOUR

Every June, the river island town of Parintins hosts Boi Bumba, Brazil's premier folklore festival. This vibrant event tells the tale of the death and resurrection of an ox, and is performed by two samba schools, Caprichoso and Garantido. Expect a typically Brazilian clash of colour, music and lavish carnivalesque hijinks. Actually, the whole festival is really a cover for a competition between the opposing schools, but don't expect to understand the complex rules, which are indecipherable to casual outsiders. Just become a slave to the rhythm and enjoy the party. Parintins can be reached by riverboat from Manaus.

NATIONAL GEOGRAPHIC SOCIETY | PHOTOLIBRARY

OPENING SPREAD Surfer Picuruta Salazar surfs the Amazon's pororoca wave in northeast Brazil. **ABOVE (L)** An Indigenous woman in Belém. **ABOVE (R)** Even jaguars want to be close to the Rio Amazonas. **LEFT** Marshland in the great river, near Manaus.

ARMCHAIR

✳ ***Survivor: the Amazon*** (2002) When the popular reality TV show did a series in the Amazon jungle, the river played a prominent role.

✳ ***Indiana Jones and the Kingdom of the Crystal Skull*** (2008) Good ol' Indy uses the Amazon as part of his quest to find the storied crystal skull.

✳ ***Aguirre, the Wrath of God*** (1972) and ***Fitzcarraldo*** (1982) The brilliant madman-director Werner Herzog is the ultimate Amazon film-maker. The first tells the story of the unhinged conquistador Aguirre and his attempt to find the legendary city El Dorado. The second tells of loopy Irishman, Fitzcarraldo, and his attempt to build an opera house in the middle of the Amazon. Both utilise the uncanny river to astounding effect, as metaphor for the dashed, elusive hopes of these flawed protagonists.

MEKONG RIVER

ONE OF THE WORLD'S LONGEST RIVERS, TO FOLLOW IT IS TO EXPERIENCE THE GREAT CULTURAL AND GEOGRAPHICAL DIVERSITY OF A CONTINENT, TO ABSORB ITS MANY REFRACTIONS OF BUDDHISM AND TO MEET RURAL ASIA AT HER MOST PICTURESQUE, ALMOST ALWAYS BATHED IN NATURAL, MYSTICAL BEAUTY.

150

The Mekong blooms from springs in the Tibetan Plateau, a huge elevated shelf in Central Asia, surrounded by mountains, and encompassing most of Tibet as well as slices of China. It rises alongside two other major rivers, the Salween and Yangtze, which run parallel through gorges in the Hengduan Mountains, before branching southeast to form the border between Myanmar (Burma) and Laos. After 100km it bends southwest to form a brief natural border with Thailand. The great river then carves through Laos, skirting its capital, Vientiane. It merges with the Mun River just before crossing into Cambodia, where it also swallows the Sap River, just prior to flowing by the Cambodian capitol of Phnom Penh. By the time it reaches the Vietnam border it is already fractured and fanning into a vast delta, with nine main channels irrigating one of the world's great rice growing regions, where floating markets, quaint rural villages and easy smiles are the norm all the way to the South China Sea.

The name, Mekong is an English perversion derived from the Thai and Lao: Mae (mother), Nam (water) and Khong (from Sanskrit for Ganges). Millions count on the river for water, power and agriculture, but despite the dams the Mekong basin is rich in biodiversity, second only to the Amazon, with 20,000 plant species, 430 mammals, 1200 birds, more than 800 reptiles and amphibians and an astonishing 850 fish species, including the Mekong freshwater stingray. In 2009 alone, 145 new species were discovered along the Mekong.

The river's oldest settlements trace back to 2100 BC, and the Khmer Empire bloomed on the banks in the 5th century. The Portuguese were the first Europeans to explore the Mekong, while the French took Saigon in 1861 and established a protectorate around Cambodia in 1863. In 1893, the French expanded into Laos, their influence fading after WWII and the Vietnam War.

ESSENTIAL EXPERIENCES

* **Wandering along the headwaters in the unforgettable Tibetan Plateau where cultures collide in the shadow of the Himalayas.**

* Exploring China's mystical and enchanting Yunnan Province, dotted with limestone peaks and carved with deep river gorges.

* **Mingling with the hill tribes of northern Laos, some of the most fascinating terrain along the Mekong.**

* Being seduced by the saffron-robed monks, shady streets, colonial buildings, handicrafts and patisseries of charming and delicious, Luang Prabang.

* **Relaxing on the islands and beaches that make Si Phan Don, southern Laos' best tourist destination.**

* Exploring the vast, colourful water world that is the Mekong Delta.

DISTANCE - 4909KM | **COUNTRIES COVERED** - CHINA, LAOS, CAMBODIA, VIETNAM | **IDEAL TIME COMMITMENT** - TWO WEEKS **BEST TIME OF YEAR** - DECEMBER TO APRIL | **ESSENTIAL TIP** - TAKE YOUR TIME AND YOU'LL HAVE A DEEPER EXPERIENCE WITH COMMUNITY TOURISM IN LAOS, CAMBODIA AND VIETNAM.

MEKONG BE DAMMED

With energy demands spiralling ever upwards, it is tempting for poor countries such as Cambodia (in which only 20% of households have electricity) and its upstream neighbours, to build hydroelectric dams on the Mekong and its tributaries. Environmentalists fear that damming the mainstream Mekong may be catastrophic for the migratory patterns of fish, and the survival of the freshwater Irrawaddy dolphin. Then there's the potential impact of dams on its annual monsoon flooding, which deposits nutrient-rich silt across vast tracts of land used for agriculture. Plans now under consideration include the Sambor Dam, a massive project 35km north of Kratie, and the Don Sahong (Siphandone) Dam just north of the Cambodia–Laos border.

MEKONG DISCOVERY TRAIL

It's worth sticking around Kratie for a few days to get into some outstanding adventure along the Mekong Discovery Trail, a new initiative established to open up stretches of the Mekong River to community-based tourism. You can go freshwater dolphin-watching or mountain biking, hop aboard horse carts pulled by local villagers, bunk on houseboats or stay in local homes or temples, visit markets or trek through the forest. The project is still in its infancy, but deserves support, as it provides fishing communities an alternative income in the hope of protecting the Irrawaddy dolphin and other species on this stretch of river.

THE JOURNEY TODAY

Your journey begins in the realm of boy-masters, Buddhist saints and nomadic shepherds: the Tibetan plateau, a high-altitude steppe surrounded by Himalayan peaks, glimmering with lakes, and undulating with grasslands. China's palpable mystery deepens as you follow the Mekong south through the length of the stunning Yunnan Province, one of China's wildest, with its lush limestone mountains and deep river gorges. You'll skirt the city of Lijiang in the north and bisect the sultry, tropical (sex) tourism vortex of Jinghong in the south before running into Laos, a slowly opening Southeast Asian flower that has quickly become a favourite bohemian destination. In the north you'll mix with the hill tribes and their palpable Tibetan influence.

The Mekong's middle reach is navigable year-round, from Heuan Hin (north of the Khemmarat Rapids in Savannakhet Province) to Kok Phong in Luang Prabang. However these rapids, and the brutal falls at Khon Phapheng in Si Phan Don, have prevented the Mekong from becoming a regional highway, which partly explains why the country has maintained its mellow, rural pace even in exquisite Luang Prabang, and why it has maintained so much biodiversity. At its widest, near the 4000 luscious islands of Si Phan Don in the south, the river can expand to 14km across during the rainy season, spreading around thousands of islands and islets on its inevitable course south where you can pick up the Mekong Discovery Trail, glimpse the rare freshwater dolphin near Kratie, and explore historic temples and the lush countryside of relaxing Kompong Cham in eastern Cambodia.

The river's ultimate grace is near the 'mouth of the dragon' in the Mekong Delta, an idyllic landscape carpeted in a dizzying variety of greens, where boats, houses and even markets float upon the endless canals and streams. Jousting with nature and the seasons, the people produce one of the most bountiful rice harvests on earth.

SHORTCUT

The Mekong Delta is a labyrinth all on its own, and if your goal is to take a snapshot of the mighty Mekong, then bring your lens here and explore quaint riverside towns, floating markets, bird sanctuaries and rustic beach getaways.

DETOUR

Angkor Wat, the eighth wonder of the world, is an easy and unforgettable detour. The temples, built between the 9th and 13th centuries, are the perfect fusion of creative ambition and spiritual devotion. The three most magnificent are eerie Bayon, romantic Ta Prohm – which is being swallowed by nature – and immense Angkor Wat.

153

OPENING SPREAD A boat woman doing what she does best: plying the Mekong. **ABOVE (L)** 'Mother, teach me to sew'. A street scene in Lijiang, Yunnan Province, China. **ABOVE (R)** A woman pans for Mekong gold. **LEFT** It's sunrise on the Mekong and the riverboat houses are also bathed in gold.

ARMCHAIR

* ***Phadaeng Nang Ai*** (translated by Wajuppa Tossa) Traditional Lao folktale about a love triangle set during a local festival and involving a king, a prince and a princess. It's an epic tale with all the big themes (love, honour and violence), partially set along the Mekong.

* ***Chang & Eng*** (Darin Strauss) This critically acclaimed debut novel, grounded in historical fact, follows conjoined twins born to a poor fisher family along the Mekong, to the King of Siam's court, PT

Barnam's New York City, and finally rural North Carolina.

* ***Apocalypse Now*** (1979) The spectacular film by Francis Ford Coppola, based on Joseph Conrad's *Heart of Darkness*. It follows a special agent, who travels up the fictional Nung River, based on the Mekong, to assassinate a legendary, renegade commander.

THE RIVER ROAD (RÍO GRANDE)

HUGGING THE RÍO GRANDE THROUGH SOME OF THE MOST SPECTACULAR AND REMOTE SCENERY IN THE COUNTRY, THE RIVER ROAD TAKES YOU UP, DOWN AND THROUGH A RUGGED TEXAS LANDSCAPE OF LOW DESERT ARROYOS, SWEEPING VISTAS AND STONY MOUNTAINS.

154

For almost 200km, the River Road (Camino del Río) snakes north along the great Texas river, the Río Grande, beginning near the Big Bend National Park. It's a wonderfully dramatic route and one you'll never forget, with vast desert and mountain landscapes, hot springs, hiking and horseback riding to enjoy. It's pretty rugged – at one point there's a 15% grade, the maximum allowable. The start point of the road is the Terlingua-Study Butte region. Here, 5km east of the park, two dusty little towns – Study Butte and Terlingua – run together at the junction of the River Road and Hwy 118. Leaving Terlingua to the west, the river road passes through the desert and through Lajitas, which looks like a town but is actually a resort – a shock to the system after Terlingua's desert appeal.

Past Lajitas, the road continues to the Big Bend Ranch State Park. It's much less explored than its big brother, but it has easily accessible turnouts for hiking or picnicking along the river road. These shouldn't be ignored. Make the easy 1.2km trek into narrow, dramatic Closed Canyon, where the cliffs rise above you to block out the sun. The road through this region is equally as spectacular. Around 70km further is the tiny town of Ruidosa, between the Río Grande and the stunning mountains. Blink and you'll miss it, although that would be too bad because if you keep going past Presidio and around 50km west, just past Ruidosa, you'll come to the turn-off for Chinati Hot Springs, where locals adore the isolation of the outdoor tubs, camping grounds and cabins. Turn north at Presidio for the famous UFO-spotting town of Marfa, 96km up US 67. If you plan to go back along the River Road, travel as least as far as Colorado Canyon (32km from Lajitas) for the best scenery.

ESSENTIAL EXPERIENCES

* **Hiking the Big Bend National Park, one of the most remote spots in North America.**
* Visiting the evocative ghost towns west of Big Bend.
* **Chasing the Marfa lights for as long as it takes, or at least until a local tells you to give up.**
* Eating as much chilli as you can stand, while watching competitors in the Terlingua chilli championships burn tongues, mouths and minds.
* **Looking for Willie Nelson everywhere you go.**
* Bird-watching in the Río Grande Valley.
* **Rafting and canoeing along the Río Grande, among North America's best river trips.**

DISTANCE - 200KM | COUNTRIES COVERED - USA | **IDEAL TIME COMMITMENT** - ONE WEEK | **BEST TIME OF YEAR** - APRIL TO EARLY JUNE AND SEPTEMBER TO NOVEMBER | **ESSENTIAL TIP** - TAKE NECESSARY SAFETY PRECAUTIONS IN THE NATIONAL PARK. DRINK WATER AND TAKE PLENTY WHEN HIKING.

CHILLI CHALLENGE

Every November, Terlingua is invaded by chilli freaks who are after the very best in homemade chilli. But it's no small-town festival they seek – the Terlingua Chili Cookoff is so big, there are actually two events to accommodate the hundreds of entrants. There's the International Chili Championship, organised by the Chili Appreciation Society International – you need to qualify to enter it. And then there's the Original Terlingua International Frank X Tolbert-Wick Fowler Championship Chili Cookoff, a name that's almost as much of a mouthful as the chilli. It's less competitive and more like a big party.

■ THE JOURNEY TODAY

It's been a great road trip, one of the best. You pulled off the highway and scrambled to the top of a huge butte. Exhilarated, you squint your eyes until you can actually see a waterline: the ghost of an ancient ocean that has deposited many years' worth of corals, skeletons, shells and sediment. You have been overloaded with new experiences, driving through this blistering and beautiful landscape but to be here in West Texas is the quintessential Texan experience, with miniature towns, even ghost towns, and lots of dust and scorching heat transforming the landscape into a shimmering haze.

The highlight of your River Road experience has been the Big Bend National Park, vast enough for a lifetime of discovery. It's a white-water rafting, mountain-biking and hiking paradise, and also one of the country's least visited national parks. You found out for yourself why that is so: it's hot – hotter than hell! But you put up with it because it's just so wonderful, with so much to do. The area around the park is also enticing, and home to many artist retreats, historic hotels and quaint mountain villages. The park's diverse geography means an amazing variety of wildlife, while the 177km of paved road and 241km of dirt road make scenic driving even more exciting.

West of Big Bend, you pull into Terlingua, which happens to be a favourite haunt of none other than Mr Willie Nelson himself, and you can see why: its relaxed vibe never fails to attract travellers and artistic souls. Then you're on your way to stay at the Hotel Paisano in Marfa, where you hope to spot a 'Marfa light' or two. From there, you to travel to Marathon, an artsy hamlet with art galleries, great eateries and the best hotel in the region: the Gage Hotel, with rooms straight out of the Wild

ARMCHAIR

Unsurprisingly, with such a dramatic landscape, Texas has featured in a number of iconic movies. The following are bound to pop into your mind as you travel the River Road:

✳ ***El Mariachi*** (1992) Made by Robert Rodriguez for $7000, this film became an inspiration to film-school students everywhere. It's about an unlucky travelling mariachi and is shot on the Texas–Mexican border.

✳ ***No Country for Old Men*** (2007) The Coen Brothers' harrowing adaptation of Cormac McCarthy's novel is about a west Texas welder who finds drug money and decides to keep it.

✳ ***Lone Star*** (1996) A compelling drama set against the unsettled racial atmosphere of a Texan border town.

✳ ***Traffic*** (2000) Filmed in part on the El Paso-Juarez borderlands, this multilayered thriller explores the US government's 'war on drugs'.

West: wide wooden blinds, saddles as furniture and cowhides on the bed.

Yep, that's doin' it easy, River Road style.

▪ SHORTCUT

If scenic driving is your thing, concentrate on the Big Bend National Park roads for a mini-experience of West Texas landscapes. Maverick Dr (35km) is notable for its scenery and wildlife. Ross Maxwell Scenic Dr (48km) takes you past the grand panorama of the Chisos Mountains, and a magnificent view of Santa Elena Canyon's 457m sheer rock walls. Río Grande Village Dr (32km) is best at sunset, when the mountains glow brilliantly with different red and orange hues.

▪ DETOUR

The middle of West Texas has some of North America's clearest and darkest skies, a legacy of being so far away from city life and its attendant light pollution. That's why the University of Texas's McDonald Observatory is here. With some of the biggest telescopes in the world, it's perched on top of 2069m Mt Locke, 30km northwest of Fort Davis on Hwy 118. The observatory offers guided tours and 'Star Parties', when professional astronomers give tours of the night sky.

WITOLD SKRYPCZAK | LONELY PLANET IMAGES ©

OPENING SPREAD The Santa Elena Canyon at sunset, Big Bend National Park. **ABOVE** Ghostworld? Just another historic cemetery in Terlingua. **BELOW** The River Road and the Rio Grande, just as they should be: side by side.

MARFA LIGHTS

What are the fabled Marfa lights? Strange atmospheric conditions? Certainly, they are 'UFOs' in the literal sense – unidentified flying objects – and they've been sighted by numerous people over the years, appearing, disappearing and moving around the sky, and often changing colour. Accounts go back to 1883, when a cowboy first reported them, believing they were Apache signal fires. Today, reports keep streaming in although a large proportion turn out to be car headlights. Aside from these, there is a genuine phenomenon here and it still hasn't been fully understood, a mystery making the Marfa lights one of West Texas's top attractions.

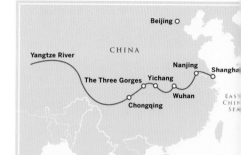

THE YANGTZE BY SLOW BOAT (THREE GORGES)

A CRUISE DOWN THE YANGTZE, THE WORLD'S THIRD-LONGEST RIVER, IS ONE OF THE MOST MEMORABLE WATER-BORNE JOURNEYS ON EARTH. WHEN THE RIVER THREADS THROUGH THE THREE GORGES, FLOWING BETWEEN ROCK FORMATIONS AND STUNNING CLIFFS, IT'S NOTHING LESS THAN MAGICAL.

158

The superlative Three Gorges are among China's most magnificent scenic wonders: few river panoramas are as awe-inspiring as these vast chasms of rock, sculpted over the ages by the Yangtze's ceaseless flow. Commencing just east of Fèngjié in Chóngqìng and levelling out west of Yichang in Hubei province, they cover an incredible 200km and cruising them by riverboat is all the more memorable, given that China's traditional penchant for waterborne travel is rapidly being eclipsed by faster, more convenient modes of transport

The 6300km river begins its reign as melting snow in southwestern Qinghai. It then spills from Tibet, before swelling through seven Chinese provinces, sucking in water from hundreds of tributaries and powerfully rolling into the East China Sea north of Shanghai. En route, it surges past some of China's greatest cities: Chóngqìng, Wuhan and Nanjing, but the Three Gorges are the jewels in the Yangtze's well-studded crown, spanning from 300m at the widest point to less than 100m at the narrowest. The journey today has the attendant, noisy hype of a marketing machine operating at fever pitch, but no one with a pulse can fail to be moved by the gorgeous panorama unfolding in real time.

The Three Gorges also host China's biggest engineering project since the construction of the Great Wall: the controversial Three Gorges Dam. The world's largest dam, it's redolent with symbolism: communist will, man's dominance over nature, China as 21st-century superpower. The dam was completed ahead of schedule in May 2006 and at the time of writing will have backed the Yangtze up for 550km and flooded an area the size of Singapore. It's 185m high and 2km wide, started generating power in 2005, and has a potential hydroelectric production capacity equivalent to 18 nuclear power plants.

ESSENTIAL EXPERIENCES

❋ **Watching the Three Gorges peek into view through a shroud of mist.**

❋ Gorging your senses on the sheer panorama unfolding before you.

❋ **Changing boats at Wushan for the Little Three Gorges.**

❋ Enjoying the ancient town of Fèngjié overlooking Qutang Gorge, the entrance point to White King Town.

❋ **Taking it easy as the boat slowly wends its way.**

❋ Wondering about the Three Gorges Dam and its future impact on this timeless region.

❋ **Trying very hard to get Monty Python's maddening song about the Yangtze out of your head for the duration of your journey.**

DISTANCE - 6300KM | **COUNTRIES COVERED** - CHINA | **IDEAL TIME COMMITMENT** - THREE NIGHTS AND FOUR DAYS
BEST TIME OF YEAR - IN THE OFF-SEASON, AWAY FROM THE CROWDS, WHEN THE TRIP IS SERENE AND YOU'RE ABLE TO OBSERVE LIFE ON THE RIVER FROM A RELAXED PERSPECTIVE | **ESSENTIAL TIP**: BRING A GOOD PAIR OF BINOCULARS.

THE THREE GORGES DAM

Although the Three Gorges Dam is improving navigation on the Yangzte and is instrumental in preventing catastrophic floods, it's not all plain sailing. In fact, the dam has generated some of the most outspoken criticism of government policy since Tiananmen Square. Environmentalists are perhaps the most vocal, as it's thought that as the river slows so will its ability to oxygenate. The untreated waste that pours into the river from over 40 towns and 400 factories, as well as toxic materials from industrial sites, could create another world record: a 550km-long septic tank, the largest toilet in the world.

▓ THE JOURNEY TODAY

You're on the boat, thinking about how the journey so far has been slow going and unremarkable. You settle back and enjoy the motion of the boat, and then you see the first of the canyons. You can't believe your eyes. Qutang Gorge rises into view – vivid, spectacular, towering into huge vertiginous slabs of rock, its cliffs jutting out in jagged and triangular chunks. It's the shortest of the three gorges, just 8km, and ends as brusquely as it starts, and yet later as you reflect on the trip, you can't help but feel it's the most awe-inspiring, with its dizzying perspective onto huge strata and vast sheets of rock. After Qutang, the terrain gives way to 20km of low-lying land. Then boats pull in at the riverside town of Wushan, high above the river, where some passengers transfer for the Little Three Gorges.

Then the boat is on the move again and you're back on the Yangtze, entering the penultimate Wu Gorge, and it is more than wondrous, a cloak of green carpeted in an abundance of shrubs, its sharp, jagged cliffs disappearing into ethereal mist. The journey continues, floating eastward out of Wu Gorge, into Hubei province and on to Xiling Gorge, the longest (80km) and perhaps least impressive of the gorges.

The trip ends at the monumental Three Gorges Dam, where you shuttle across to the observation deck for a bird's-eye view of this mammoth project, reflecting on the confusions and contradictions of the modern age.

▓ SHORTCUT

What's the opposite of a slow boat through the Yangtze? A hydrofoil, of course. The fastest route through the gorges, hydrofoil journeys take around 11 hours: three hours for the bus trip from Chóngqìng to Wanzhou, seven hours for the hydrofoil journey from Wanzhou to Yichang and an hour by bus from the Yichang hydrofoil terminal into town. Remember: hydrofoils are passenger vessels so there's no outside seating. Stand by the door for the best views.

▓ DETOUR

At Wushan, many boats stop for five hours, allowing passengers to transfer to smaller boats for trips along the narrow Little Three Gorges on the Daning River, where the landscape is so impressive that some travellers insist the gorges little gorges are more beautiful than their larger namesakes.

MASSIMO RIPANI | SIME | 4CORNERS IMAGES

OPENING SPREAD The Three Gorges: a natural wonder, and truly a feast for each and every one of the senses. **ABOVE** Qutang Gorge: possibly the king of all the gorges.

ARMCHAIR

✳ ***Yangtse Incident*** (1957) An old-time action film about the adventures of the British frigate HMS *Amethyst* during the Chinese Civil War, when it sailed up the Yangtze.

✳ ***Up the Yangtze*** (2008) A poignant, elegiac documentary about the Three Gorges Dam and how its rising waters have drowned towns and displaced two million people.

✳ ***The Romance of the Three Kingdoms*** (Luo Guanzhing) In this 14th-century historical novel, the King of Shu, Liu Bei, entrusts his son and kingdom to Zhu Geliang. The location for this occasion is White King Town, above Qutang Gorge.

ALTERNATE TRAVEL

An alternative to travelling the river is to board one of the Chinese cruise ships that depart Chóngqìng and take three days to reach Yíchāng. Some stop at all the sights, others at just a few (or none). Another alternative is to board a passenger ship from Chóngqìng to Yíchāng. These are cheap but can be disappointing as you may end up sailing through the gorges in the dead of night.

ANCIENT TRADE ROUTES

GREAT JOURNEYS

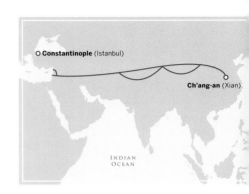

SILK ROAD

TAKE AN EXOTIC JOURNEY ACROSS CENTRAL ASIA, THREADING THROUGH
FORMER SOVIET REPUBLICS AND PAST ISLAMIC ARCHITECTURAL MARVELS,
ON ROADS ONCE TRAVERSED BY CARAVANS CARRYING SILK WORTH ITS
WEIGHT IN GOLD.

162

Containing as many strands as silk itself, the 'Silk Road' was no single road but rather a fragile network of shifting intercontinental caravan tracks that threaded through some of Asia's highest mountains and bleakest deserts.

Silk first began moving westward from China more than 2000 years ago, when the Parthians, on the Iranian plateau, became enamoured with the soft, fine fabric – the first exchange was supposedly an ostrich egg for a bolt of silk. The Romans developed an expensive fixation with the fabric after their defeat at Carrhae in 53 BC, and within a few centuries it would become more valuable than gold.

Though the road map expanded over the centuries, the route had its main eastern terminus at the Chinese capital Ch'ang-an (now Xian), and finished at Constantinople (now Istanbul), with caravanserais every 30km or so acting as hotels for traders. It took many months to traverse the 8000km route and, while it gave rise to unprecedented trade between Asia and Europe, its glory lay in the intellectual interchange of ideas, technologies and faiths that formed the world's first 'information superhighway'. Ironically as the bulk of trade headed west, religious ideas primarily travelled east.

The Silk Road was delivered its first major body blow when China abandoned the cosmopolitanism of the Tang dynasty and retreated behind its Great Wall. The trading route was eventually abandoned when the new European powers discovered alternative sea routes in the 15th century. Central Asia remained largely forgotten by the East and the West until the arrival of Russian and British explorers in the 19th century. Ironically it was only then, 20 centuries after the first Chinese mission to the West, that the term 'Silk Road' was dreamed up, coined by the German geographer Ferdinand von Richthofen. Today, almost any overland crossing through Central Asia will follow strands of the Silk Road.

ESSENTIAL EXPERIENCES

❋ **Standing atop Xian's surviving city walls and contemplating an epic journey ahead towards Europe.**

❋ Getting a taste for Silk Road–style trading at Kashgar's Sunday market, when the somnolent town is invaded by bleating animals.

❋ **Silk-shopping in Margilon, the centre of Uzbekistan's modern silk production. You can buy silk by the metre at the Yodgorlik Silk Factory, where the fabric is still mostly produced sans electricity, just like in the good old days.**

❋ Medressa-hopping through Samarkand and Bukhara in Uzbekistan, the silkiest of Silk Road countries.

❋ **Touring the scattered ruins of Merv, once a linchpin of the Silk Road, rivalling Damascus, Baghdad and Cairo as great centres of Islam.**

DISTANCE - 8000KM | **COUNTRIES COVERED** - CHINA, KYRGYZSTAN, UZBEKISTAN, TURKMENISTAN, IRAN, TURKEY | **IDEAL TIME COMMITMENT** - THREE TO FOUR MONTHS | **BEST TIME OF YEAR** - JUNE TO OCTOBER | **ESSENTIAL TIPS** - ARRANGE VISAS BEFORE YOU DEPART.

MARCO POLO

The most famous traveller on the Silk Road was Marco Polo (see p94). The son of an itinerant trader, Marco was 20 when his father and uncle took him on a journey in the 1270s to the court of the Kublai Khan, whom they had met on a previous trading expedition. The Kublai took a great liking to Marco, who was exceptionally intelligent and observant, and he was soon made a trusted adviser and representative of the ageing khan. The three Polos spent around 16 years in China, with Marco travelling far afield. Later in his life, Marco dictated the story of his travels – the resulting book became the world's most widely read travel account.

A SILKY SECRET

Shortly after the time of Christ, Roman writer Pliny the Elder speculated on silk's origin and processing, falling wide of the mark, believing the fabric to literally grow on trees in a land called Seres or Serica (in modern Central Asia). The Chinese, had they known, would most likely have done little to disillusion him. For centuries China guarded the secret of silk-making jealously, making it illegal to take silkworm eggs or mulberry seeds out of the country. Today the secret has spread, though production remains focused on Silk Road regions: China remains by far the world's largest silk producer, with Uzbekistan the third-largest and Iran the fifth-largest.

■ THE JOURNEY TODAY

Preparations for your Silk Road journey – visas, vehicles – may have taken longer than your actual travel time, but suddenly it feels more than worth it. After a few weeks through China and Kyrgyzstan, you have reached the country where all strands of the Silk Road converged: Uzbekistan.

The capital, Tashkent, may look much like the communist behemoth that rebuilt it, but after a morning on the road, Samarkhand is approaching and few places still emit such an aroma of the ancient Silk Road as does Uzbekistan's most glorious city.

There's much here that feels like a history book, from the skyline of domes and minarets to the monuments created by Timur (also known as Timur the Lame), who, in the functioning days of the Silk Road, ruled his vast empire from here.

But what you really want to see is the Registan, Samarkand's still-beating heart. Hemmed in by the grand edifices of three medressas (Muslim schools) – the world's oldest preserved medressas – it's easy to picture the plaza in its Silk Road heyday, functioning as a wall-to-wall bazaar.

Standing in the plaza is like being in an artificial canyon, with the tiled facades of the three medressas rising above you. They are intricate mosaics, and you're most struck by the roaring felines atop Sher Dor Medressa, their tiger-like lions flouting Islamic prohibitions against the depiction of live animals. It's a reminder that even through history, Uzbekistan has been a practical and sometimes irreverent practitioner of its religion, which the modern incarnation of the medressas continues to show. There is still commerce here, around this plaza, though it has retreated to the souvenir stores inside the rooms and cells of the medressas. You head inside to see if there's still silk on the tables of this most Silk Road of cities.

■ SHORTCUT

To cut down on red tape and time, many travel companies offer tours along individual segments of the Silk Road. The most evocative sections are those through China's Xinjiang province and the Uzbekistan cities of Samarkand and Bukhara.

■ DETOUR

Any Silk Road journey will land you at some point in the Xinjiang city of Kashgar. From here it's possible to veer away onto another of the world's most spectacular and adventurous roads, the Karakoram Highway (p226). Following a branch of the Silk Road itself, the highway climbs through the Himalaya, crossing 4730m Khunjerab Pass into Pakistan and the semi-mythical Hunza Valley. It ends 1300km from Kashgar in the Pakistani city of Rawalpindi.

165

OPENING SPREAD All the action of the Kashgar street market. **ABOVE** Redolent with history: Xian's ancient city wall. **LEFT** Welcome to the Shir Dor Medressa, Samarkand.

ARMCHAIR

✳ **Life along the Silk Road** (Susan Whitfield) A scholarly yet intriguing book that brings alive the Silk Road through a variety of characters.

✳ **Shadow of the Silk Road** (Colin Thubron) A prolific travel author follows the tread of the Silk Road, travelling third-class.

✳ **Silk Road: Monks, Warriors & Merchants on the Silk Road** (Luce Boulnois) Wonderful reworking of a classic text, with chapters on Silk Road museum collections, websites and travel information.

✳ **The Silk Road: Art & History** (Jonathan Tucker) Large-format art book for the connoisseur.

✳ **The Great Game** (Peter Hopkirk) Learn about the rediscovery of Central Asia, as Russia and Britain stealthily charted unknown regions.

SALT TRAIN IN THE SAHARA

SINCE THE MIDDLE AGES, CAMEL CARAVANS HAVE HEADED NORTH FROM THE STORIED CITY OF TIMBUKTU IN MUSICAL MALI, INTO THE WINDSWEPT SAHARAN SANDS IN SEARCH OF A MOST VALUABLE MINERAL THAT COULD BE TRADED FOR GOLD AND EVEN SLAVES. THEY WERE AFTER SALT, OR 'WHITE GOLD'.

At its peak, caravans of more than 100 camels would navigate the nearly 800km north from Timbuktu up and over massive dunes, through sandstorms, and in spite of wild fluctuations in temperature, eventually reach the salt mines of Taoudenni. They were discovered in the 12th century, a time when West Africa was flush with gold and ivory but in dire need of salt. Suddenly the Sahara became vitally important and soon trails bloomed from Timbuktu in all directions, connecting present day Mali with West and southern Africa, Morocco and Europe, Ethiopia, Egypt and Arabia. And it wasn't just salt, ivory and gold moving through the desert, but people, ideas, music and eventually Islam. During the 12th and 13th centuries, Timbuktu was not only wealthy, but a vortex of Islamic thought. Scholars trekked across the desert sands for months from as far as Persia, to teach and study with one another.

The salty salad days came to an end when Portuguese explorers opened the West African coast to European trade. Soon Timbuktu held less promise for the West Africans since the sail from Europe was now relatively easy and safe, and the Saharan crossing still arduous. Timbuktu and the rest of North Africa suffered a gradual political and economic decline. The Moroccans dealt the caravan trade a near fatal blow when in 1591–92 they attacked Timbuktu and other important cities like Gao. The soldiers destroyed buildings, stole property and turned even prominent citizens into refugees.

Although most of the traditional caravan routes are now largely camel-free, a shorter route from Timbuktu to Taoudenni in Mali is still operational as a largely localised salt trade. However, some of the indigenous Tuareg people still cross the Sahara by camel, travelling for as far as 2400km and as long as six months. Salt remains their most valuable commodity.

ESSENTIAL EXPERIENCES

* **Walking the sandy streets of Timbuktu, once a great city, now haunted by dusty memories, with a few epic 14th-century buildings still standing.**

* Venturing into the Sahara, aboard a camel, where you can see sunset over dunes, and sleep in Taureg camps beneath the stars.

* **Venturing into the moonscape salt mines of Taoudenni.**

* Following the salt downriver to the port markets and boatyards in Mopti.

* **Bouncing over to Bamako where you can revel in some of Africa's best and most soulful music.**

DISTANCE - 1600KM | **COUNTRIES COVERED** - MALI | **IDEAL TIME COMMITMENT** - FOUR WEEKS | **BEST TIME OF YEAR** - OCTOBER TO FEBRUARY | **ESSENTIAL TIP** - CHECK THE CURRENT SECURITY SITUATION BEFORE VENTURING FROM TIMBUKTU.

THE TUAREG

The Tuareg are a nomadic people who, until relatively recently, have roamed the Sahara for generations and make up a small 6% minority in Mali. Their domain stretches into Niger and they are traditionally responsible for the remaining salt caravans that once dominated Saharan commerce. Tuareg tribes meet once a year in the Sahara for the Festival in the Desert, which remains a sublime musical and cultural experience open to all. They also have a history of insurgency, beginning in 1916 and surfacing again between 2007 and 2009 when Tuareg groups, reportedly acting independently, launched guerilla attacks against Malian and Nigerian forces.

■ THE JOURNEY TODAY

It all begins in Timbuktu, its streets filled with sand blown in from the desert. The oldest of Timbuktu's mosques, dating from the early 14th century, is Dyingerey Ber Mosque. Its mud minaret with wooden struts is one of the city's most enduring images. For the best view of the mosque, climb to the roof of the Bibliotheque Al-Imam Essayouti opposite the mosque's eastern entrance. Timbuktu remains home to some of the best Islamic libraries in the world, including the Centre de Recherches Historiques Ahmed Baba, with 23,000 Islamic religious, historical and scientific texts.

The salt mines of Taoudenni, 800km north of the city in the desert, are still attended by camel caravans, and you can visit them by camel or 4WD. The mines are cut out of an ancient seabed that seems to stretch in all directions. Hundreds of men work the mine, some reportedly as indentured servants, cutting slabs of salt and loading them on camels for the 14-day trip back to town through a seemingly limitless monochrome of sand that stretches your depth of perception to untested limits. In Timbuktu, the slabs are loaded onto riverboats, which cruise up the Niger River to Mopti, the largest salt market in West Africa. It's possible to join the three-day journey in either direction.

In Mopti's port you'll see the requisite salt bricks, dried fish, firewood, pottery, goats, chickens and a wonderful cast of characters building boats. Historically the Sahara caravan trail continued east through the city of Gao, 350km beyond Timbuktu in one of Africa's most forgotten corners graced with a stunning riverside dune, and into Niger. If you time it right, you can still manage to travel with twice-yearly camel caravans from Agadez to Bilma in Niger, although most of

ARMCHAIR

❋ **Men of Salt** (Michael Benanav) A thrilling account of a 40-day journey across the Sahara as part of a camel caravan from Timbuktu to the salt mines of Taoudenni.

❋ **Sahara Unveiled** (William Langewiesche) Written by a correspondent for the Atlantic Monthly, this travelogue documents the author's almost 2000km journey across the Algerian Sahara.

❋ **Timbuktu: The Sahara's Fabled City of Gold** (Marq de Villiers & Sheila Hirtle) A copiously researched and enthralling history of an ancient and evocative city.

❋ **Bamako** (2006) Directed by Abderrahmane Sissako, this film is set in Mali's capital city, where the International Monetary Fund and World Bank are on trial for being the source of African poverty, while village life goes on.

this territory is dominated by 4WD these days. You'll also need a hefty 4WD vehicle to make a full trans-Sahara passage from Bilma, northeast to Cairo or Addis Ababa in Ethiopia, or from Timbuktu to marvellous Marrakesh.

SHORTCUT

Short trips are the most popular Saharan excursions and can be easily organised in Timbuktu. The most popular include sunset trips by camel to nearby dunes or overnight trips to the same dunes at sunset, followed by a night under the stars, often at a Tuareg encampment. You can also shorten the Taoudenni trip by taking a 4WD.

DETOUR

Bamako, Mali's capital, is sprawling and gritty, and can be overwhelming if you let the streets full of people, cars, buzzing flocks of mobylettes (mopeds) and clouds of pollution get to you. And yet, most are drawn in by the chance to hear some of Africa's best music featuring indigenous *kora* (harp)-driven melodies, and those gritty Malian blues. If you like your markets colourful, clamorous and spilling into the surrounding streets, and if you appreciate pulsing night-time energy, Bamako might just get under your skin.

JUAN MEDINA | CORBIS

OPENING SPREAD A Tuareg nomad in the Sahara, Niger. **ABOVE** Amadou and Mariam, the internationally-renowned blind singing duo from Mali. **BELOW** A Tuareg nomad camel train crosses the Sahara's Air Mountains, Agadez, Niger

SOUL MUSIC

For centuries, Mali's *griots* (also called jelis), a hereditary caste of musicians, have served as the praise singers and storytellers of Malian society and continue to play an important role. Toumani Diabaté, the undisputed master of the 21-string *kora* (harp), is himself a 71st-generation kora player and griot. Other renowned Malian kora players, such as Ballaké Sissoko and Mamadou Diabaté, also come from griot families. The blues are another Malian speciality – some scholars believe that the roots of American blues lie with the Malian slaves who worked on US plantations. The genius of Ali Farka Touré, who died in 2006, was largely responsible for Mali's musical migration beyond Africa's shores.

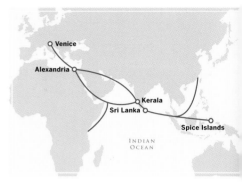

SPICE ROUTE

WITH ALL THE DRAMA AND MYSTERY OF THE ANCIENT WORLD, THE SPICE
ROUTE THREADED ITS WAY THROUGH INDONESIA, MALAYSIA, SRI LANKA,
INDIA, GHANA, IRAQ, EGYPT AND ITALY, TRANSPORTING VALUABLE SPICES
FROM THE EAST TO ARABIAN, ROMAN, EGYPTIAN AND GREEK WORLDS.

170

In ancient times, the spice trade was a highly lucrative commercial
enterprise that transported and merchandised huge volumes of spices
as well as incense and drugs such as opium. The spices included
cinnamon, cassia, cardamom, ginger and turmeric, with the first two
being transported to the Middle East as far back as 2000 BC. Arab
traders and merchants built up improbable legends around the origins of
spices – they were guarded by phantasmagorical beasties, went one such
story – in order to increase their mystique and allure and consequently
their retail price. Alexandria in Egypt was also in on the action. When
the Romans began travelling from Egypt to India, they transformed
Alexandria into the world's most powerful commercial centre,
distributing Indian spices to Greek and Roman markets.

Trade from spice regions to Arabian lands was conducted mainly by
sea routes, as it was in East Asia, when the Chinese travelled to the
Spice Islands in Indonesia and Ceylon (Sri Lanka). In medieval times,
Europeans developed advanced ships and new navigation technology,
and could cross oceans in search of wealth. The prizes that drew the
great Portuguese explorers in the 16th century were cloves, nutmeg and
mace, all native to Maluku, the Spice Islands of eastern Indonesia, and
all in high demand because they made food taste more interesting and
because nutmeg was supposed to cure the plague.

Dutch merchants set sail for the Spice Islands in 1595 and 1598,
both expeditions returning with lucrative spice cargoes, leading to the
formation of the Dutch East India Company in 1602. In 1664, the French
East India Company was formed and Portugal was becoming displaced in
the region after dominating for a century. By the 19th century, the British
were in India and Ceylon while the Dutch controlled the East Indies.

ESSENTIAL EXPERIENCES

✳ **Visiting the amazing Spice Islands
in Indonesia.**

✳ Travelling to Melaka in Malaysia, one of the
most important Asian stops on the Spice
Route and today a top-drawer destination
with historical treasures and a rich character.

✳ **Visiting a spice garden in Sri Lanka,
another important stop on the Spice
Route, to discover the alternative uses
of familiar spices.**

✳ Visiting Ghana's extraordinary coastal forts,
originally established as trading posts to store
goods brought to the coast including gold,
ivory and spices.

✳ **Imagining yourself a spice trader in the
evocative old alleyways of Al-Quseir, Egypt.**

DISTANCE - APPROXIMATELY 12,000KM | **COUNTRIES COVERED** - INDONESIA, MALAYSIA, SRI LANKA, INDIA, GHANA, IRAQ, EGYPT,
ITALY **IDEAL TIME COMMITMENT** - AS LONG AS YOU CAN MANAGE | **BEST TIME OF YEAR** - ANY TIME | **ESSENTIAL TIP** - DON'T FOOL
YOURSELF INTO THINKING YOU'LL MAKE MONEY OFF NUTMEG.

If you really want to go back in time, the earliest physical evidence of an international spice trade can be found in the wall reliefs of the Funerary Temple of Hatshepsut in Luxor, Egypt. The temple rises majestically from the desert in a series of terraces before merging dramatically with the sheer limestone cliffs of the Theban walls. The effect is uncanny, almost as if it was organic, making the partly rock-cut, partly free-standing structure one of ancient Egypt's finest monuments. It must surely have been even more spectacular in its original form.

SPICY KERALA

The spices grown in Kerala, India, have drawn traders for more than 3000 years. The coast was known to the Phoenicians, Romans, Arabs and Chinese and was a transit point for spices from Maluka in Indonesia. The kingdom of Cheras ruled much of Kerala until the early Middle Ages, competing with kingdoms and small fiefdoms for territory and trade. The arrival of Vasco da Gama (see p174) in 1498 opened up European colonialism, as Portuguese, Dutch and English interests fought Arab traders and each other for control of the lucrative spice trade. Today, tours of spice gardens and plantations can be arranged.

THE JOURNEY TODAY

The Maluku Islands, Indonesia's original Spice Islands, are an untouristed gem. Spices now have no economic clout and the islands are protected from mass tourism by the 'tyranny' of distance, erratic transport and the residue of a destructive period of conflict between 1999 and 2002. But that's society's loss and your gain, for you know there's something here money cannot buy: idyllic islands, charming culture, amazing snorkelling, beautiful beaches...

But you want to follow the trail of the original Spice Route so you head for the Banda region, a tiny yet fascinating cluster of 10 islands. In medieval times, nutmeg was produced almost exclusively on the Bandas and was highly prized. It was traded for food and cloth with Arab, Chinese, Javanese and Bugis merchants, but when Europeans arrived (the Portuguese in 1512 and the Dutch from 1599) things changed quickly, with the new arrivals demanding a monopoly. After the Bandanese began trading with the English, the governor general of the Dutch East India Company in 1621 ordered the virtual genocide of the local people. Just a few hundred survivors escaped to the Kei Islands.

Walking around Bandaneira, you reflect on this tragic history as you take in the sleepy, flower-filled streets, colonial-era houses, mouldering ruins and glorious cloudscapes over Gunung Api. But that tragic past can't take the gloss off what is a wonderful place to visit. That sense of joy is uppermost in your mind as you take a speedboat to the Kei Islands, following the exiles of old and finding at that destination stunning, yet almost entirely empty, white-sand beaches, and the chance to begin again...

SHORTCUT

There's plenty to do on the Spice Islands alone: unwinding on white sand at Ohoidertawun or Pasir Panjang; watching the sunset from Pulau Ternate beam golden hues onto the jungle-covered volcanic cone of neighbouring Pulau Tidore; and discovering idyllic empty beaches as well as WWII remnants on the desert islands around Morotai.

DETOUR

In the Middle Ages, before the rise of Portugal and Holland, Venice was Europe's primary player in the spice trade, building a maritime empire importing precious spices. This had a big bearing on Italian food that can still be tasted today. Once ordinary Italians knew what was cooking in noble homes, they felt less enthusiastic about their dubious meats and unsalted bread. With bumper crops from the 11th to the 13th century meeting basic food needs, Italians could afford to get creative, curing meats, cave-ageing cheeses and developing speciality wines to complement increasingly sophisticated local foods.

OPENING SPREAD The Funerary Temple of Hatshepsut, where the earliest extant remnants of the Spice Route can be found. **ABOVE** The Spice Trade today: preparing ginger at Fort Cochin, India. **LEFT** In Kerala, a cheerful beach-cloth vendor carries her wares in inimitable style.

ARMCHAIR

✳ **This Earth of Mankind** (Pramoedya Ananta Toer) Toer, Indonesia's best-known novelist, spent over 14 years in jail because of his criticism of the New Order government. This is the first of his quartet of historical realist novels set in the colonial era; the others are Child of All Nations, Footsteps and House of Glass.

✳ **Twilight in Djakarta** (Mochtar Lubis) This novel is a scathing attack on corruption and the plight of the poor in Jakarta in the 1950s. The book, Lubis' most famous, was banned and he was subsequently jailed.

✳ **Puisi Tak Terkuburkan** (The Poet; 2000) This film, by Indonesia's best-known contemporary director Garin Nugroho, tells the story of poet Ibrahim Kadir, who was imprisoned by the Suharto government.

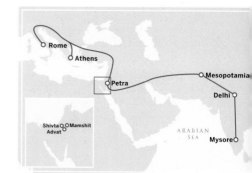

THE INCENSE ROAD OF ANTIQUITY

MASSES OF FRANKINCENSE, A SUBSTANCE ONCE WORTH MORE THAN GOLD, WERE TRANSPORTED ALONG THE INCENSE ROAD EACH YEAR FROM SOUTH ARABIA TO THE MEDITERRANEAN, INSPIRING COUNTLESS MYTHS AND LEGENDS AND PLAYING A MAJOR PART IN SHAPING HUMAN HISTORY.

174

From around the beginning of the 3rd century BC until the 2nd, the Incense Road was a major system of trade routes from Egypt through the Middle East and into India. Its purpose was to link the Mediterranean world with Arabic sources of frankincense and myrrh and eastern sources of incense and spice. The route went into decline when the Greeks and Romans decided to deal directly with India via ancient sea routes, although it was still used for a good few centuries after. Travelling the Incense Road was fraught for the ancients, who moved over very difficult, harsh and unforgiving terrain in long camel trains containing thousands of people. Due to the lack of maps or navigational systems, the presence of robbers and the fact that the kingdoms they passed through tried to tax the travellers at every opportunity, the route wasn't fixed and new ones were often devised, forcing some towns along the way into decline and others into prosperity, depending on the path of the camel train.

The goods were precious indeed: rare, exotic spices for cooking; myrrh and frankincense for women to pamper themselves with; and salts for preserving and cooking. All told, the journey took around six months and covered around 50 stops, and was a constant struggle for all concerned to keep fit, healthy and alive for the duration. To fully appreciate the historic importance of the route, bear in mind that during antiquity frankincense was as valuable as gold, as evidenced by the gifts given to baby Jesus and mother Mary: none other than gold, frankincense and myrrh.

Truly, the Incense Road speaks of a journey full of intrigue and riddled with history, larger-than-life characters and the mysterious allure of the desert and what lies beyond.

ESSENTIAL EXPERIENCES

✳ **Travelling to Mysore from Bangalore in India for a glimpse of its storied incense factories and famous palace.**

✳ Shopping for eye-popping handicrafts, spices and tea, and of course *agarbathi* (incense) from Chandni Chowk, Old Delhi's famous shopping street of bazaars.

✳ **Visiting amazing Petra in Jordan, a vast city hewn from towering rock walls of multicoloured sandstone and a key player in the trade of frankincense, myrrh and spices transported by camel caravan here.**

✳ Trekking to Al-Khamasin in Saudi Arabia, on an ancient caravan route and particularly famous for its *bachoor* (incense) and the quality of its camels.

DISTANCE - 2400KM | COUNTRIES COVERED - GREECE, KUWAIT, YEMEN, OMAN, SAUDI ARABIA, JORDAN, ISRAEL, INDIA | IDEAL TIME COMMITMENT - THREE MONTHS | BEST TIME OF YEAR - FOR ISRAEL, APRIL AND MAY OR SEPTEMBER AND OCTOBER, WHEN TEMPERATURES ARE MILD IN MOST AREAS. | ESSENTIAL TIP - DON'T CONFUSE 'FRANKINCENSE' WITH 'FRANKENSTEIN'.

UBAR

In 1992, British explorer Ranulph Fiennes and a group of US researchers announced they'd found the remains of Ubar, otherwise known as the 'Atlantis of the Sands', which according to legend had been the crossroads of the ancient frankincense trail. Legend is one thing, but even scholars are reasonably certain that Ubar existed and that it controlled the frankincense trade and became highly prosperous because of it. According to the Quran, God smote Ubar because of its decadent populace. However, excavations have proceeded slowly with nothing sufficient to verify any such claims.

■ THE JOURNEY TODAY

The Negev desert covers over half of Israel yet despite its vast, yawning emptiness, you're seduced by its low sandstone hills, rocky peaks and fertile plains. But you're not here for the scenery. You've come to the desert because it was the heart of the Nabataean empire, once forming a highly significant part of the ancient incense route. Indeed, the remnants of that trade are more visible in this part of the world than anywhere else.

You hire a bus to take you to the Nabataean strongholds of Mamshit, Avdat and Shivta, built along the ancient incense and spice route to protect travelling caravans bringing their hugely profitable trade from south Arabia to the port city of Gaza on the Mediterranean coast. At Avdat, a well-preserved city on a hill dominating the desert sky, the ruins are impressive and the vistas amazing. It's a steep climb but worth it.

Your next stop is Shivta, the most isolated Nabataean town, where ruins are visible from when it was an important Byzantine town on the caravan route between Egypt and Anatolia. Finally, the bus drops you at Mamshit. Although visually less impressive than Shivta, Mamshit is the best-preserved of the ancient towns, and you marvel at entire streets that have survived intact and the excavated Nabataean remains including reservoirs, watchtowers, Roman military and Byzantine cemeteries, jewellery and coins, churches and mosaics. You are filled with admiration, for despite the hostile desert, these towns flourished as the remains of forts, caravanserai and agricultural systems testify.

Then it's time to leave. You feel satiated that your knowledge of the incense route is now just that little bit deeper, that little bit more

ARMCHAIR

❋ **The Bridal Canopy** (SY Agnon) In the mid-20th century, Agnon, Israel's first Nobel Literature Prize winner, emerged as a powerful force on the international literary scene. This 1931 novel secured his stellar reputation.

❋ **Frankincense & Myrrh: A Study of the Arabian Incense Trade** (Nigel Groom) Vividly relates how these exotic fragrances made Arabia rich.

❋ **Plants of Dhofar** (Anthony Miller & Miranda Morris) In this beautifully illustrated scientific guide to the plants of the Dhofar region, there's a wonderful account of the social and historical importance of the frankincense tree.

❋ **Ha Buah** (*The Bubble*; 2006) For a modern perspective on Israel, this film, directed by Eytan Fox, showcases Tel Aviv and the 'bubble' life its residents lead. Things turn upside down when one of the main characters becomes romantically involved with a Palestinian.

intense and keenly felt after your excursion into the wondrous Negev.

SHORTCUT

Dhofar, the southernmost province of Oman, can give an exciting buzz to the traveller keen on connecting with the old incense days. It's an historic region strongly associated with the old frankincense route, plus it has great beaches, a laidback atmosphere and a stimulating ethnic mix. Visit Mughsail, famed for the violent blowholes in the undercliff and for nearby groves of wild frankincense, and tread in the path of ancient traders by purchasing a small bag of locally harvested frankincense from Al-Husn Souq.

DETOUR

If you're visiting Avdat, don't miss Ein Avdat National Park, one of the highlights of the Negev. Ein Avdat is truly a freak of nature – a pool of icy water in the hot desert fed by waters flowing through intricate channels. You can reach it by taking a gentle hike through incredible scenery dominated by a steep, winding canyon. You can also reach the top of a waterfall that transforms into a spectacular sight during winter – all well worth the effort and expenditure.

TIM BARKER | LONELY PLANET IMAGES ©

OPENING SPREAD At Avdat, this is all that remains of a road station for Nabataean caravans. **ABOVE** Ancient, mysterious and hewn from rock: the Treasury at Petra. **BELOW** Massive, awesome and seductive: the Negev desert.

FRANKINCENSE

Along the road from Salalah to the Yemeni border, look out for one of the most important markers in the Arabian Peninsula's history. Sprouting from the limestone rock, and leafless and lifeless for much of the year, Boswellia sacra, the frankincense tree, is a singularly unspectacular 'monument' with its peeling bark and stumped branches. Yet its sacred sap sustained entire empires across the peninsula, inveigled its way into the temples of Egypt, Jerusalem and Rome, is recorded in the Bible and Quran, and is still used today in many sacred ceremonies around the world. In the 1st century AD, Pliny wrote that the frankincense trade made the people of southern Arabia the richest on Earth.

THE BALTIC AMBER ROAD

YOU DON'T NEED TO BE AN AMBER GAMBLER TO ENJOY THIS JOURNEY, JUST A SEEKER OF CULTURALLY RICH AND UNIQUE EXPERIENCES. THE AMBER ROAD TRACES THE BALTIC'S SINGULAR AMBER SIGHTS AND EXPERIENCES, WINDING ALONG THE COASTS OF THE KALININGRAD REGION, LITHUANIA AND LATVIA.

178

Amber – fossilised tree resin – was formed in the Baltic region 40 to 60 million years ago and has been traded since before Jesus was a boy, but it wasn't until the mid-19th century that the trail for so-called 'Baltic gold' began to take off. In 1854–55 and 1860, substantial amounts of amber were excavated near Juodkrantė on the Curonian Spit in Lithuania. Three separate clusters weighing 2250 tons in total were uncovered during the 'amber rush' to the sleepy seashore village, yet by 1861 the supply had dried up. Since 1869, it has been excavated at the Yantarny mine in the Kaliningrad region, and it's still the place where most amber sold in the Baltics today comes from.

The Baltic Amber Road, an EU-funded tourism route, stretches for 418km and is designed to steer travellers to and through the Baltic's most amber-dextrous attractions, following the shores of the Baltic Sea from Kaliningrad in the south to Latvia in the north. Indeed, there's nowhere more suitable for savouring its subtle magic than in the Russian-controlled Kaliningrad Region, source of most Baltic amber. Here, stunning jewellery and the world's second-largest amber hunk are features of the Kaliningrad Amber Museum. A tour of the industrial Yantarny Amber Mine is a must, while the region's finest amber gallery in Nida, Lithuania, is just across from the Russian province.

In Lithuania, amber treasure was found in Juodkrantė in the 1850s but today only specks are washed up on the shore after fierce storms. Instead, professional amber-fishers frequent Karklė and Šventoji beaches. Palanga has a palatial amber museum. Latvia's Liepāja boasts the world's largest piece of amber art (a dangling tapestry) and an amber sundial, and there are displays inside the Livonian Order castle in Ventspils, at the end of the Amber Road.

ESSENTIAL EXPERIENCES

❋ **'Fishing' for amber on the beach – if the locals will let you.**

❋ Exploring the Old Towns of Riga and Vilnius, which sum up everything good and great about the Baltic region.

❋ **Admiring magnificent, superlative Baltic and art nouveau architecture in Riga.**

❋ Exploring the magnificent archaeological site of Kernavė near Vilnius, which will take you back on a trip through time.

❋ **Enjoying the many superb Baltic song and dance festivals dotted around the region – real, live Baltic culture.**

DISTANCE - 418KM | **COUNTRIES COVERED** - KALININGRAD REGION (RUSSIA), LITHUANIA, LATVIA | **IDEAL TIME COMMITMENT** - FOUR DAYS TO ONE WEEK | **BEST TIME OF YEAR** - MAY TO SEPTEMBER | **ESSENTIAL TIP** - EXPLORE THE HISTORY OF AMBER BEFORE YOU LEAVE; THE REGION WILL THEN UNFOLD ITSELF TO YOU.

THE JOURNEY TODAY

Although curious about amber, you also want to see the sights and so you let the 'Baltic gold' guide you to quirky places that you would never have visited otherwise. Travelling the Baltic Amber Road, you think about the uses to which amber has been put: primitive humans burnt it for heat; in the Middle Ages it was used as cash; around 12,000 BC, tribal Prussians rubbed it to create static electricity; and during the 12th century it was said to contain mystical qualities, allowing one to become closer to the spirits. Gazing upon the enormous Yantarny Amber Mine in Kaliningrad, you recall how foreigners were not allowed into the region as recently as 1991. Here, at the world's largest open-pit amber mine, a frontier atmosphere sometimes prevails, as amber-hunters compete with commercial concerns.

You leave for Lithuania and arrive at the Palanga amber museum, where you admire the deeply seductive hues of the object of your journey, marvelling at displays featuring amber jewellery encasing ancient mosquitoes and other insects. Then you hit the long, Baltic shoreline, watching professional 'fishers' scour for amber. It's sunset and you can't help but imagine the orange skyline as an amber casing covering the earth and you as the insect trapped inside.

The final experience in a triumvirate of amber ecstasies occurs at Nida. You're at the Gaigalas family homestead on a wild stretch of coastline, open to the public and decorated with trash washed up from the sea (life buoys, toothbrushes) retro-fitted as sculptures.

Yes, it's a real home, where the owners survive by selling 15kg amber specks washed up on the beach after storms.

SHORTCUT

An abridged version could just include Latvia. There are a variety of amber sellers in Riga's old town to explore, but generally it's an excellent country to be in: a sensory delight containing magical ingredients like pine forests with castle ruins, onion-domed cathedrals and spicy beaches. And the cosmopolitan capital, Riga, is the region's liveliest.

DETOUR

Explore Latvia and Lithuania's Unesco-protected treasures – Riga has a phenomenal collection of medieval and neoclassical buildings, and boasts Europe's best art nouveau buildings. Vilnius is riddled with medieval, Gothic, Renaissance and classical churches and Europe's biggest baroque Old Town. The archaeological site of Kernavė near the Lithuanian capital is worth a side trip, as is the Curonian Spit, the extraordinary slither linking Lithuania with Kaliningrad, a natural wonder sculpted over millennia by the Baltic Sea.

BRENT WINEBRENNER | LONELY PLANET IMAGES ©

OPENING SPREAD A fine sight: a 19th-century orthodox cathedral in Riga. **ABOVE (L)** Seducing with its colour, texture and form: amber pieces in Nida. **ABOVE (R)** Parklife: Kaliningrad domino players enjoying some outdoor action.

ARMCHAIR

* ✳ *The Child of Man* (1992) and *The Mystery of the Old Parish Church* (2000) Two Latvian films that skilfully deal with the Soviet occupation of Latvia and, in the case of the latter, the Nazi invasion, including background to the theories surrounding the Amber Room (see boxed text p179),

* ✳ *A Woman in Amber: Healing the Trauma of War and Exile* (Agate Nesaule) A semi-autobiographical novel about the author's exile from Latvia after the Soviets invaded, and her emigration to the US.

ALL ABOUT AMBER

Amber comes in 250 colours. White amber contains one million gas bubbles per cubic millimetre. Some pieces for sale are heated or compressed, some are combined, while others are polished. Test amber by placing it in salt water – if it sinks, it's fake. Rubbing unpolished amber yields a pine smell. The most valuable pieces are those with 'inclusions': grains, shells, vegetation or prehistoric insects.

LITERARY
JOURNEYS

❧

GREAT JOURNEYS

THEROUX IN THE PACIFIC

PAUL THEROUX HAD A SPECIAL AFFINITY FOR THE PACIFIC, RESULTING IN ONE OF HIS BEST-KNOWN TRAVEL BOOKS, THE HAPPY ISLES OF OCEANIA – PADDLING THE PACIFIC. IT RECOUNTS A KAYAKING ODYSSEY THAT TOOK HIM FROM NEW ZEALAND TO PAPUA NEW GUINEA AND ON TO HAWAII.

182

The background to *The Happy Isles of Oceania* is one of anxiety and stress. Theroux was waiting for results of a cancer test at the same time as he was dealing with the break-up of his first marriage, so he decided to get as far away from it all as possible: the South Pacific ocean. Taking with him a collapsible kayak and a tent, he visited Australia, New Zealand and 51 Pacific Islands. His mood was sombre and sullen, often putting him in conflict with the local people and into some rather dangerous situations. Theroux is at his best relating anecdotes about the people he meets and his descriptions of Australians, New Zealanders, islanders and Hawaiians are cantankerous and cynical.

His visits to the small islands (the Solomons, Samoa, the Cooks) are the most memorable. Theroux really gets to the heart of what it is that makes these places so mythical (their status as archetypal paradise) and so tarnished at the same time (war, Western exploitation, poverty and pollution). On top of it all is the sheer adrenalin thrill of a man travelling via kayak around these remote places. But Theroux also hikes the wild Fiordland in New Zealand and the desert around Alice Springs in Australia. He lives among the Trobriand Islanders of New Guinea, with their unique sexual mores. He visits the megapode egg-diggers of the Solomon Islands and the cargo cults of Vanuatu and drops in on Fiji and Tonga, even summoning an audience with Tongan King Taufa'ahau Tupou IV. Theroux is either fearless or oblivious – or too jaded to care – about the danger he's in: sleeping near crocodile-infested jungle; washing up on a deserted island; camping on private, tribal land.

People have described this book as 'acerbic', 'caustic', even racist. However, as he moves to some sort of personal fulfilment at the journey's end so, you sense, does he hope the Pacific finds peace too, after all it's been through.

ESSENTIAL EXPERIENCES

✱ **Tramping through the Fiordland, New Zealand's rawest wilderness area.**

✱ Watching the charming brand of cricket played on the Trobriand Islands in Papua New Guinea, which has no limit on the amount of players per side and often features more singing and dancing than actual game play.

✱ **Paddling a traditional canoe and watching wildlife in the huge World Heritage–listed Lake Te'Nggano in the Solomons.**

✱ Enjoying the superb and wildly exuberant 'island' nights – like minifestivals – in Rarotonga, in the Cook Islands.

DISTANCE - APPROXIMATELY 8000KM | **COUNTRIES COVERED** - NEW ZEALAND, AUSTRALIA, PAPUA NEW GUINEA, SOLOMON ISLANDS, VANUATU, FIJI, TONGA, WESTERN SAMOA, AMERICAN SAMOA, TAHITI, MARQUESAS, COOK ISLANDS, EASTER ISLAND, HAWAII **IDEAL TIME COMMITMENT** - 18 MONTHS | **BEST TIME OF YEAR** - PREFERABLY NOT AFTER A MAJOR TRAUMA IN YOUR LIFE. **ESSENTIAL TIP** - BE THE ANTI-THEROUX: ENJOY YOURSELF!

■ THE JOURNEY TODAY

'Am I mad?' you think to yourself. 'Why am I doing this?' You are in your folding kayak, out somewhere in the South Pacific sea, and you can't see any land. What if there are sharks? What if you've gone off course? What if the islanders don't want you on their turf, when – if – you do wash up somewhere? But then you realise Theroux has corrupted your imagination, that moody, grumpy man in *The Happy Isles of Oceania*, wary of everyone, down on his luck and, seemingly, actively seeking squalor. And yet the rugged appeal of Theroux's ocean voyage remains, even though you're not really out in the wide ocean, merely hopping from lagoon to lagoon in the Cooks. Still, there are moments such as now, when you've lost sight of land, that you start to tingle with equal parts fear and excitement. It's that adrenalin rush that adventure-sports lovers know, the feeling of being a hair's breadth from danger.

You're travelling at little over 5km/h. It's slow going and the waves are choppy. You couldn't outrun a shark if you tried. But think of the things you've seen already. You followed much of Theroux's itinerary. You've been to Tonga and kayaked through the Wunderkammer of waterways and inlets in the Vava'u islands. You've kayaked around Kadavu and Yasawas and the beautifully calm Fijian lagoons. In Samoa, you piloted your little waterborne vessel through the Upolu mango groves and around the deserted Aleipata Islands. In the Cooks, you sailed around Rarotonga's sheltered lagoon. Soon you'll be on your way to Hawaii and the superb river kayaking there. As for the locals, you have no idea what Theroux was on about. No one has chased you with a rusty spear! You've been welcomed with open arms.

Let's hope the sharks play nice, too...

ARMCHAIR

Theroux's book hasn't been filmed as yet, but if you want a perspective on the Pacific that's different to his 'unique' world view, try the following:

✳ **The Thin Red Line** (1998) Terrence Malick's war drama, based on a novel by James Jones, showcases the beautiful singing of the Solomon Islanders and stunning scenery of Guadalcanal (which Theroux visited).

✳ **Tatau Samoa** (2001) In this documentary, German director Glsa Schleelein retraces the life of Samoan tattoo master Paulo Sulu'ape (whom Theroux visited when he was in Samoa)

✳ (1998) This documentary about traditional voyaging and the Hawaiian Hokule'a double canoe showcases a far different beast to Theroux's dinky folding kayak.

GOD IS AMERICAN

The Jon Frum Movement is one of the Pacific's true oddities. Theroux visited Tanna, home of the movement, writing that it was 'the oddest outside-time island in Vanuatu'. It's a prime example of a Pacific cargo cult, formed after islanders saw American troops during WWII with expensive, exotic US cargo and goods. So the story goes, Jon Frum is an American spirit who came from the sea at Green Point and announced himself to the locals, telling them that if the Europeans left Tanna there would be an abundance of wealth. Today, the locals still yearn and wait for his return.

SHORTCUT

Of course, Theroux didn't paddle the entire South Pacific by kayak. For the most part, he took planes, hired cars and hopped on freighter ships. So if you want to get a flavour for Theroux's Pacific without the hard work, try those methods between selected islands (although travelling by freighter is of course not 'short' at all in terms of duration). Travelling between the Cook Islands, for example, could easily make a nice little shortcut if you don't fancy the full ocean odyssey.

DETOUR

Theroux didn't make it to the North Pacific in *The Happy Isles of Oceania*, but if you're in the mood for more kayaking, the Micronesian region possibly trumps the south in that regard. Palau's amazingly photogenic Rock Islands, for example, are absolutely made for this sport. Surreal and majestic, studding the cobalt sea like jewels, they're a series of mushroom-shaped limestone islets undercut by erosion. They're uninhabited, some with tiny beaches, so you can camp out and pretend you're Theroux without getting too far out of your comfort zone – the Rock Islands are only 20km or so from civilisation.

GÖRAN BURENHULT | PHOTOLIBRARY

OPENING SPREAD Heading towards Mitre Peak, Fiordland, New Zealand.
ABOVE Doing the Pole Dance, local style, on Kiriwana Island in the Trobriands.
BELOW Here's looking at you – Easter Island's uncanny moai statues.

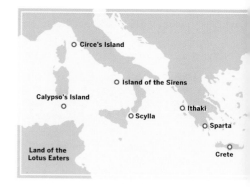

HOMER'S THE ODYSSEY

THE ODYSSEY IS ONE OF THE MOST BELOVED WORKS IN THE WESTERN LITERARY
CANON. TODAY, IT STILL STIRS PASSION IN THE HEARTS OF TRAVELLERS WHO
YEARN TO TRACE THE TORTUROUS ROUTE, WITH ALL ITS TRICKS AND CHALLENGES,
THAT THE HERO, ODYSSEUS, TOOK TO RETURN HOME AFTER THE FALL OF TROY.

186

Homer, the first and greatest writer of ancient Greece, was renowned for his
epic poems *The Iliad* and *The Odyssey*, which together told the story of the
Trojan War and the subsequent wanderings of Odysseus. *The Odyssey*, in
today's terms, can be seen as a sequel to *The Iliad*, which detailed the final
year in the Greek siege of the city of Ilion. The Odyssey picks up the story
after the Trojan War, with Odysseus commencing his lengthy journey home
to Ithaki after Troy fell. While he is away, his wife Penelope must fend off
the attentions of multiple suitors, all of whom believe him to be dead, while
his son Telemachus tries to assert his dominion over the household.

This stirring tale takes place throughout ancient Greece and along
the Mediterranean coast. It begins with Odysseus being held captive by
the nymph Calypso, who has kept him prisoner for seven years. When
he is released on a raft, it is destroyed by the god Poseidon, seeking
revenge after Odysseus blinded his son, Polyphemus. Odysseus ends up
on Scherie, where he entertains the Phaeacians living there with stories
of his adventures. As they listen intently, he spares them and the reader
no detail: after being captured, he relates, he blinded Polyphemus in
his efforts to escape. Poseidon condemned him to wander the sea for
10 years as penance, before finally wrecking his raft. Odysseus then ran
into the Laestrygonians, a giant cannibal race, but escaped again only
to encounter the witch Circe, who turned his men into swine. He also
encountered the infamous Sirens, met the ghosts of famous people, and
ran foul of Scylla, the monster with six heads. Somehow, after all that,
he managed to borrow a ship and set sail for Ithaki, where he killed the
suitors and returned to the arms of the adoring Penelope.

Was Odysseus telling lies to the Phaeacians? Perhaps, but whatever your
take, it's a fascinating and gripping tale – one of the best travelogues ever told.

ESSENTIAL EXPERIENCES

* **Relaxing in tranquil Ithaki while on the trail of Odysseus.**

* Exploring ancient Tamassos in Cyprus, the favoured trading port for the goddess Athena in *The Odyssey*.

* **Relaxing in Sicily, called Thrinakrie in *The Odyssey*, a name meaning 'trident shaped', appropriate for Sicily, which is also known as 'the island of three promontories'.**

* Looking for traces of King Minos in beautiful Crete, an island described in *The Odyssey* as 'Out on the dark blue sea...a rich and lovely land [where] King Minos ruled and enjoyed the friendship of the mighty Zeus'.

DISTANCE - APPROXIMATELY 1300KM | **COUNTRIES COVERED** - GREECE, ITALY, TURKEY, TUNISIA | **IDEAL TIME COMMITMENT** -
TEN YEARS | **BEST TIME OF YEAR** - APRIL TO MID-JUNE, SEPTEMBER TO OCTOBER | **ESSENTIAL TIP** - AVOID SIRENS AND NYMPHS.

AROUND THE MEDITERRANEAN

Jerba, an island in southern Tunisia, was the land of the lotus-eaters in *The Odyssey*, so seductive it was impossible to leave (especially after consuming the drugged honey). Turkey's Troy is referenced in *The Iliad* and *The Odyssey*, while Izmir, Turkey's third-largest city, claims to be Homer's birthplace. It was in the Italian waters of Sorrento that the mythical Sirens, who so tempted Odysseus, lived. The island of Ponza, between Rome and Naples, was also mentioned in *The Odyssey*.

■ THE JOURNEY TODAY

You arrive on Ithaki via ferry from Kefallonia, and immediately fall in love with the sheer cliffs, precipitous mountains, swathes of olive groves and cypresses, attractive villages, hidden coves, pebbly beaches and Byzantine monasteries. You want to find the sites associated with *The Odyssey*, but with no signs and little transport it won't be easy. Undeterred, you hire a moped and ride through narrow lanes wriggling inland from the waterfront. Zipping along, you reach the south of the island and the Fountain of Arethousa, where Eumaeus, Odysseus' swineherd, is believed to have brought his pigs to drink. You park the bike and set off on an exposed and isolated hike. It takes you two hours to get there and back from the turn-off, and you are amply rewarded by the unspoilt landscape and amazing sea views along the way.

As with most of the Homeric locations, the physical coordinates of Odysseus' palace have been much disputed between archaeologists. Some say it was on Pelikata Hill near Stavros, which seems as good a place to begin as any. After riding there on the moped, you're none the wiser, however you discover what many travellers on the Homer trail have: that the vaporous locations of Homeric myth, even if they prove to be nowhere to be found, turn out to be portals into amazing real-world locations.

So, as a result of looking for the palace that cannot be found, you discover the little village of Stavros above the Bay of Polis, and from there the lovely seaside village of Frikes, and then magical Kioni, which spills down a verdant hillside into a miniature harbour with bars, taverna and a beautiful beach...

■ SHORTCUT

Southwest of Athens, ancient Mycenae, near the modern village of Mycenae, is a condensed Homeric delight. Homer described it as 'well-built Mycenae, rich in gold', and the ruins, with their fortified citadel and surrounding settlement, make for an absorbing visit. Due to the sheer size of the citadel walls (13m high, 7m thick), the Ancient Greeks believed a Cyclops, one of the giants described in *The Odyssey*, must have built them.

■ DETOUR

Italy's Aeolian Islands are just like paradise, with stunning cobalt sea, splendid beaches, fantastic hiking and an incredible volcanic landscape. The Aeolians figured prominently in *The Odyssey* and evidence of the distant past can be seen everywhere, especially in Lipari's fabulous archaeology museum. The seven World Heritage– listed islands form part of a massive 200km volcanic ridge that runs between the smoking stack of Mt Etna and the threatening mass of Vesuvius above Naples.

188

OPENING SPREAD A solitary lighthouse sits atop volcanic rock on Stromboli Island, Sicily. **ABOVE (L)** A typical scene from the legendary Jerba Island. **ABOVE (R)** Scintillating Cefalù, Sicily. **RIGHT** Ios island, home to fleas – and the mystery that did Homer in.

ARMCHAIR

* **Odyssey** (Nikos Kazantzakis) A modern-day epic loosely based on the travels of Odysseus.

* **O Brother, Where Art Thou?** (2000) The Coen Brothers humorously transfer key scenes from *The Odyssey* to Depression-era Mississippi.

* **2001: A Space Odyssey** (1968) Stanley Kubrick surmised the vastness of space must engender similar existential feelings in astronauts as the sea did in the ancient Greeks, and so astronaut Bowman's travails closely parallel Odysseus's.

* **Apocalypse Now** (1979) The adventures of Willard in Francis Ford Coppola's epic Vietnam War saga also loosely echo Odysseus's mission.

* **Ulysses** (James Joyce) Each episode of Joyce's 1922 modernist classic closely follows themes and scenes from *The Odyssey*.

* **Le Mépris** (1963) Jean-Luc Godard's film features German director Fritz Lang as himself attempting to film *The Odyssey*.

R.I.P. HOMER

It's said that Homer died on the island of Ios, distressed because he was unable to solve a riddle posed by the fishermen there that 'what they caught they discarded and what they could not catch, they kept' (fleas, of course). Ios has long claimed the site of 'Homer's Grave', but his alleged resting place, a rather forlorn little mausoleum, is unimpressive. The views are worth it, though, with Sikinos, Naxos, Iraklia and Schinousa forming a nicely balanced crescent of islands across the sea.

CHE GUEVARA'S MOTORCYCLE DIARIES

ERNESTO 'CHE' GUEVARA WAS, IN HIS YOUNGER DAYS, A HARDY AND INSATIABLE TRAVELLER. HIS MEMOIR, THE MOTORCYCLE DIARIES, DOCUMENTS AN 8000KM RIDE ACROSS SOUTH AMERICA ON A BATTERED NORTON MOTORCYCLE, A JOURNEY FILLED WITH REVOLUTIONARY DERRING-DO.

190

Ernesto Guevara de la Serna – 'Che' to his friends – divided public opinion more deeply than just about any figure in the 20th century. There are many 'Ches': hero of the third world and the Sierra Maestra; the CIA's most wanted man; a handsome and often misunderstood pop figure. His image can still be seen all over Cuba (and beyond), on everything from key rings to billboards.

Che graduated from the University of Buenos Aires in 1953 with a medical degree, but the year before, he embarked on a transcontinental motorcycling odyssey with his friend Alberto Granada. The pair's nomadic wanderings were documented in *The Motorcycle Diaries*, which, when published in 1996 by Verso, carried the flip, though appropriate, tag: 'Das Kapital meets Easy Rider'. It was a momentous journey because it planted the seed that would change irrevocably the course of Latin American history. When it was over, Che was convinced that Latin America needed to be united as one super state, a belief that drove him to play a critical role in the Cuban revolution.

Che and Alberto travelled through Argentina, Chile, Peru, Ecuador, Colombia, Venezuela, Panama and Miami, before returning to Buenos Aires, the trip opening his eyes to the grinding poverty and stark political injustices prevalent in Latin America. When he later travelled to Guatemala in 1954 on the eve of a US-backed coup against Jacobo Arbenz' leftist government, he was enthusiastically devouring the works of Marx and nurturing a deep-rooted hatred of the US. In 1955, he was deported to Mexico for his pro-Arbenz activities, falling in with a group of Cubans that included Moncada veteran Raúl Castro, a longstanding Communist Party member impressed by Che's sharp intellect and unwavering political convictions. Raul introduced him to his charismatic brother, Fidel, and the rest, as they say, is history.

ESSENTIAL EXPERIENCES

❋ **Paying homage at the apartment building at Entre Ríos 480 in Rosario, Argentina, where Che was born in 1928.**

❋ Visiting Cuba – enough said.

❋ **Travelling to the Museo Casa Ernesto 'Che' Guevara in Alto Gracia, Argentina, which focuses heavily on Che's early life.**

❋ Crossing the Cruce de Lagos, as Che did, in Parque Nacional Vicente Perez Rosales.

❋ **Taking up the trail of Che in Chile's Lakes District.**

❋ Locating the exact spot where Che was killed in the village of La Higuera, Bolivia.

DISTANCE - 14,000KM | **COUNTRIES COVERED** - ARGENTINA, CHILE, PERU, ECUADOR, COLOMBIA, VENEZUELA, USA, PANAMA
IDEAL TIME COMMITMENT - SIX MONTHS | **BEST TIME OF YEAR** - WHENEVER REVOLUTIONARY FERVOUR GRIPS YOU
ESSENTIAL TIP - LEAVE YOUR REVOLUTIONARY IDEALS AT HOME.

THE CHE TRAIL

In 2010, tourism authorities in Argentina, Cuba and Bolivia announced they were working on an international historic tourist route that follows Che's trail through the three countries. Cuba's Che sites are legion, of course, while in Argentina stops include Rosario, where he was born, and the Guevara family mate plantation in Misiones. Bolivian highlights include the jungle location where Che was killed and his burial place at Valle Grande. The trail will eventually widen out to include many of the places Che and Alberto visited on their motorcycle odyssey.

THE JOURNEY TODAY

You've made it to Chile, arriving from Argentina through the Parque Nacional Vicente Perez Rosales, a zone of celestial lakes and soaring volcanoes. You're following the route Che and Alberto took, except they had to lake hop when and where they could, helping out with bilge-pumping.

On your hired motorbike, you arrive in Petrohué, with its majestic lakeside setting and all-enveloping serenity, then you take the road skirting the enormous Lago Llanquihue and past the huge Volcan Osorno, a prime destination for mountain climbers and skiers, with its perfect conical peak towering above azure glacial lakes. You pause for a while, struck by its idyllic shape, a serendipitous result of the 40 craters around its base, ensuring that the volcano's eruptions have never taken place at the top. You imagine Che similarly lost in thought, perhaps thinking of the volcano's unique structure as a metaphor for the united nations of Latin America, a superstructure working to preserve the whole...

From Osorno, Che and Alberto rode to the lively, handsome port of Valdivia, the most attractive city in Chile's Lakes District, with its touches of German influence, mist and rain. You pause there, suitably relaxed and refreshed, and then you push on for Temuco, where they paid homage to poet Pablo Neruda, although it was at this point that their ancient motorbike reached the end of its life. Che and Alberto then rode a truck to the beautiful colonial city of Valparai, and again you follow their lead, minus the truck, before travelling further north to see Chuquicamata's breathtaking copper mine and to explore the nitrate ghost towns around the city of Iquique. These towns were still functioning

ARMCHAIR

✱ **The Motorcycle Diaries** (Che Guevara) Became the basis for the acclaimed 2004 film of the same name, directed by Walter Salles.

✱ **Traveling with Che Guevara: The Making of a Revolutionary** (2004) Che's companion, Alberto Granado wrote his version of the journey, which would also serve as a reference for Salles' film.

✱ **Che** (2008) Steven Soderbergh's two-part epic is an exhaustive account of Che's life, from his first meeting with Fidel to his

death in Bolivia. This timeline was also covered in the 1969 film *Che!*, with Omar Sharif in the lead role, widely considered an ill-conceived production.

✱ **Chasing Che: A Motorcycle Journey in Search of the Guevara Legend** (2000) Details Patrick Symmes' efforts to retrace Che's journey.

THE IMAGE

Che was immortalised in a 1960 Alberto Korda photograph that skilfully captured his iconic qualities: that now-famous defiant expression and wistful eyes gazing far into the future. It's perhaps the world's best-known photograph, but it wasn't until seven years after Che's death that it took off, when an Italian publisher cropped it and reworked it into a poster to publicise Che's Bolivian diaries. Ever since, everyone from Andy Warhol to Smirnoff and rock band Rage Against the Machine has been riffing off it, and ripping it off. Korda, a lifelong socialist and Che supporter, steadfastly refused to ever take a cent in payment for his photograph and even sued Smirnoff for commercial exploitation.

when Che visited, and their psychic trace is heavy in the air – as is his, everywhere you go.

Finally, you wash up at beachside Arica, the end of your Chilean adventure. There, as you watch the sea and sand, you take it easy for a while, contemplating the next country in your Guevarian adventure.

▪ SHORTCUT

If don't have time for the whole Motorcycle Diaries journey, try the Chile loop as outlined in the previous section. Allow one to two weeks.

▪ DETOUR

It wasn't part of the original journey, but a visit to Cuba should be compulsory, seeing as though you're already in that part of the world. Cuba is full to the brim with bombastic Che iconology as well as Santa Clara's Monumento Ernesto Che Guevara, a monument, mausoleum and museum complex in a vast square guarded by a bronze statue of 'El Che.' The mausoleum below contains 38 stone-carved niches dedicated to guerrillas killed in the failed revolutionary attempt in Bolivia that cost Che his life, along with the remains of 17 of them, including the man himself. The adjacent museum holds Che ephemera.

CHRISTINA SIMONS / CORBIS

OPENING SPREAD A sight to inspire revolution? Osorno volcano, Chile.
ABOVE In Havana, Cuba, Che's iconic gaze watches over a 1950s Chevrolet Bel Air.
BELOW Lucky llamas grazing in Chile's Lauca National Park.

AROUND THE WORLD IN 80 DAYS

ALTHOUGH FICTIONAL, JULES VERNE'S CLASSIC STORY IS ONE OF THE BEST-KNOWN TRAVEL JOURNEYS OF ALL. FROM LONDON TO SUEZ TO INDIA TO ASIA TO AMERICA, AND BACK TO LONDON, THE TRIP, CONDUCTED VIA RAIL AND STEAMER, IS MUCH LOVED BY DREAMERS AND TRAVELLERS ALIKE.

194

Jules Verne's classic novel *Around the World in 80 Days* (1873) has colonised the popular consciousness. Even if you haven't read it, doubtless you'll know the basic story. There's a Londoner with a strange name, Phileas Fogg, who has a French valet called Passepartout. Fogg accepts a bet from his posh friends at the exclusive Reform Club that he can travel around the world in 80 days. The prize is £20,000. They decide to do the journey by rail and steamer.

Along the way, many japes, cases of mistaken identity and thrilling adventures ensue. A detective on the hunt for a bank robber trails them. They ride elephants in India. They rescue an Indian woman who is about to be sacrificed, by having Passepartout pretend to be a zombie and carry her away. In Calcutta, the detective catches them, now with the rescued woman in tow, and arrests them, although they skip bail and flee to Hong Kong. The detective tries to get Passepartout drugged up and drunk in order to manipulate him to turn against his master, although he escapes and catches a steamer to Yokohama, which Fogg misses. Fogg turns up later and finds Passepartout in a circus, trying to earn enough money to make it back home. Reuinted, they fight off bison and Sioux Indians in America. They start mutinies, lose all their money and think they've lost the bet. They bribe crews and captains, and so it goes, on and on, misadventure upon misadventure piling up to create chaotic comedy. Back home, they think they've lost the bet but realise that since they crossed the International Date Line, they have in fact won.

What's most remarkable about this very tall tale is that for all the high farce, it's highly accurate about the realities of travelling. Didn't we all start a mutiny, get wasted on drugs with strangers and bribe the last of our cash away during our days as desperate, thrill-seeking backpackers?

ESSENTIAL EXPERIENCES

✳ **Visiting the Reform Club in London and wishing you could afford to become a member.**

✳ Trying to circumnavigate the world as best you can without flying.

✳ **Visiting the 14th-century Gothic Corvin Castle in Transylvania, also visited by Fogg.**

✳ Taking a hot-air balloon from Paris, as Fogg did in the 1956 film (such a trip wasn't in Verne's novel, although it has entered popular culture due to the film's abiding popularity).

✳ **Riding elephants in India.**

✳ Watching super-tankers seemingly gliding through the desert at the Suez Canal.

✳ **Searching for a circus and your own private Passepartout in Yokohama, Japan.**

DISTANCE - APPROXIMATELY 9000KM | **COUNTRIES COVERED** - ENGLAND, INDIA, CHINA, JAPAN, USA | **IDEAL TIME COMMITMENT** - 80 DAYS | BEST TIME OF YEAR - ANY TIME | **ESSENTIAL TIP** - IF YOU HAVE TO RESCUE SOMEONE, DON'T TRY THE ZOMBIE TRICK.

CALCUTTA

Why not spend some time in Calcutta (Kolkata), where Fogg and the gang were arrested? Kolkata, India's second-biggest city, is shrugging off its old image in the West as a repository of human suffering – doubtless one that Verne was aware of – to regain its place as a vibrant city considered by the Bengalis to be India's intellectual and cultural capital. As the former capital of British India, it instantly invokes Fogg and his time, especially the fine old buildings with their colonial architecture in a state of permanent semicollapse.

THE REFORM CLUB

London's Reform Club, a classic old-school 'gentlemen's club', is where it all began for Fogg. With subscription fees among the highest in London, it's not for the faint-hearted – not even Michael Palin could get in. When Palin recreated Fogg's journey for TV, he refused to wear a jacket and tie, having just endured a long and arduous journey, and so ended his quest on the steps outside the club. As Palin wrote: 'Shabby, tired, rushed and ruffled I stand before the steps of the Reform Club...Would love to have bought Passepartout [his film crew] a drink, but we weren't allowed inside.'

■ THE JOURNEY TODAY

Your time starts...now! You've decided to emulate Fogg's epic journey as best you can. Verne wanted to celebrate the technological marvels of the 19th century, namely the new ability for people to travel quickly around the world via transcontinental railways and the Suez Canal. In hindsight, this was the beginning of mass global tourism as we know it today: anyone could travel long distances in comfort and with relatively fixed schedules to follow. Obviously, to honour that impetus in Verne's writing, you'd have to subscribe to the modern-day equivalent: air travel. However, you decide that it's far more interesting and adventurous to honour the spirit of Verne, namely the desire for adventure, escapism and new horizons, and the manner in which it was executed – without flying.

You can't catch a steamer so you hitch a ride on a cargo ship from London to Suez. Out at sea, you realise that travelling this way is outrageously expensive, yet hopelessly romantic. After a few days away from land, you forget about the expense and even begin to think about writing a novel! Maybe an update of Verne...maybe a response to Verne...

And then one day, you are informed that the ship is making an unscheduled stop at a country that will take you far away from your well-planned itinerary. You think for a while and even consider offering the captain a bribe, as Phileas did, although you eventually decide to just go with the flow.

After all, our hero was presented with innumerable unscheduled challenges along the way, and if he could surmount them, so can you.

■ SHORTCUT

The simplest, quickest way to do Verne's journey is air travel. The rise of low-budget airlines means that the trip can be done even cheaper and quicker than traditional round-the-world air trips. It requires a bit of planning, though, as you'll need to book a series of one-way flights. Theoretically, it's possible to follow Fogg's route closely – London, Bombay, Hong Kong and San Francisco, returning to London – in just over 24 hours.

■ DETOUR

Although not on Fogg's original route, there are plenty of other Verne detours the intrepid traveller could make. Here are just a few options: the Jules Verne House in Amiens, France, where he lived for 18 years; the Museé Jules Verne in Nantes, France; the Pazin Cave in Croatia, the setting for Verne's Mathias Sandorf (Pazin also has the annual Days of Jules Verne festival, featuring races and re-enactments from the novel); and Iceland's mighty ice-cap Snæfellsjökull, the setting for Verne's *A Journey to the Center of the Earth*.

OPENING SPREAD Fogg had no time to meditate, but this holy man in Kolkata does. **ABOVE** Camels and cruise ships – a scene unique to Suez. **LEFT** A hot-air balloon in Paris, among the favoured modes of transport for the film version of Fogg.

ARMCHAIR

❋ *Around the World in 80 Days* (1956 & 2004) Verne's book has been filmed twice, with the best-loved version from 1956, with David Niven as Fogg and Cantinflas as Passepartout. The 2004 version stars Steve Coogan as Fogg and Jackie Chan as Passepartout, and was criticised for taking liberties with the original story.

❋ *Around the World in 72 Days* (Nellie Bly) About Bly's journey in 1889 to be the first person to do Verne's journey in the real world.

❋ *The Three Stooges Go Around the World in a Daze* (1963) A knockabout parody of Verne's story, starring the eponymous chuckle-brained dunderheads.

❋ *Michael Palin's Around the World in Eighty Days* (1989) TV series following the beloved traveller's retracing of Fogg's journey.

ITALY'S LITERARY LANDMARKS

ITALY HAS HAD A DEEP IMPACT ON WRITERS, AND THIS JOURNEY JOINS THE DOTS FOR THOSE SEEKING KNOWLEDGE OF THIS HISTORY. LEARN WHAT ROME DID FOR KEATS, HAWTHORNE AND SHELLEY; WHY FLORENCE CAPTIVATED THE BROWNINGS; AND WHY VENICE INSPIRED MELVILLE, MANN AND HEMINGWAY.

198

In a country blessed with exquisite cities, few would argue that Rome – addictive, charming, exasperating – towers above all. In the 18th century, historians and Grand Tourists stampeded in from northern Europe, and Rome also proved irresistible for the English Romantics: John Keats, Lord Byron, Percy Bysshe Shelley, Mary Shelley. American author Nathaniel Hawthorne wrote his classic *The Marble Faun* after two years in Rome, using a sculpture in the Capitoline Museums as the hook to explore his thoughts on art and culture.

Venice has also proved a beguiling backdrop for foreign authors. Once again, Byron and Shelley were ever-presents, while Henry James set *The Wings of the Dove* in the lagoon city in the 1880s. Herman Melville, author of *Moby Dick*, was also enraptured. Passing through, he wrote in his diary: 'Rather be in Venice on rainy day than in any other capital on fine one.' Ernest Hemingway's maudlin *Across the River and into the Trees* was set in postwar Venice, but perhaps the archetypal Venetian fiction is Thomas Mann's *Der Tod in Venedig* (Death in Venice), in which the city itself seems to be conspiring to crush the last remaining life out of the main character, Aschenbach.

Through the years of the Grand Tour, Florence was also in vogue, with the French (Stendahl, Germaine de Staël) outnumbered by the English and Americans. Byron popped up again, as did the Shelleys – Mary gave birth to Percy's son here, naming him Percy Florence Shelley out of affection for the town. In 1847, Robert and Elizabeth Barret Browning came to Florence for many years. Elizabeth died here in 1861. In 1868-69, Dostoevsky washed up in Florence, debt-ridden and without a word of Italian but smitten by the city he called 'Paradise'. The year he left, Henry James showed up, a stay that inspired *The Portrait of A Lady*. And on it goes into the modern era, with European and American writers still flocking to the three cities to find inspiration.

ESSENTIAL EXPERIENCES

✳ **Being awestruck by the grandeur of St Peter's Basilica and the Vatican Museum in Rome.**

✳ Imagining the roar of the crowd at the Colosseum, and peering at the heavens through the Pantheon's oculus.

✳ **Enjoying a vaporetto ride down the Grand Canal in Venice, then heading to Giudecca for a romantic dinner with waterfront views.**

✳ Exploring artisans' studios in Santa Croce, Venice.

✳ **Savouring a coffee in one of the historic cafes in the Piazza della Repubblica, Florence.**

✳ Visiting the masterpiece-packed Uffizi in Florence.

✳ **Admiring the sunset from the Ponte Vecchio, Florence.**

DISTANCE - APPROXIMATELY 400KM | **COUNTRIES COVERED** - ITALY | **IDEAL TIME COMMITMENT** - THREE WEEKS | **BEST TIME OF YEAR** - APRIL TO JUNE | **ESSENTIAL TIP** - READ AS MUCH AS YOU CAN!

MODERN ROMAN INSPIRATION

In recent years, it's again become fashionable for novelists to use Rome as a backdrop. Dan Brown's 2001 thriller *Angels and Demons* is set there, as is Kathleen A Quinn's *Leaving Winter* (2003). In her 2006 historical novel *The Borgia Bride*, Jeanne Kalogridis weaves a sensual account of Vatican scheming and dangerous passions. Robert Harris re-creates 1st-century-BC Rome in *Imperium* (2006), his fictional biography of Cicero. Lindsey Davis has had great success with her Roman detective stories, including *Two for the Lions* (1999), in which her hero Marcus Didius Falco investigates the curious murder of a man-eating lion.

■ THE JOURNEY TODAY

You arrive in Rome, and you know it is a contradictory place. You recall reading about Byron, who described Rome as the city of his soul even though he'd only been there briefly. Keats, too, was smitten, coming here in 1821 and hoping that his ill health would be cured, only to die of tuberculosis in his lodgings at the foot of the Spanish Steps. Still, you don't hold that failure against the city – you know it's going to save your soul.

You look around you but the city centre overwhelms, with 3000 years of ad hoc development snaking all around. There seems little order to the patchwork urban quilt of ruins, mansions and piazzas, so you just follow your nose. 'Keats,' you say to a gregarious local who stops to ask you if you need help. 'Shelley...' 'Ah,' she replies, pointing east, and you're on your way. Following the local's rudimentary directions, you're sure you'll get lost, but that, you realise, is half the charm.

Somehow, after going round in what seems like endless circles, you reach the Piazza di Spagna – and the fabled Spanish Steps. In the 1700s,

this Roman zone of intensity was beloved by the English on the Grand Tour, and the steps were built to connect the piazza with the eminent people living above it. The area became a meeting point for Rome's most desirable men and women, who gathered hoping to be chosen as artists' models, but today all you see are Roman teenagers flirting theatrically with each other.

Next to the Spanish Steps, you spy the Keats-Shelley House, where Keats died at the age of 25. He'd hoped the Italian climate would improve his health, and although you don't have tuberculosis as he did, you look around at the vibrant scenes surrounding you, and already you're feeling better than ever.

ARMCHAIR

Enjoy the following location-specific films by foreign directors:

※ In Rome, William Wyler's **Roman Holiday** (1953) and **Ben-Hur** (1959); Jean Negulesco's **Three Coins in the Fountain** (1954); Jean-Luc Godard's **Le Mépris** (1963); Peter Greenaway's **The Belly of an Architect** (1987); Jane Campion's **Portrait of a Lady** (1996); Anthony Minghella's **The Talented Mr Ripley** (1999).

※ In Venice, Alexandre Volkoff's **Casanova** (1927); Ernst Lubitsch's **Trouble in Paradise** (1932); Orson Welles's **Othello** (1952); David Lean's **Summertime** (1955); Nicolas Roeg's **Don't Look Now** (1973); Paul Schrader's **The Comfort of Strangers** (1990).

※ In Florence, William Dieterle's **September Affair** (1950); Guy Green's **The Light in the Piazza** (1962); Brian De Palma's **Obsession** (1976); James Ivory's **A Room with a View** (1985); Ridley Scott's **Hannibal** (2001); David Leland's **Virgin Territory** (2007).

SHORTCUT

If you only have time for one city, perhaps it should be Florence, a place you can visit many times and not see everything. Florence's favoured son, Dante Alighieri, wrote quintessentially Florentine poetry that is still considered Italy's finest. Florence, too, is the cradle of the Renaissance – the home of Machiavelli, Michelangelo and the Medici. It's magnetic and romantic, with towers and palaces evoking a thousand tales of its medieval past.

DETOUR

Trieste is another great Italian city that proved irresistible to foreign writers, notably James Joyce. He was poor and unpublished and did much of his writing in Trieste's atmospheric *fin de siècle* cafes and bars, allowing the surrounding street theatre to trigger his imagination. To recreate the peculiar atmosphere of Joycean Trieste, you can follow a specialised walking tour that leaves from the tourist office in Piazza dell'Unita d'Italia. The tour visits the Berlitz school where Joyce taught English, his former residences, the Joyce museum, key bars and cafes and the iconic statue of him that overlooks the Canal Grande.

IZZET KERIBAR | LONELY PLANET IMAGES ©

OPENING SPREAD The Holy version of the Beatles' Abbey Road? A nun crosses the street in front of St Peter's Basilica, Vatican. **ABOVE** Only half there but double the excitement: the Colosseum in Rome. **BELOW** The grandeur of St Mark's Basilica, Venice.

MODERN VENETIAN

Venice continues to inspire writers from abroad, for example, as a backdrop for the evil sexual games in Ian McEwan's *The Comfort of Strangers* (1981). In Robert Dessaix's *Night Letters* (1997), a man with an incurable disease writes a letter every night for 20 nights while on a journey from Zurich to Venice, the City of Water providing the setting for some elements in the story, in which figures such Marco Polo and Casanova emerge. Donna Jo Napoli's *Daughter of Venice* (2002) tells the story of a rich young girl in 16th-century Venice. Sally Vickers' *Miss Garnet's Angel* (2002) is about a retired teacher and communist who decides to live in Venice for six months.

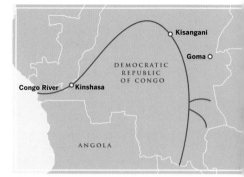

JOSEPH CONRAD'S HEART OF DARKNESS

THE CONGO, THE WORLD'S SECOND LARGEST RIVER, SNAKES THROUGH THICK RAINFOREST, THUNDERS OVER THREE MAJOR FALLS, IS A LIFELINE FOR PYGMY VILLAGERS AND WILDLIFE, AND HAS SUPPORTED THE MOST VIOLENT OF MEN. AND IN 1889 IT INSPIRED ONE OF THE GREAT WORKS IN ENGLISH LITERATURE.

202

Forever an explorer, Joseph Conrad dreamt as a child about visiting the most remote heart of Central Africa, and in 1889, at the age of 32, he realised that dream when he became the captain of a steamboat that cruised the Congo River in what was then, rather subversively, called the Congo Free State. Pieced together by legendary explorer Henry Morgan Stanley and purchased by King Leopold of Belgium, the only thing free in this colony was Leopold's bounty as he set about fleecing it. Hideous crimes were committed against the Congolese by Leopold's rubber traders. These included raiding villages and taking women and children captive as an incentive for the men to bring back ever-greater supplies of rubber. Those who did not return with their quota had their hands chopped off. Meanwhile, Leopold promoted his Congo venture as benevolence.

But Conrad found the truth when he began steaming up the Congo from Kinshasa to Kisangani, and what he witnessed informed his most acclaimed book, *Heart of Darkness*. Published in 1902, it's a dark tale about Captain Charles Marlow's journey up an African river where he witnesses unspeakable atrocities and gains insight into the potential for evil inside all of us through his interactions with the once great and god-like Colonel Kurtz. Before Conrad left the Congo he met British diplomat Roger Casement, whose 1904 report detailing Leopold's abuses led to Leopold finally relinquishing his holdings. The Belgian government ended forced labour, built schools and roads, but largely excluded Congolese from roles in the government or economy. Conrad, meanwhile, settled with his wife in England, and although prolific, he remained relatively unknown. He didn't achieve much popular success until his 1913 novel *Chance*, which boosted his notoriety and brought him rewards of wealth and fame, and literary friends such as Henry James.

ESSENTIAL EXPERIENCES

✳ **Cruising down the Congo through untamed jungle on an open barge – travel doesn't get much wilder.**

✳ Admiring each of the seven steps of Democratic Republic of the Congo's signature Boyoma Falls.

✳ **Spotting wildlife and the ageless villages of Pygmy tribes along the Congo.**

✳ Settling into the Kinshasa chaos and joining a soukous dance party at one of the city's many nightclubs, where Congolese rhumba reigns and you can experience a strain of Africa's unparalleled musical heritage.

✳ **Snapping photos of mountain gorillas, still the star attraction in the Democratic Republic of the Congo, near the Rwandan and Ugandan borders, while on a guided trek.**

DISTANCE - 1730KM | **COUNTRIES COVERED** - DEMOCRATIC REPUBLIC OF THE CONGO | **IDEAL TIME COMMITMENT** - THREE WEEKS
BEST TIME OF YEAR - DECEMBER-MARCH | **ESSENTIAL TIP** - EXTENSIVE PLANNING IS KEY. TRAVEL WITH EXTRA FOOD AND WATER; YOU MAY GET STRANDED SOMEWHERE. NOT A TRIP TO ATTEMPT ON A LARK.

LAST DESCENT

In December 2010, South African Hendrik Coetzee, a legendary paddler, put in on the Lukuga River in the Democratic Republic of the Congo, after warning his mates to 'stay out of eddies...because there are three-ton hippos that will bite you in half. Stay off the banks because the crocs are having a bake and might fancy you for lunch.' Yet on 9 December 2010 reports came in that Coetzee had been pulled from his kayak by a large croc and was presumed dead. His mates were able to paddle to safety and alert the International Rescue Committee for evacuation.

LIFE AFTER LEOPOLD

First there was the charismatic revolutionary Patrice Lumumba, and then the army chief Joseph Mobutu who renamed the country Zaire in 1965, ruled with an iron fist and pocketed an estimated US$5 billion before he was ousted in 1997. Next, Laurent Kabila rose to power, outlawed political opposition, and was assassinated in January 2001. His son, Joseph Kabila welcomed UN troops and presided over a 2002 peace agreement that paved the way for a transitional government. But in 2005 war returned to the mining regions where rape has been used as a brutal weapon of war. Forty years of civil war has claimed more than five million lives.

THE JOURNEY TODAY

The journey in *Heart of Darkness* is upriver, but as a boat captain, Conrad made the trip in both directions. You can too, but the trip will last up to five or six weeks. The classic path across the Congo includes a 1730km boat ride down the Congo River to Kinshasa through still-untamed jungle.

These days the trip must begin at Kasindi on the Ugandan border, near Beni, in the shadow of the Rwenzori Mountains, since this road, passing through the heart of pygmy country, is the only safe route (there are still some bandits, so it's best not to drive your own vehicle). Follow it to badly war-scarred, but recovering, Kisangani, the last point ships can travel upriver from Kinshasa before being blocked by spectacular Boyoma Falls. You'll probably spend a lot of time in this legendary town; not because it's so appealing but because boats are still quite infrequent. There are usually one or two departures a month and the trip typically takes two weeks. Bear in mind that, unlike in Conrad's day, there are no longer steamers with passenger cabins, although you can try to rent one from a crew member. Otherwise, you'll be living out on the deck of the barges with hundreds of other people, plus all their cargo and livestock. Villagers sell food from *pirogues* (traditional canoes) along the way, but this trip still requires careful preparation for cooking, water and shelter.

The voyage ends in Kinshasa, sprawling seemingly forever from the banks of the Congo River. Like most African cities it's big, fast and loud, but this one swings to the intoxicating sound of *soukous* (African rumba), the click-clack of the shoeshine boys and the spontaneous song-and-dance of its citizens.

SHORTCUT

The only way to get a quick Congo experience, upriver, where Conrad was most affected and inspired, is to arrange transport from Kasindi on the Uganda border, to Kisangani where you can experience Boyoma Falls, a 100km stretch with seven major water falls. The final drop, just east of town, is a gorgeous spot, with a rocky stage and a jungle backdrop.

DETOUR

Most visitors to the Democratic Republic of the Congo pop over the Rwandan border ever so briefly to track mountain gorillas and climb Nyiragongo Volcano in Parc National des Virunga, one of Africa's most diverse parks, but also one of its most threatened. The nearest habituated gorilla families are at Bukima, about 40km north of the border city of Goma where you can make all the arrangements. The volcano's appeal is the incredible lava lake nested in the crater. It can be seen on a day trip, but an overnight stay is best.

OPENING SPREAD Scenes from the Congo I: a hippo yawning at full stretch. **ABOVE (L)** Scenes from the Congo II: a Western Lowland gorilla in reflective mood. **ABOVE (R)** Nyiragongo Volcano, Parc National des Virunga. **LEFT** Libinza women making a thatch roof in the Congo's Ngiri river region.

ARMCHAIR

* ***Heart of Darkness*** (Joseph Conrad) The book that inspired the journey that inspired the book. The classic novel didn't sell well at first, but in the end, along with Lord Jim, confirmed Conrad's place among literary giants.

* ***Apocalypse Now*** (1979) Francis Ford Coppola's spectacular adaption of Conrad's novel, where the Congo becomes the Mekong, and Leopold's brutal Free State is traded for the Vietnam War.

* ***Blood River*** (Tim Butcher) In 2000, with the Democratic Republic of Congo in the midst of civil war, against the warnings of everyone in his life, and from more than a few corrupt border officials, journalist Tim Butcher spent six horrifying weeks tracing explorer Henry Morton Stanley's footsteps through the Congo. Desperate and mesmerising.

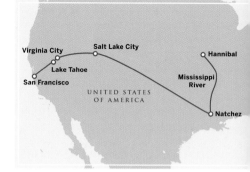

MARK TWAIN'S USA

HOP ABOARD A MISSISSIPPI RIVERBOAT, BUNK IN THE VERY ROOM ABOVE THE VERY SALOON THE ONE-TIME STEAMBOAT PILOT PATRONISED. NAVIGATE THE WESTERN USA TO EXPERIENCE THE CHILL OF A SAN FRANCISCO SUMMER FOG, AND GET INTO THE HEAD OF THE OFT QUOTED GENIUS, MARK TWAIN.

206

To follow in Mark Twain's footsteps is to journey south and west from his home state of Missouri with spurs floating down the Mississippi River (see p138) into America's deep south, and another rambling to San Fransisco, California's first great, and most beautiful, city. Armed with the proper reading material, your mind will be opened and your point of view sharpened by the same land and waters that moulded Twain's humour and insight, and inspired within him a literary mischief that bottled a still young and wild America in the 19th century.

Whether he was writing about the small towns and thick wilderness along the Big Muddy from Missouri to New Orleans, hopping the first steamship to the Sandwich Islands or wandering the streets of San Francisco, Twain made his adventures, real and imagined, leap from the page and take anchor in a reader's mind and heart, as well as America's cultural zeitgeist forever.

Born Samuel Clemens, in Florida, Missouri in 1835, Twain moved to Hannibal when he was four. Missouri was a slave state and Hannibal's characters, scenery and politics would later inspire the fictional town of St Petersburg, home of Tom Sawyer and the mischievous orphan hero, Huckleberry Finn. After a stint as a printers' apprentice, Twain became a riverboat pilot and made dozens of trips up and down the Mississippi River before heading west into the Nevada Territory in 1861. He spent two weeks in a stagecoach rolling through the Great Plains, and over the Rocky Mountains, before stopping briefly in the new Mormon community of Salt Lake City. After trying his hand at gold mining in Virginia City, Nevada, he became a journalist and moved to San Francisco in 1864. From here, local newspapers funded his sojourn to the Sandwich Islands (now Hawaii) and Europe. His most creative period was the 17 years he lived in Hartford, Connecticut, with his family.

ESSENTIAL EXPERIENCES

❋ **Exploring Twain's own Hannibal, Missouri, and mingling with other Twain devotees.**

❋ Listening to a banjo strumming, and the Big Muddy sloshing against the bow, on a ride on a real Mississippi riverboat.

❋ **Surveying the Mississippi River from the atmospheric Under-The-Hill Saloon, a glorious dive with bluegrass bands jamming on weekends.**

❋ Setting out on one of the most beautiful drives in the American West, following the route Twain took through the Utah high desert, up and over the Sierra Nevada, past Lake Tahoe to the San Francisco Bay.

DISTANCE - 2303KM | **COUNTRIES COVERED** - USA | **IDEAL TIME COMMITMENT** - ONE WEEK | **BEST TIME OF THE YEAR** - JUNE TO AUGUST | **ESSENTIAL TIP** - FROM NATCHEZ, DRIVE TO NEW ORLEANS THEN FLY TO SALT LAKE AND YOU CAN DO THIS TRIP IN ONE SHOT.

■ THE JOURNEY TODAY

The first leg of your journey begins in Hannibal, Missouri, where you can visit the Mark Twain Boyhood Home & Museum, a complex of seven buildings including two houses Twain lived in, and the home of Laura Hawkins, the true-life inspiration for Tom's great love, Becky Thatcher. In his 20s, Twain was a commercial steamboat pilot on the Big Muddy, and he got to know all the bends and eddies, towns and outlaws, islands and sandbars that made Huck's grand escape with Jim, the runaway slave, so true to life. You don't have to pilot a driftwood raft to honour that legacy, just join a dinner cruise aboard the Mark Twain Riverboat. Further downriver, historic antebellum mansions will greet you in Natchez, Mississippi. In the 1840s, there were more millionaires per capita here than anywhere in the world. When Twain passed through, he crashed in a room above the Under-The-Hill Saloon, which remains the best bar in town, with terrific live music on weekends. You can still sleep upstairs at what is now called Mark Twain Guest House. Reserve your bed at the bar.

It would be unreasonable to recreate the entire overland stagecoach journey he depicted in his 1872 tome, *Roughing It*. Instead, pick up the Mark Twain trail in Salt Lake City. Once a Mormon camp and homestead, Utah's largest city remains one of the American West's best-kept secrets. From here, drive I-80 to the foot of the Sierra Nevada and Virginia City, where you can tour the Mark Twain Museum, set in the offices of the Territorial Enterprise where Twain honed his skills as a journalist.

Stay on Interstate 80 and wind your way into the Sierra Nevada and Lake Tahoe. Tahoe trout was one of Mark Twain's favourite foods, and you can still fish here in a deep cobalt lake

ARMCHAIR

❋ *The Celebrated Jumping Frog of Calaveras County* (Mark Twain) His first important work, originally published in the *New York Saturday Press* in 1865, is about a gold-rush gambler named Jim Smiley.

❋ *A Connecticut Yankee in King Arthur's Court* (Mark Twain) In what is considered one of the original time travel tales, a 19th-century Yankee mingles and meddles in the lives of King Arthur, Sir Lancelot and Guinevere.

❋ *The Adventures of Tom Sawyer* (Mark Twain) This American classic drew upon Twain's experience growing up along the Mississippi River.

❋ *Adventures of Huckleberry Finn* (Mark Twain) Widely considered his greatest work, Huck Finn, a poor orphan teen slips from the 'sivilizing' confines of St Petersburg, and escapes his violent, drunken father to float down the Mississippi with runaway slave Jim.

ringed with jagged granite peaks, but it's all catch and release. San Francisco bay oysters were another favourite of Twain's. Although they still exist, bay pollution is far too severe to consider them a viable protein. But you can slurp safely at Hog Island Oyster Bar in the Ferry Building.

■ SHORTCUT

Mark Twain will always be synonymous with the mighty Mississippi River. Start in Hannibal at the Mark Twain Boyhood Museum, hop on the Mark Twain Riverboat, and if you crave more road miles, follow the river down to Memphis and over to the Natchez Trace Parkway, which will lead you to the Under-The-Hill Saloon, an old Twain haunt in Natchez, Mississippi.

■ DETOUR

Twain cut his teeth as a journeyman writer on a nine-month sojourn through the Hawaiian Islands (then known as the Sandwich Islands) in 1966 for the Sacramento Union. Twain-era Honolulu is long gone, but you can still taste wild 19th-century Hawaii on the Big Island, which the 31-year-old explored on horseback. He also paddled with local surfers and rode to the edge of the Kilauea caldera, its lava flowing then and now.

PHILIP GOULD | CORBIS

OPENING SPREAD Instantly recognisable: San Francisco and the Golden Gate Bridge. **ABOVE** New Orleans' best-known tuba player, Tuba Fats, busts a gut as only he can. **BELOW** Lake Tahoe, home to the eponymous trout, some of Mark Twain's favourite food.

STILL MAKING WAVES

Twain is still making waves. First came the publication of his autobiography in November 2010, which despite middling reviews became an unexpected bestseller, making Twain the only author ever to publish bestsellers in the 19th, 20th and 21st centuries. Then in January 2011 NewSouth Books annouced plans to release a new edition of *Huckleberry Finn*, in which the 200-plus mentions of the 'n-word' have been replaced with 'slave'. NewSouth's argument is that Huckleberry Finn and Tom Sawyer have been disappearing from school curricula in the US due to their offensive language. This is not the first attempt to cleanse Twain. Huckleberry Finn was banned or altered by institutions and media outlets across the country in 1885, 1905, 1955 and 1998.

ROBERT LOUIS STEVENSON'S TRAVELS WITH A DONKEY

BEFORE TREASURE ISLAND, KIDNAPPED AND THE STRANGE CASE OF DR JEKYLL AND MR HYDE, ROBERT LOUIS STEVENSON WAS JUST A WANNABE WRITER WITH A DONKEY, CROSSING FRANCE'S WILD CÉVENNES REGION ON FOOT, IN WHAT WOULD BECOME ONE OF THE WORLD'S CLASSIC TRAVELOGUES.

210

Robert Louis Stevenson was a sickly child, with a consumptive condition that led to winters spent in Torquay, on the Devon coast, and, most tellingly, in the south of France. It was to here, in the Cévennes, that he returned in 1878, spending a month in the town of Le Monastier-sur-Gazeille, around 15km south of Le Puy-en-Velay, preparing to walk across the mountains of Cévennes. Deciding he wanted the freedom provided by having the 'means of camping out in my possession', he then needed to find a way to carry so much gear, which led to the purchase of a small donkey named Modestine, bought for 65 francs and a glass of brandy (costing him less than his sleeping sack). Loading Modestine up with a curious set of provisions – a leg of cold mutton, an egg beater, a revolver, a bottle of Beaujolais, an empty bottle to carry milk – he set out to walk 190km south through approaching winter to St-Jean du Gard, west of Alès, seemingly picking the highest possible routes as he went. After the walk he sold Modestine – and wept – before sitting down to write about his journey. The story, *Travels with a Donkey in the Cévennes*, was published the next year, becoming Stevenson's first successful book. Why he made the journey, he never said.

In 1978, exactly a century after Stevenson's walk, his route was retraced and marked with the cross of St Andrew, prompting renewed interest in the remote and wild Cévennes and in literary pilgrimages replicating his 12-day hike – with or without donkey. In 1994, the trail, which now stretches from Le Puy-en-Velay to Alès, was designated as the GR70 route, making it part of France's official long-distance *grande randonnée* path network.

ESSENTIAL EXPERIENCES

❋ **Crossing the Loire, France's longest river, near its headwaters, just out of Le Monastier-sur-Gazeille.**

❋ Spending a night at Pradelles, one of France's listed *plus beaux* (most beautiful villages).

❋ **Soaking up the views from Mont Lozère, the highest point along the trail.**

❋ Munching on chestnuts as you wander through the Parc National des Cévennes.

❋ **Fuelling up at the Notre-Dame-de-Neiges monastery, best known not for its veneration but for its liquor.**

❋ Admiring the 17th-century bridge, across the 'glaring river-bed' of the Tarn, that gives Pont-de-Montvert its name.

DISTANCE - 225KM | **COUNTRIES COVERED** - FRANCE | **IDEAL TIME COMMITMENT** - 12 DAYS | **BEST TIME OF YEAR** - JUNE TO SEPTEMBER | **ESSENTIAL TIP** - DONKEYS CAN CARRY 30KG TO 50KG.

THE JOURNEY TODAY

Many people walk in Robert Louis' wake, along this route now christened the Stevenson Trail, but you want to do it most faithfully. And that requires a donkey. Luckily, several companies hire donkeys, mostly in St-Martin de Lansuscle, and they've even booked your accommodation along the way.

Your donkey is more willing than the mouse-coloured Modestine, the animal that made true that old statement, 'as stubborn as an ass'. Soon you are leaving the Auvergne region and heading up into the Parc National des Cévennes, its lands drier, hotter and generally leafier than those back in the Auvergne.

Even today the Cévennes is like a French outback: wild and sparsely populated, though rippled with mountains. Though you outwardly curse Stevenson's choice of route – he seemed to pick off every mountain top he could – secretly you are pleased, for the views are stupendous. And, besides, it's the donkey that's the true beast of burden here. You are just walking; it's carrying all the gear.

Towards Florac, the largest town you're going to see, Stevenson tests you as the shadow of his journey ascends to Mont Lozère, the 1699m-high lump of granite that's the highest point of the trail. Streams pour past and the slopes are covered with heather, blueberries and peat bogs. On the summit you stand and, like Stevenson, take 'possession…of a new quarter of the world…a view into the hazy air of heaven, and a land of intricate blue hills below my feet'.

Looking down you can't help but smile. Down there in the valley awaiting you is the town of Pont-de-Montvert, where, over dinner, Stevenson was briefly infatuated by the waitress Clarisse with her 'heavy placable nonchalance, like a performing cow'. After so many days of walking and climbing, you suspect you'll be more interested in the food than any of the waitstaff once you reach the town.

SHORTCUT

Much of Stevenson's journey was made along roads and drovers' tracks, many of which are now sealed roads, making it possible to get a feel for his walk through the windscreen of a car. Key spots include Bouchet St Nicolas, Notre-Dame-de-Neiges, Pont-de-Montvert and Florac.

DETOUR

From the walk's starting point in Le Monastier-sur-Gazelle, make the short trip north to Le Puy-en-Velay, the modern trailhead for the Stevenson Trail. Three volcanic pillars thrust skywards from the town's terracotta rooftops, crowned with a trio of ecclesiastical landmarks – Le Puy has been a focal point for pilgrims for over a millennium – while the town itself is filled with shops selling Le Puy's trademark exports: lace and lentils.

OPENING SPREAD Formations everywhere: sheep and rocks in Parc National des Cévennes. **ABOVE (L)** Rare wild horses – Przewalski 's horses – in the Causse Méjean region. **ABOVE (R)** The picturesque village of Cantobre.

ARMCHAIR

❋ *Travels with a Donkey in the Cévennes* (Robert Louis Stevenson) Your bible.

❋ *The Robert Louis Stevenson Trail* (Alan Castle) A well-informed companion.

❋ *Robert Louis Stevenson: A Biography* (Claire Harman) More about the man.

❋ *To Travel Hopefully: Footsteps In The French Cévennes* (Christopher Rush) A fellow Scot following in Stevenson's donkey steps.

❋ *The Collected Works of Robert Louis Stevenson* (Robert Louis Stevenson) Go beyond the donkey and read the full set of Stevenson's immortal yarns.

ROBERT LOUIS STEVENSON

Robert Louis Stevenson was born in Edinburgh in 1850. He studied engineering and law, but was obsessed with writing. *An Inland Voyage*, was published in 1873 but he didn't meet with any success until *Travels with a Donkey*. He'd go on to write some of the most recognisable titles in English literature. A tuberculosis sufferer, he moved to Samoa in 1890 but died in 1894 aged 44.

ROAD

GREAT JOURNEYS

ARGENTINA'S PATAGONIAN HIGHWAY

IF YOU WANT TO SEE A SIDE TO ARGENTINA THAT MOST TRAVELLERS NEVER DO, THE PATAGONIAN HIGHWAY IS A MUST. IT TRAVELS ALMOST THE LENGTH OF THE LAND AND THROUGH SOME OF ARGENTINA'S MOST REMOTE REGIONS.

214

Known officially as Ruta Nacional 40 (RN 40), the Patagonian Highway travels nearly the length of Argentina, a distance of more than 5000km. In the north of the country, it begins just south of the Bolivian border and continues nearly to Tierra del Fuego in the south. To do the full trip requires a combination of vehicles, as much of the road is unpaved. Some stretches you will need your own car and others a 4WD. Of course, walking is an option for part of the way, in which case good walking shoes, plenty of food and water and an appetite for adventure are essential.

Save for the travel hubs of El Calafate and El Chaltén, rutted RN 40 is every bit a no-man's-land. It parallels the backbone of the Andes, where ñandú birds flit through sagebrush, trucks whip up huge storms of whirling dust and gas stations dominate the horizon like oases. Nonetheless, the paving of RN 40 is underway, with long stretches of the road smooth enough for cycling. Still, if you want to experience this lonely highway at its most evocative, get in quick before the renovations are complete. Its raw state is, after all, the mythical road to nowhere that has stirred the loins of many, including the writer Bruce Chatwin and outlaw Butch Cassidy.

The paving of RN 40 will clearly end this identity, which has defined a generation. When the reconstruction is finished, chances are most motorists will whiz from sight to sight, bypassing the quirky, unassuming settlements that provide so much joy for connoisseurs of the trip. For the moment, public transport stays limited to a few summer-only tourist shuttle services, and driving requires both preparation and patience.

ESSENTIAL EXPERIENCES

* **Becoming completely mesmerised by the magical, blue-hued Moreno Glacier, and entranced by icebergs crumbling with an almighty boom.**

* Stepping back in time to explore the wonderful, eternal millennial forest in the Parque Nacional Los Alerces.

* **Accepting the challenge and trekking the exciting Fitz Roy range near El Chaltén.**

* Communing with nature and enjoying the sight of southern right whales right up close in the waters of Reserva Faunística Península Valdés.

* **Pretending you're a gaucho by riding the wide-open range and feasting on firepit-roasted lamb at an *estancia* (ranch).**

DISTANCE - 5000KM | COUNTRIES COVERED - ARGENTINA | **IDEAL TIME COMMITMENT** - ONE TO TWO MONTHS | **BEST TIME OF YEAR** - DECEMBER TO MARCH | **ESSENTIAL TIP** - STOP TO HELP ANYONE STRANDED ON THE SIDE OF THE ROAD; THERE'S NO ROADSIDE ASSISTANCE AND CELL PHONES DON'T WORK IN THE AREA.

THE WELSH

Welsh settlers first came to Patagonia in 1865, though they quickly found themselves out of their depth. Few had farmed before and the arid steppe was a completely alien contrast to verdant Wales. After nearly starving, they survived with the help of the native Tehuelche, coming to occupy the entire lower Chubut valley and founding the towns of Rawson, Trelew, Puerto Madryn and Gaiman. Today, around 20% of Chubut's inhabitants have Welsh blood and Welsh culture has made a revival, with yearly British Council appointments of Welsh teachers and exchanges for Patagonian students.

■ THE JOURNEY TODAY

You've been on the road for a week and everything about the trip has been monumental, including the repairs. Gravel punctured your gas tank a while back, and you dodged flying rocks and sheep that think they own the road. You've negotiated blind curves on windy days when it seemed your car would fly right off the road, and all the while you've been struggling to process the sheer amount and variety of experiences that have come your way. You've seen massive frontier horizons dwarfing the gauchos that ride their horses on the steppe, and you've imbibed the monumental silence that accompanies such a space, a wild, barren emptiness as thrilling and as awesome as the craggy peaks and unspoiled rivers.

Now you've arrived in Patagonia itself, this unusual land. The map tells you it's a very large place and you've seen that for yourself. It's almost a country within a country with its oil boomtowns, ancient petrified forests, spectacular Península Valdés and splendidly isolated Welsh settlements.

You've heard about the trendy Patagonia, too: the tourist hubs with their designer shops, which seem worlds apart from the RN 40.

But it's been hours since the last town. You've been driving forever. The weather is cunning and the gravel dastardly. You're not in a hurry because the conditions won't allow you to be. The road seems to go on forever and your car is rattling, as are your teeth, as you trundle along this bumpy stretch. But then magic strikes: the view ahead suddenly cracks apart with brilliance and radiance as glacial peaks and gem-coloured lakes make their presence felt with preternatural charm. And then it hits you, like a flying rock from the side of the road. This is why you came.

ARMCHAIR

❋ **In Patagonia** (Bruce Chatwin) This classic is something of a tourist bible in this part of the world. It's a book of errant wanderings and musings on everything from hiking from Estancia Harberton to Viamonte, taking tea in Gaiman and visiting the sacred mylodon cave.

❋ **La Historia Oficial** (The Official Story; 1985) Luis Puenzo's film is about a privileged couple who gradually realise that their adopted child was born to a victim of Argentina's 'Dirty War'.

❋ **The Old Patagonian Express** (Paul Theroux) This is the author's acclaimed account of his journey from Massachusetts, across North America by train, through to Mexico, and into South America and the remote Andes.

❋ **Nueve Reinas** (Nine Queens; 2000) Fabián Bielinsky's film about a chance meeting between two criminals won numerous awards.

SHORTCUT

The Patagonian stretch of the RN 40 provides a potted summary of everything that makes the journey great. Through inland Patagonia, highlights include the Perito Moreno and Los Glaciares National Parks, the rock art of Cueva de las Manos and remote ranches. The iconic character of the road is also intact – from Esquel, it continues paved until south of Gobernador Costa, where it turns to gravel. From there on it's mostly gravel, with slowly increasing numbers of paved sections, mainly near population centres.

DETOUR

On the eastern seaboard, take the RN 3 south to Patagonia's famous Welsh settlements. Gaiman is a favourite, a quintessential Welsh river-valley village ... in Argentina. A third of Gaiman's residents claim Welsh ancestry and teahouses are popular for traditional afternoon fare of cream pie, teacakes, fruit cake and pots of black tea. Dolavon, 19km west of Gaiman, is an authentic historic Welsh agricultural town, and less touristy than its neighbour. Its pastoral appeal derives from the waterwheels lining the irrigation canal, framed by rows of swaying poplars, and a historic centre full of brick buildings.

FABIAN VON POSER | IMAGEBROKER

OPENING SPREAD A lovely dawn breaks over Los Glaciares National Park. **ABOVE** A glorious southern right whale, Chubut province, Patagonia. **BELOW** Stop, look and listen: you're at the awesome Moreno Glacier.

THE MORENO GLACIER

The Moreno Glacier (Glaciar Perito Moreno), the amazing centrepiece of the southern sector of Patagonia's Parque Nacional Los Glaciares, is a stunning natural wonder. It measures 30km long, 5km wide and 60m high and is exceptional for its constant advance, creeping forward up to 2m daily and causing icebergs the size of buildings to calve from its face. Watching it is thrilling, an auditory and visual adventure as the huge icebergs collapse into the Canal de los Tempanos (Iceberg Channel) and the glacier's appearance changes as shadows progress during the day.

ROUTE 66

THIS IS IT: THE GRANPAPPY OF ALL ROAD TRIPS. NOTHING BEATS THE 'MOTHER ROAD', AS NOVELIST JOHN STEINBECK DUBBED IT IN THE GRAPES OF WRATH. IT'S LIKE A TIME-TUNNEL INTO RETRO AMERICA: THINK DINERS, SODA FOUNTAINS AND MOTOR COURTS.

218

Route 66 snakes across the very heart of America. It first connected Chicago with Los Angeles in 1926, and in between gave rise to a flurry of small towns that provided all the comforts of home to those perpetually on the move: drive-ins, motor courts – the whole transient, garish bit. Everything around here has to have a nickname, and the Oklahoma entrepreneur Cyrus Avery was no exception. Known as the 'Father of Route 66', he came up with the idea for a new national highway linking the Great Lakes with the greater Pacific Ocean and formed an association to promote and build it. The new highway, itself earning the handle the 'Main Street of America', was to link existing roads, many of them through rural areas. It proved immensely valuable during the Depression, allowing countless migrants to escape the Dust Bowl for more salubrious climes such as California. Conversely, the jubilant postwar boom saw newly cashed-up Americans taking their newfound optimism out for a spin on the wide, open road, which ran through Illinois, Missouri, Kansas, Oklahoma, Texas, New Mexico, Arizona and California. This is where the well-worn cliché 'get your kicks on Route 66' kicked in.

But an ambitious new interstate system spelt the end, paving over much of Route 66 while bypassing the rest of it and its collection of kinky roadside artefacts. Entire towns began to disappear and Route 66 was officially decommissioned in 1984, although preservation associations began to spring into action. Today, what remains of the gravel frontage roads and blue-line highways connects you to places where the 1950s never ended – and that's the journey's enduring appeal. But even if retro Americana doesn't start your motor, it's still an awesome trip, with big horizons and superb natural beauty: the Grand Canyon, the Mississippi River, Arizona's Painted Desert and Petrified Forest National Park and the Pacific beaches of Santa Monica.

ESSENTIAL EXPERIENCES

❋ **Enjoying that essential Route 66 small-town flavour in McLean, Tucumcari, Santa Rosa and Needles.**

❋ Counting off the unique parade of Mother Road icons including the Gemini Giant; Black Madonna Shrine; Meramec Caverns; Red Oak II; Arcadia's Round Barn; Cadillac Ranch; Big Texan Steak Ranch; Rainbow Rock Shop and WigWam Motel; Jackrabbit Trading Post; Elmer's Place and Bob's Big Boy.

❋ **Stopping off to enjoy some of America's best national parks, natural monuments and vast outdoor recreation areas, all close to the road, including the Chain of Rocks Bridge; Wilson's Creek; Sandia Tramway; Sky City; El Morro and El Malpais; Petrified Forest and Painted Desert; Grand Canyon; Wupatki Monument; the Mojave Desert and Santa Monica State Beach.**

DISTANCE - 3862KM (2400 MILES) | **COUNTRIES COVERED** - USA | IDEAL TIME COMMITMENT - TWO WEEKS | **BEST TIME OF YEAR** - BETWEEN MAY AND SEPTEMBER TO AVOID WINTER SNOW | **ESSENTIAL TIP** - GO WITH THE FLOW.

LAS VEGAS

It would be a crime to drive all that way without seeing wild and wonderful Las Vegas. Really, if Route 66 is tacky (and we mean that in a good way, of course), then it's got absolutely nothing on Vegas. Casino gambling, hot nightlife and plastic glamour – all of that and more can be yours on 'The Strip' (otherwise known as Las Vegas Blvd). If that doesn't appeal, why not get spontaneously hitched by one of the multitude of Elvis impersonators at Vegas' drive-thru wedding chapels. Starting west of Needles, Vegas is almost 257km (160 miles) north on US95.

■ THE JOURNEY TODAY

The car top's down, 'Route 66' is pumping on the radio, and your mind is free, easy and wild. You've only been on the road a short while but already 'The Main Street of America' has delivered the goods. Let's see, now: join an automobile club – check; make sure the car has a spare tire and tool kit – check; good map in the glovebox – check; tank full of gas – check; jettison preconceptions of small-town American life – check!

Route 66 has been an eye-opener. You've drunk Jack Daniels with country-and-western stars in Missouri. Old-timers in Oklahoma assailed your ears with tall tales of cowboys and Indians. You've visited Native American tribal nations and contemporary pueblos across the Southwest. You've followed the trails of miners and desperados deep into the Old West. And you've been to Cadillac Ranch, the subject of many a rock song, a surreal art installation where old-school Caddys are buried nose-down in the dirt.

It hasn't all been plain sailing though, and despite your map you've gone and got yourself lost trying to find one more roadside curio town. You've suffered through realignments of the route, dead-ends in farm fields and tumbleweed-filled desert patches, and rough driving conditions. But getting lost is what makes it all so interesting. And besides, ending up in an unplanned stop at a small town is really what it's all about: the taste of the Mother Road is often most piquant in such places, where the vintage neon signs flicker after sunset and there's only one bar to mix it with the locals. And then the next morning, you can cure your hangover with a greasy, full breakfast at one of those old-time diners you've seen so often on TV. What's not to love?

■ SHORTCUTS

If you're in a hurry, take the interstate through most of southern Illinois, Missouri and Texas, and concentrate on New Mexico and Arizona. As long as the weather holds, the shoulder months (April, May and September) can be good, especially for avoiding crowds, but most events happen in summer. Also, some attractions are closed (or at least keep shorter hours) during the off-season.

■ DETOUR

The Grand Canyon is arguably the USA's most famous natural attraction. An incredible spectacle of coloured rock strata and the many buttes and peaks within the canyon itself, the meandering South Rim gives you access to amazing views. It can be visited as a day trip from Flagstaff or Williams. The foremost attraction is the canyon rim, paralleled by a scenic drive east, and a 15km hiking trail west to Hermit's Rest.

220

OPENING SPREAD An old sign for a vintage land, near Chambless with the Marble Mountains providing the backdrop. **ABOVE** 'Get your kicks on Route 66' – enough said. **RIGHT** Caddys every which way at the famous Cadillac Ranch.

ARMCHAIR

❋ **The Grapes of Wrath** (John Steinbeck) This is the classic Route 66 novel, set during the Dust Bowl years. It was made into a film in 1940 by John Ford, who won an Oscar (Best Director), as did Jane Darwel (Best Supporting Actress) in the role of Ma Joad.

❋ **For more recent American fiction**, try these: *Bright Lights, Big City* (Jay McInerney), *Less Than Zero* (Bret Easton Ellis), *Slaves of New York* (Tama Janowitz), *What We Talk about When We* *Talk about Love* (Raymond Carver), *Infinite Jest* (David Foster Wallace) and *Underworld* (Don DeLillo)

❋ **Bound for Glory** (Woody Guthrie) A road-trip autobiography about life during the Depression.

❋ **On the Road** (Jack Kerouac) A beatnik hymn to the open road, as is Walt Whitman's *Song of Myself*.

ROADSIDE WEIRD

If you're a lover of kitsch, Route 66 is most definitely your kind of trip. Some of the best loved include Illinois's Gemini Giant, a fibreglass astronaut with a rocket in his hand, and the Black Madonna Shrine in Eureka, built by a Polish émigré Franciscan monk. It features a series of folk-art grottoes hand-decorated with shells, glass and statuary surrounding an open-air chapel. Inside hangs a copy of the 'Black Madonna' painting, associated with miracles in the Old World. Other oddities include Holbrook's WigWam Motel in Arizona, where you can stay in concrete tepees filled with cosy 1950s furniture.

THE DAKAR RALLY

THE WORLD'S LONGEST AND MOST DANGEROUS MOTORING EVENT TRADITIONALLY BEGAN IN PARIS, CROSSED THE SAHARA DESERT, AND FINISHED IN SENEGAL. RECENTLY IT'S BEEN HELD IN SOUTH AMERICA. WHATEVER THE LOCATION, IT'S NOT FOR THE FAINT HEARTED.

222

The rally, also known as 'Le Dakar', was the brainchild of French racing driver Thierry Sabine. First held in 1978–79, it occurs annually in January. Despite its popular name – the 'Paris to Dakar Rally' – it usually started in Paris, although it sometimes began in Barcelona and Lisbon, and it always crossed the Sahara Desert to Dakar. The race takes about 20 days to complete and the pace, heat and terrain are so arduous that of the 400 or so vehicles that start each year, less than half cross the finish line and sometimes only a quarter. Categories include motorbikes, cars and trucks, and international auto manufacturers such as Citreön and Yamaha spend millions of dollars on drivers, machines and support teams. Then there are the 'privateers', individuals or amateur teams with tiny budgets; many reckon they embody the true spirit of the race.

Adding to the danger, Le Dakar, from the beginning of its existence, has always been under threat from bandits, rebellion and terrorists, although it, like other famous historical routes through the desert, such as the Incense Road of Antiquity, had always rerouted and survived. However, in 2008, on the eve of the event, organisers cancelled the race for the first time, shocking long-time observers and admirers of the event. The organisers had been spooked by French intelligence reports of direct threats to the race and the deaths of four French tourists and three soldiers in Mauritania, apparent victims of terrorism. They decided to relocate the race to South America in 2009, traversing Argentina and Chile, where it has remained ever since.

The fact that the race is still called the 'Dakar Rally' holds out hope that it will return to Africa should the security situation improve, but even if it does, its mythical aura will have been tarnished. The race always had an invincible air and a seemingly unbreakable bond to the African continent, but now all that has gone, ending the era of glamorous adventurism in West Africa.

ESSENTIAL EXPERIENCES

✳ **Soaking up everything Paris has to offer to the seasoned traveller.**

✳ Enjoying addictive mbalax music in Dakar, a mash-up of Latin and Caribbean sounds with African drumming.

✳ **Taking the ferry to relaxed Goree Island to escape Dakar's crowds.**

✳ Visiting the fishing village of Soumbedioune, west of Dakar's city centre, to watch pirogues beach themselves.

✳ **Coaxing your old banger across the line in the Plymouth–Banjul Challenge.**

✳ Travelling to South America to watch the exiled Dakar Rally.

✳ **Driving to Lac Rose and wishing the rally would return to Africa.**

DISTANCE - 10,000KM │ COUNTRIES COVERED - FRANCE, SPAIN, MOROCCO, MAURITANIA, MALI, SENEGAL │ **IDEAL TIME COMMITMENT** - ONE MONTH │ **BEST TIME OF YEAR** - JANUARY │ **ESSENTIAL TIP** - LEAVE NOTHING TO CHANCE!

PETROL WARS

When the Dakar Rally was still in Africa, some questioned the morality of a million-dollar monument to Western consumerism blasting through the poverty-stricken Sahel: the sponsorship money the rally generated equalled 50% of Mauritania's total aid budget and each stage went through 10% of Mali's total annual fuel consumption. In fact, competitors needed so much petrol that 'host' countries ran short and some aid and relief operations were unable to move their trucks for weeks. Competitors were killed most years, and even innocent villagers were run over by speeding cars. Given all that, with scenes resembling the sci-fi film *Death Race 2000*, some are praying the rally never returns.

■ THE JOURNEY TODAY

You are not so crazy as to drive across the Sahara, but you do want to see Dakar, famous end point of the legendary race, for yourself. You hire a car in Dakar central with the aim of driving to Lac Rose in Greater Dakar, where the race traditionally ended. But first, the urban downtown, which is chaos personified – a raw, exhilarating experience that hits you immediately like a strong blast of wind-blown, hot Saharan air. For respite, you visit the IFAN Museum of African Arts, among West Africa's best museums, with imaginative displays of masks and lively, traditional dress from Mali, Guinea-Bissau, Benin and Nigeria, and beautiful fabrics and carvings, drums and tools.

Suitably chilled, you head back to the street to eat delicious *fajayas* (like samosas) and drink the local beer as you watch night-time come, when you begin to hear percussive beats and soaring, swooping vocals pulsating from buildings and nightclubs, gaining momentum as Dakarois start to party their way through until the sun rises the next morning. You visit a nightclub or two to see for yourself and it is a relentless, electrifying, high-energy experience, a continuation of the buzz outside on the streets. You feel battered like a punch-drunk fighter, down for the count. This is your Dakar dreamtime as seen through a veil of gauze.

You retire to your hotel bedroom to lick your wounds and try to get some rest. The next day, as you nurse your hangover from hell, you're tired, thirsty, cranky and impatient, exactly how the rally drivers must feel as they enter Dakar after 20 days travelling through the Saharan desert.

You walk towards your hire car, ready for the drive to Lac Rose, 25km along the coast...

ARMCHAIR

* **Moolaadé** (2004) A moving story about female circumcision from Senegalese director Ousmane Sembene.

* **Yeleen** (1987) This lavish generational tale, by Malian director Souleymane Cissé, is set in 13th-century Mali.

* **Tilaï** (1990) Burkinabé director Idrissa Ouedraogo's exceptional cinematic portrayal of life in a traditional African village.

* **Buud Yam** (1997) Also from Burkinabé, director Gaston Kabore's film is concerned with childhood identity and superstition.

* **Dakan** (1997) In this film, Guinean director Mohamed Camara daringly uses homosexuality to challenge social and religious taboos.

* **Clando** (1996) A film about Africans seeking a better life in Europe, by Cameroonian director Jean-Marie Teno.

* **The Blue Eyes of Yonta** (1992) Flora Gomes' film, made in Guinea-Bissau, captures the disillusionment of young Africans.

■ SHORTCUT

The offbeat Plymouth-Banjul Challenge is not really a 'shortcut' in terms of physical distance, however it is more accessible to the average traveller. The challenge often runs at the same time as the Dakar Rally, and to enter, cars – dubbed 'bangers' – must cost less than UK£100, with the maximum budget for preparation a paltry UK£15. At the end, vehicles are auctioned off to support Gambian and Senegalese charities.

■ DETOUR

Dakar can serve as a launching pad for a very stimulating West African adventure along the beautiful coastal region. To the north, Saint-Louis is like stepping back into pre-colonial Africa. To the south, Sierra Leone has some of the continent's best beaches. Neighbouring Gambia is small but its beaches, especially those around Serekunda, make it worthwhile. Off the coast, the islands of Cape Verde are West Africa's loveliest surprise with soulful music, unspoiled beaches, a mountainous interior and relaxed locals. The islands of Santiago, Sao Vicente and Santo Antao are particularly beautiful, and visiting during Mardi Gras is a sheer delight.

GUZOU FRANCK / PHOTOLIBRARY

OPENING SPREAD Drummers and dancers laying down the beat, Goree Island, near Dakar. **ABOVE** Timbuktu, Mali: bringing water from the well – and a few kids, too. **BELOW** The Sahara, Mauritanian syle.

THE HAPLESS MARK THATCHER

When Mark Thatcher, son of former British prime minister, Lady Margaret Thatcher, took part in the Dakar Rally in 1982, he, his co-driver and mechanic promptly got lost for six days in the desert after becoming separated from the convoy they were travelling in. Unable to fix the damage, they set up camp and waited, and were found 50km off the race route by an Algerian search plane. This was the first in a series of incidents that made the bumbling boy Thatcher an enduring target for British tabloids and comedians.

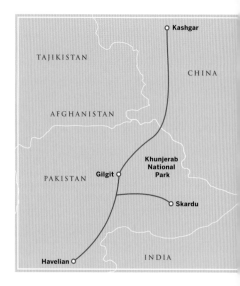

KARAKORAM HIGHWAY

PEOPLE HAVE BEEN CROSSING THE CHINA–PAKISTAN BORDER SINCE TRAVEL BEGAN, WEAVING AROUND SOME OF THE WORLD'S MIGHTIEST MOUNTAINS TO SPREAD CARGO AND NEW IDEAS. TODAY AN ICONIC ROAD MAKES THE JOURNEY EASIER, BUT NO LESS OF AN ADVENTURE.

Today's physical Karakoram Highway, the daring 1200km slither of road connecting Havelian in Pakistan with Kashgar, China, was finally completed in 1982. But its historical roots stretch back millennia. Religious teachers, laden traders, marching armies – all have used approximations of this peak pathway to negotiate some of the world's most inhospitable yet jaw-dropping terrain. This branch of the fabled Silk Road permitted the spread of everything from Buddhism to jade and gemstones: camel caravans would inch along the Indus Valley, weaving between three mighty mountain ranges – the Karakoram, Himalaya and Hindu Kush converge here – to move their items and ideologies.

From the 14th century, the overland route fell into decline – it became quicker and easier to do business by boat. But following Partition in 1947, when Pakistan's Northern Areas were left virtually adrift thanks to the new nation's disputes with India over Kashmir, the route was revived. To connect this cut-off expanse to the rest of Pakistan, a two-lane highway would be hacked into the mountains. The Chinese were on board, too. They would build south from Kashgar over the Khunjerab Pass, linking the countries to facilitate cross-border trade. Sounds simple, but from the first chisel strokes in 1966, it was clear this was an engineering effort of monumental proportions, one of the biggest since the Pyramids, involving the transformation of what was barely a donkey track into dual carriageway – with the added challenge of negotiating 8000m-plus mountains. And gigantic glaciers. In a monsoonal zone, prone to earthquakes...

That the Karakoram Highway took 'only' 16 years to build is something of a miracle, though completion came at a cost – it's thought that one worker lost their life for every 1.5km of road. But when the China–Pakistan border subsequently opened to tourism in 1986, a modern travel classic was born. It's a journey that has everything.

ESSENTIAL EXPERIENCES

❋ **Hiking from the trailhead, a short drive off the Karakoram Highway, to magical Fairy Meadow for grassy knolls, polo-playing locals and breathtaking views of 8125m Nanga Parbat.**

❋ Admiring Karimabad's wonderfully restored Baltit Fort, a 13th-century stronghold amid the mountains.

❋ **Crossing the Khunjerab Pass, the most historic of international borders; detouring into Khunjerab National Park, home to the rare Marco Polo sheep and snow leopard.**

❋ Staying in a Kyrgyz yurt by the shores of deep-blue Kara Kul Lake (3700m), and exploring the area riding a horse or camel.

❋ **Rolling into Kashgar in time for the Sunday market, the most mind-boggling of Asian bazaars.**

DISTANCE - 1200KM | COUNTRIES COVERED - PAKISTAN, CHINA | **IDEAL TIME COMMITMENT** - THREE TO FOUR WEEKS | **BEST TIME OF YEAR** - MAY TO JUNE, SEPTEMBER TO OCTOBER | **ESSENTIAL TIP** - DO NOT TRAVEL AT NIGHT.

RESIDENTS OF THE ROAD

Buddhism spread along the Silk Road from around
250 BC – see its legacy in the petroglyphs near
Chilas and cave frescoes of San Xian. Islam arrived
in the 11th century: locals living along the southern
Karakoram Highway today are mainly Sunni;
the Indus Kohistan region is especially strict. Gilgit
is a melting pot of peoples from all over Central and
South Asia; further north in Hunza, the prevailing
religion is Ismailism, a more liberal form of Islam
in which women are less secluded. China's Xinjiang
Province is a mix of nearly 50 ethnic minorities,
though Turkic Muslim Uighurs dominate: Kashgar's
Id Kah Mosque is the largest in China.

THE KHUNJERAB'S CATS

According to Wakhi people of northern Pakistan, mergichan are female spirits that live in the highest mountains. They can assume the guise of animals, and choose to help or hinder farmers at will, leading them to good grazing or ruin. Powerful, beautiful, potentially deadly – just like the spirits themselves – the snow leopard is considered a mergichan incarnation. This has complicated the relationship between Pakistanis and these rare cats: there are 200 to 400 of them lurking around the Khunjerab region, but they live in conflict with locals, whose livestock they frequently kill. The Snow Leopard Conservancy aims to educate the people and encourage them to help preserve the fast-diminishing leopard population.

THE JOURNEY TODAY

Do you laugh or cry? Actually, it seems you dance. You've been on the road for 10 scenic hours and have finally hit a landslide even your gung-ho driver can't get around. As darkness deepens, the traffic amasses – queues of jangling trucks, vans and overloaded sedans. You'd think there'd be anger – rampant rockfall-rage – but no. As you look out of the window a group of white-robed men have started singing, clapping and doing backflips between the cars. Just another day on the Karakoram Highway, where hold-ups are common – the terrain is too tricky, the potholes too big, the other drivers too scary – but it's always a fascinating ride. From nomads herding yaks to apricots drying on rooftops, from ancient Buddhist rock art to pimped-up Bedford trucks wheezing along like aged showgirls, there is always something to look at. Think of the delays not as inconveniences but opportunities.

Super-cheap buses run all along the Highway, attempting to keep to a semblance of a timetable; smaller minibuses that leave when full are more comfy and more expensive. Private tours offer the most flexibility, but if you're brave you can cycle (best done north to south, between September and October, when the weather is kinder).

Sailing became an option in 2010, when a landslide north of Karimabad resulted in the flooding of a huge stretch of highway. Much damage was done to bridges and the only way to access China was via small boat. Will this be fixed by the time you read this? *Inshallah* – God willing. Such is the nature, and part of the allure, of this most iconic of roads.

SHORTCUT

Arguably, the best bits of the Karakoram Highway are north of Gilgit, so those short on time could fly to this point. Two flights connect Islamabad and Gilgit daily, taking around 70 minutes. However, they are prone to delay and cancellation due to adverse weather; always check, and confirm your reservation, before departure.

DETOUR

From Gilgit there are two fine forks off the Karakoram Highway. Just south of town, turn east to Skardu (six to seven hours from the highway). The drive is dramatic, but nothing compared to the landscape around Skardu itself, the base for some of Pakistan's best treks.

Alternatively, head west from Gilgit, across the 3810m Shandur Pass, for Chitral (16 hours) and the ethnically unique Kalasha Valleys. It's a scenic ride, via wide valleys, fishing lakes, yaks and petroglyph-scribbled rocks. Visit in July to see the annual Chitral-versus-Gilgit polo match, fiercely contested on Shandur's high-altitude pitch.

WES WALKER | GETTY IMAGES

OPENING SPREAD Karakoram: a picture tells a thousand stories. **ABOVE (L)** Doing a brisk trade in fruit along the Highway. **ABOVE (R)** 'What's your problem, human?' A snow leopard lays down the law. **LEFT** Yurts at Karakul Lake, with the wonderful Pamir Mountains behind.

ARMCHAIR

✳ **Three Cups of Tea** (Greg Mortenson) The K2 climber's account of trying to provide schooling in remote Pakistan and Afghanistan.

✳ **Magic Bus** (Rory MacLean) A humorous retracing of the old Hippy Trail, from Istanbul to Kathmandu, via Kabul and the Karakoram.

✳ **Karakoram Highway 1:1,000,000** (Open Road Guides) Excellent map, including roads, places of interest and some detailed town plans.

✳ **Himalaya** (2004) Affable Python-turned-TV-traveller Michael Palin traces the roof of the world, meeting Pakistani polo players and mighty K2 en route; a book accompanied the BBC TV series.

✳ **The Travels of Marco Polo** (Marco Polo) No one is sure if the 13th-century explorer's tales are true, but his account of crossing the Hindu Kush and arriving in Kashgar inspires anyway.

ICELAND'S RING ROAD

ICELAND IS A MAGICAL COUNTRY, AND THE BEST WAY TO SEE IT IS VIA THE RING ROAD, WHERE YOU'LL ENCOUNTER SHEEP AMBLING OUT OF THE WAY OR HERDS OF HORSES GALLOPING ACROSS THE TARMAC. IT ALL ADDS TO THAT UNIQUE ICELANDIC CHARACTER.

After the Cold War, Iceland went through a period of growth, rebuilding and modernisation. Among the outcomes was the Ring Road, completed in 1974. Carrying the official designation Route 1, it signified the dawning of a new era, opening up transport links to the remote southeast that finally allowed drivers to make a full circuit of this most dramatic of islands. It was a very popular move, given that the Ring Road is 1339km of spine-tingling volcanic scenery, attracting big tourist dollars every year.

You'll notice you're in a very different land straight away, with the drive from Kevlavík airport to Iceland's capital, Reykjavík, an eye-popping introduction as you pass through a barren landscape of jagged, black lava fields. Then, the Ring Road: the perfect road trip. Not only is traffic light anywhere you go, but camping opportunities abound, and many of Iceland's highlights can be found right by the roadside including Jökulsárlón, a pristine glacial lake on the south coast filled with huge icebergs that calve from Vatnajökull, the mammoth glacier forming Europe's largest ice cap.

Other Ring Road highlights include Northern Mývatn's geological gems, which also lie conveniently along the road as it weaves through the harsh terrain between the north end of Lake Mývatn and the turn-off to steaming Krafla. Here, you'll do well to stop the car, pull over and explore the many paths in the area on foot. At Jökulsá á Dal, the outcrop called Goðanes, about 3km west of the farm Hofteigur, was the site of an ancient pagan temple where some ruins are still visible. The iron-stained spring Blóðkelda (Blood Spring) carries an apocryphal legend that the blood of both human and animal sacrifices once flowed into it.

Indeed, the ice won't be the only thing that'll make you shiver: some of the scenery alongside the Ring Road is said to be haunted by mischievous leprechauns and bloodthirsty Norse deities.

ESSENTIAL EXPERIENCES

* **Wallowing in the Blue Lagoon, Iceland's most famous geothermal pool.**

* Walking up the icy blue surface of the Svinafellsjokull glacier.

* **Splashing around in geothermal water in Iceland's so-called 'hot pots'.**

* Hiking in magical Skaftafell National Park.

* **Diving in to Reykjavík's exhilarating, nonstop nightlife.**

* Photographing immense glaciers and wiggling fjords.

* **Exploring unspoiled wilderness areas and visiting tiny fishing villages.**

* Admiring the clean and icy sea, where humpback whales surface, roll and dive into the depths.

* **Thrilling to Iceland's cinematic beauty and fascinating Viking past.**

* Hoping to bump into Björk somewhere along the way.

DISTANCE - 1339KM | **COUNTRIES COVERED** - ICELAND | **IDEAL TIME COMMITMENT** - ONE TO THREE WEEKS | **BEST TIME OF YEAR** - JUNE TO AUGUST | **ESSENTIAL TIP** - DETOUR OFF THE ROAD FOR MANY OF ICELAND'S MORE UNHERALDED SIGHTS.

A RING ROAD MEMORIAL

The section of the Ring Road that passes across Skeiðarársandur was the last bit of the national highway to be constructed. Long gravel dykes have been strategically positioned to channel floodwaters away from this highly susceptible artery. They did little good, however, when in late 1996 three Ring Road bridges were washed away like matchsticks by the massive glacial flood released by the Grímsvötn eruption. There's a memorial of twisted bridge girders and an information board along the Ring Road just west of Skaftafell National Park.

■ THE JOURNEY TODAY

In your hire car, you beetle down the Ring Road towards Iceland's southeast. Mighty Vatnajökull, the largest ice cap outside the poles, dominates the region and you pass a multitude of wonderful settlements: Hveragerði, famous for its geothermal fields and hot springs; Hvolsvöllur, the launch pad for Þórsmörk, one of Iceland's most popular hiking destinations; Skógar, home to one of Iceland's best folk museums; and Vík, surrounded by glaciers, vertiginous cliffs and black beaches. You are giddy with the sheer bliss-bomb overload, but giddiness is replaced with suspense as you negotiate the narrow, unpaved lanes. Every time you cross an icy bridge, the perilous nature of the adventure increases your adrenalin levels.

Then a desert of dark glacial sand unrolls beside you, damage caused by the Grímsvötn and Öræfi volcanoes beneath Vatnajökull. When they blow, huge areas of the ice cap melt, sending powerful rock-filled rivers smashing onto the coast. The most recent *jökulhlaup* (glacial flood) was only a decade or so ago: perhaps too recent, you reflect.

Back in your car, you trundle through a flat, wide coastal plain full of horse farms and greenhouses, before the landscape suddenly begins to spasm and grow jagged. Mountains thrust upwards on the inland side of the road and the first of the awesome glaciers appears. You stop the car, awestruck by the glacial lagoon, Jökulsárlón, with its huge rivers of frozen ice pouring down steep-sided valleys towards the sea. Now it's official: Iceland really is a photographer's idea of heaven.

You snap off a succession of shots, capturing the chilly, ice-blue, phantasmagorical shapes that have been sculpted by wind and water. No wonder they thought there were

ARMCHAIR

* ***Independent People*** (Halldór Laxness) This dark masterpiece won the Nobel Prize for Literature in 1955.

* ***Children of Nature*** (1992) Nominated for an Academy Award for Best Foreign Film.

* ***Nonni*** (Reverend Jon Sveinsson) Sveinsson wrote old-fashioned tales of derring-do with a rich Icelandic flavour.

* ***Devil's Island*** (Einar Karason) Quality fiction about 1950s Reykjavík.

* ***101 Reykjavík*** (Hallgrimur Helgason) A black comedy about out-of-work Hlynur. Baltasar Kormakur directed the acclaimed film version.

* ***The Fifth Element*** (1997), ***Lara Croft: Tomb Raider*** (2001), ***Die Another Day*** (2002), ***Batman Begins*** (2005), ***Flags of Our Fathers*** (2006), ***Stardust*** (2007) and ***Journey to the Centre of the Earth*** (2008) Hollywood blockbusters filmed in Iceland.

supernatural creatures here in the old days. After all, this is a landscape unlike any other on Earth.

■ SHORTCUT

Northern Mývatn's selection of geological marvels sit alongside the Ring Road between the lake's north and the Krafla turn-off. As the lakeshore road circles back around towards Reykjahlíð, the marshes dry up and the terrain returns to its signature stretches of crispy lava. Travellers who continue along the Ring Road towards Krafla will discover a wicked world of orange sky and the gurgling remnants of ancient earthen cataclysms. This section can be done in a day.

■ DETOUR

In Iceland's remote northeast, Langanes is a little-visited and sparsely populated peninsula of desolate moors and wildly beautiful scenery. It has a rugged character and wonderful wilderness hiking on the remote, uninhabited headlands that jut into the sea, an experience aided by the peninsula's flat terrain, cushioned by mossy meadows and studded with crumbling remains. Expect abandoned farms, lonely lighthouses and craggy windswept cliffs with barely a tourist in sight.

KRISTJAN MAACK | PHOTOLIBRARY

OPENING SPREAD The lush, sensual delights of the Blue Lagoon geothermal spa. **ABOVE** Let off some steam – volcanic eruption at Vatnajökull. **BELOW** The wondrous iceberg lagoon at Jökulsárlón, with the Vatnajökull glacier in back.

SLOW FOOD

On the Ring Road, Skagafjörður is a region known principally for horse breeding. In recent times, however, it's become renowned as the hub for Iceland's slow-food movement. The restaurant at the Hótel Varmahlíð has some of the best local produce in the area, including – in a bizarre twist on the region's historical fame – foal, which is supposed to be delicious. It also does a mean lamb dish direct from the hotel manager's sheep farm. Local produce won't be hard to find: Skagafjörður has developed a 'culinary tourism' infrastructure, which requires restaurant menus to have a fork-and-knife symbol next to items made solely from locally sourced produce.

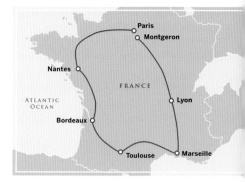

TOUR DE FRANCE – THE ORIGINAL ROUTE

LOOP AROUND FRANCE, FOLLOWING THE COURSE OF THE ORIGINAL TOUR DE FRANCE, PEDALLING THROUGH SOME OF THE COUNTRY'S MOST SPECTACULAR REGIONS. THEY DID IT IN SIX DAYS IN 1903, BUT YOU SHOULD STRETCH IT OUT FOR AS LONG AS YOU CAN.

234

The Tour de France is cycling's Everest, its Superbowl, its annual World Cup. But when it began in 1903 it was just a newspaper editor's publicity stunt. That year Henri Desgrange was searching for a money spinner to boost the circulation of his newly established *L'Auto* (now *L'Equipe*). In a florid editorial he announced that '*L'Auto*, a newspaper of ideas and action, is going to fling across France those reckless and uncouth sowers of energy who are the great professional riders of the road... "Le Tour de France", the greatest cycling test in the world.'

Despite widespread publicity, it was a difficult birth. Even Desgrange contemplated cancelling the event when, with just a week to go, only 15 riders had signed up. As few riders could afford to be away for the proposed 35 days, Desgrange reduced the Tour to 21 days, the length it remains to this day.

In the end, the inaugural Tour proved to be an overwhelming success, with 60 riders starting and *L'Auto's* circulation skyrocketing.

The race was held over six stages, each one averaging an extraordinary 400km, with up to three rest days between stages. The first stage, from the now-famous Cafe au Réveil-Matin in the Paris suburb of Montgeron to Lyon, was won by race favourite (and eventual winner) Maurice Garin. He took almost 18 hours to ride the 467km, but was still 20 hours ahead of the slowest rider; only 37 of the 60 riders completed the first stage.

The second stage was the only hilly stage of the event, slipping through the Rhône valley from Lyon to Marseille, and was won by Hippolyte Aucouturier, who'd actually abandoned during the first stage but was allowed to continue racing. The remaining stages took the riders from Marseilles to Toulouse, Toulouse to Bordeaux, Bordeaux to Nantes and finally Nantes to Paris on a monster 470km final ride.

ESSENTIAL EXPERIENCES

* **Stepping onto your bike outside Cafe au Réveil-Matin in Montgeron, the starting point of the maiden Tour.**

* Feeling the lure of Mont Ventoux, Col du Galibier or the Alpe d'Huez, the modern-day mountain icons of the Tour de France.

* **Paying homage at the Notre-Dame des Cyclistes, a chapel and museum dedicated to cyclists, in Labastide-d'Armagnac, south of Bordeaux.**

* Stopping at wineries and patisseries through Burgundy and around Bordeaux for wines and *pain au chocolates*, an experience as French as the *maillot jaune* (yellow jersey).

* **Braving your own sprint finish along the Champs-Élysées in Paris.**

DISTANCE - 2428KM | **COUNTRIES COVERED** - FRANCE | **IDEAL TIME COMMITMENT** - TWO TO THREE MONTHS | **BEST TIME OF YEAR** - MAY TO SEPTEMBER | **ESSENTIAL TIP** - SEEK OUT BIKE PATHS; FRANCE IS RIDDLED WITH THEM.

THE SECOND TOUR

If the 1903 Tour is worth following, the 1904 Tour
was worth forgetting. Following a very similar route
to the original Tour, it was a disaster. Treachery and
sabotage were rampant, with crowds of hooligans
blocking the road, beating up riders and only allowing
their favourites through. Nails were strewn on the
road, puncturing the riders' tyres, and some cyclists
were accused of having caught trains. Twelve cyclists,
including the leading four in the final classification,
were later disqualified. Desgrange declared that the
race was the death of the Tour de France, though he
was talked into continuing with it the next year.

■ THE JOURNEY TODAY

As you drop down the hills from St-Etienne to the Rhône valley, you're struck again by the thought that those first Tour riders were here on just their second morning of riding. It's been a week since you left Paris, riding on better roads and a better bike – the thought is almost as exhausting as rolling through these hills. The Rhône valley didn't look like this in 1903 – this traffic, these nuclear power plants – but at least by Viviers you're able to leave the roads, switching to a towpath beside the river. The scene here is spectacular: the river cliffs and the sharp-tipped peaks of the Défilé de Donzère giving you the feeling that you could be across the country in the celebrated Lot or Cere valleys.

A short distance downstream, the Ardèche River flows into the Rhône, and briefly you turn up along it to meander through the lower reaches of the Gorges de l'Ardèche – one of France's most spectacular roads – where the river squirms between limestone cliffs, the gorgeous village of Aiguèze watching over its finish.

Back beside the Rhône, it's a short roll into Orange, where the valley begins to open up – wide enough for you to see across to the tower-topped summit of Mont Ventoux. The first Tour cyclists didn't climb this peak they call the 'Giant of Provence', but most have since. It claimed the life of Tommy Simpson in 1967, when he keeled over with exhaustion. Its name means windy, and even down here at river level the mistral is howling through. Today, most cyclists in the area are drawn to its 1912m summit but, hey, you're a traditionalist. You're following the 1903 route – bless it – so as much as you'd love to attempt the 22km climb from Bédoin, you continue pedalling down the valley towards Avignon.

■ SHORTCUT

If you don't have the time to complete the Tour loop, there's always the Paris-Brest-Paris (PBP). The most prestigious event in the world of noncompetitive long-distance cycling, it's held every four years and sees riders pedalling 1200km nonstop from near Versailles to Brest in Brittany and back. Riders must finish the course within 90 hours, thereby averaging at least 13.3km/h – sleep deprivation is one of the major hazards.

■ DETOUR

Though not a feature of the first race, nothing embodies the Tour de France quite like the Alps. Two climbs near Grenoble stand out. In 1911 the Col du Galibier (2645m) was the first Alpine climb introduced. With an average gradient of 5.5% over 16km, this col (pass) has come to embody the toughness of the Tour. Nearby is the climb regarded as the toughest of all: Alpe d'Huez. Towering above the Romanche Valley, the 13.8km lung-searing climb from Le Bourg d'Oisans has 21 hairpin bends at an average grade of 8%.

237

OPENING SPREAD Mount Ventoux: cycle it if you dare. **ABOVE** The Champs-Élysées: an incredible end point for the most incredible cycling event of all. **LEFT** A scene so French it hurts: on the Alsatian wine road in Alsace.

ARMCHAIR

✳ *Le Tour: A History of the Tour de France* (Geoffrey Wheatcroft) Does exactly as the name on the box suggests.

✳ *Vive Le Tour!: Amazing Tales of the Tour de France* (Nick Brownlee) If the shenanigans of the 1904 Tour piqued your interest, read about all the bizarre moments from the world's greatest bike race.

✳ *The Rider* (Tim Krabbé) The classic cycling novel, inside the head of one rider's gruelling effort in the mythical Tour de Mont Aigoual.

✳ *French Revolutions: Cycling the Tour de France* (Tim Moore) The comic travel rider sets out in the wheel tracks of the Tour, only with a lot more wine involved.

✳ *Hell on Wheels* (2005) Documentary video account of Team Telekom's 2003 Tour de France – the 100th anniversary race.

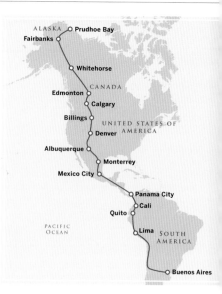

THE PAN-AMERICAN HIGHWAY

THIS DELICIOUSLY CROOKED LINE, WITH MORE WRONG TURNS THAN RIGHT ONES, CUTS THROUGH THE GREAT TEMPERATE FORESTS OF THE NORTH, SKIRTS MOUNTAIN RANGES ON TWO CONTINENTS AND JOINS ICY SEA WITH ICY SEA, FROM PRUDHOE BAY TO TIERRA DEL FUEGO.

238

Make no mistake, there is an official Pan-American Highway, its name emblazoned on (relatively) easy to follow signage. It stretches from Monterrey, Mexico's second largest city and its northern economic hub, to Buenos Aires. First imagined as a railroad as early as 1889, the idea grew legs at the Fifth International Conference of American States in 1923. Mexico was the first country to hold up its end of the bargain, but still didn't complete its branch until 1950. Gradually, all the other countries fell in line and when the original and official route was completed it ran from Monterrey through Mexico City, and down the Pacific coast of Central America until petering out at the Darién Gap – that no-man's land of swampy jungle separates as much as it links Panama with Colombia. Several attempts have been made to bridge the gap, but environmental concerns shelved it once in the early 1970s and again in the early 1990s, when armed drug smugglers were also rumoured to have roamed these jungles. The road did (and does) pick up again in Colombia before rolling through the Andes and into Quito, Ecuador where it hugs the Pacific once more before connecting Lima, Peru with Valparaíso, Chile and crossing over to Buenos Aires. Still, the route always felt incomplete, with so much beautiful country extending from either end of the highway. Gradually several unofficial routes sprung up. One extends south from Buenos Aires to Tierra del Fuego, and two more extend north from Monterrey, one heading through the Rocky Mountains via Denver and Calgary, the other veering east through Dallas and Minneapolis. Eventually the North American routes converge in Edmonton and join the Alaska Highway north to Fairbanks and the Dalton Highway to Prudhoe Bay. All told, the route is 47,958km. The fastest known trip from point to point? Just under 24 days.

ESSENTIAL EXPERIENCES

* **Rumbling through the remote Arctic north and glimpsing the Brooks Range from Atigun Pass on the Dalton Highway.**

* Glimpsing epic Mayan ruins and experiencing lush cloud forests, echoing with the call of the howler monkeys, in Chiapas and Guatemala.

* **Canyoning in Nicaragua's oft overlooked Canon de Somoto in the Northern Highlands, then staying overnight here or in the nearby college town, Estelí.**

* Rolling through grasslands and over steep Andean passes as you journey from sexy Cali, Colombia to laid-back Quito, Ecuador.

* **Moving from the tasteful cosmopolitan glamour of Buenos Aires to the exquisite desolation of Tierra del Fuego.**

DISTANCE - 47,958KM | **COUNTRIES COVERED** - CANADA, USA, MEXICO, GUATEMALA, EL SALVADOR, HONDURAS, NICARAGUA, COSTA RICA, PANAMA, COLOMBIA, ECUADOR, PERU, CHILE, ARGENTINA | **IDEAL TIME COMMITMENT** - 12 WEEKS | **BEST TIME OF YEAR** - AUGUST TO JANUARY | **ESSENTIAL TIP** - DARIÉN GAP REMAINS IMPENETRABLE; TAKE A FERRY FROM PANAMA CITY TO COLOMBIA.

THIS WAY OR THAT?

Like the Minneapolis alternative in North America, there's an alternative route through South America that's worth considering, if you are an ambitious driver who wants to see Brazil and Venezuela. Best navigated if you plan on starting from Tierra del Fuego, you'll begin by hopping on a ferry from Buenos Aires to Colonia del Sacramento, Uruguay and continue north along the coast to Pelotas, Brazil where Highway 116 leads to Rio de Janeiro. Continue north from here and you'll reach Bogota, Colombia, and eventually, Venezuela, where Highway 9 ends at Güiria on the Caribbean coast. The most important leg of this multinational run is the Simon Bolivar Highway that connects the two capitals of Caracas, Venezuela and Bogotá, Colombia.

■ THE JOURNEY TODAY

Begin on the shores of Prudhoe Bay in the Arctic Ocean, and bump along a rough, gravel road 788km south to Fairbanks. Things get more, ahem, civilised, as you carve through Canada's Midwest to the prairie town of Calgary. Cross the American border where the I-25, nicknamed the Pan-American Freeway, skirts the Rockies past Billings, Montana, through Denver, gorgeously groovy Taos, artsy Santa Fe and into Albuquerque. You'll want to move quickly through the border regions of Mexico and down to Mexico City, replete with art galleries, museums and *zócalos* (plazas). Head east on Highway 190 through the indigenous influenced state of Oaxaca, the jungles of Chiapas and into Guatemala where the 190 becomes Central American Highway 1, which zags across the Continental Divide and into the Sierra de los Cuchumatanes. Continue through El Salvador and Honduras and into Nicaragua's Northern Highlands. You'll want to soak up colonial Granada and snap photos of Lake Nicaragua on your left before buzzing through Rivas and into Costa Rica, where the highway separates two national parks and passes through the shadows of Arenal, one of the world's most active volcanoes. You'll take a ferry from Panama City to Buenaventura, Colombia 115km north of Cali. Known as a haven for drug cartels and some of Colombia's most beautiful women, the charming city of Cali is worth a stop. You can make it from here to Quito, Ecuador's Andean capital, in one long day. The city of Cuenca, a Unesco World Heritage Site, is even more charming and your last Ecuadorean stop before you hug the Peruvian coast on Peru Highway 1 through Lima to the Chilean border, where you'll continue along the coast on Chile's Highway 5. In Valparaíso, pick up Ruta 60,

ARMCHAIR

* **Road Fever** (Tim Cahill) This high-speed travelogue documents travel-writer Cahill and professional long-distance driver Garry Sowerby's record breaking run from the southernmost tip of Tierra del Fuego to the northernmost terminus of the Dalton Highway in a camper-shelled GMC Sierra.

* **Long Road South** (Joseph R Yogerst) A touch more serious and illustrated by *National Geographic* photographers, this book follows Yogerst's journey along the original and official Pan-American Highway from Mexico to Argentina.

* **Obsessions Die Hard** (Ed Culberson) Because someone had to ride a motorcycle through the Darién Gap and write a book about it.

* **Motorcycle Diaries** (Ernesto Che Guevara) Not all of Che's iconic postgraduate road trip followed the Pan-American Highway, but some of it certainly did.

which links with Argentina's National Route 7 to Buenos Aires. Regal and cosmopolitan, Buenos Aires is where you can explore 48 districts influenced by Spanish, Italian, Jewish, German, Syrian and Lebanese Argentineans. From here cut along Argentina's Atlantic Coast on Highway 3 to rugged Tierra del Fuego National Park.

◼ SHORTCUT

On a highway this expansive it's easy to find a bite that suits your schedule. The most romantic choices would be the Dalton Highway into the Alaskan Arctic from Fairbanks to Prudhoe Bay, where car rental is easy to find. The run from Buenos Aires to Tierra del Fuego is equally remote and alluring. If you want a blast of the official highway, however, pick it up in northern Colombia, rolling through Cali and into Quito.

◼ DETOUR

From Fairbanks, it's an easy drive to the Chena River State Recreational Area, where there are a number of trails, including the impressive Granite Tors Trail, a 24km loop. End the day at Chena Hot Springs Resort where you can soak those sore feet or have a cold one in the Aurora Ice Museum, the world's only year-round ice palace.

KELLY-MOONE PHOTOGRAPHY | PHOTOLIBRARY

OPENING SPREAD The Atigun Pass and the Brooks Range to the north, and the Dalton Highway all the way through. **ABOVE** Young lads at the Saturday market, Oaxaca de Juarez, Mexico. **BELOW** Cormorants enjoying their time together, Tierra del Fuego, Argentina.

NICARAGUA'S SWEET SANDINISTAS

Its namesake is a small mountain lake, around which the Area Protegido Miraflor unfurls with waterfalls, blooming orchids, coffee plantations, swatches of remnant cloud forest home to hold-out monkey troops, hiking trails, and dozens of collective farming communities that welcome tourists. Nature is glorious here, and the chance to participate in rural Nicaraguan life — making fresh tortillas, milking cows, harvesting coffee, riding horses through the hills with living, breathing *caballeros* (cowboys) — is unforgettable. But Miraflor, best accessed from Estelí, also has a past. When the US-trained Contras snuck over the Honduran border with a plan to march into Managua and seize political power, a large contingent came through these mountains, hoping to sack Estelí. But the farmers rose up in resistance, and helped win the war.

EAST COAST OF AUSTRALIA

COLOUR YOUR VIEW OF AUSTRALIA WITH A BEACH HOP ALONG ITS CELEBRATED EAST COAST, A DRIVE PINCHED BETWEEN BOTTLE-GREEN RAINFOREST, GOLDEN SANDS AND PEACOCK-BLUE SEAS.

242

Study a population density map and it looks almost as though every Australian lives hard against the east coast, between the Pacific Ocean and the Great Dividing Range. But travel this coast and something curious happens: you learn that it's not all settlements. Dotted with national parks, Australia's east coast is as green on a map as it is on the ground.

This drive, along the interconnecting Princes, Pacific and Bruce Hwys, is all about the omnipresent water. The east coast of Australia bangs into the Pacific Ocean for some 4000km – or closer to 20,000km, if you measure every notched crag and sinuous strand. Sydney is the nucleus of the east coast, and Sydney and water are inextricably linked. The harbour. The opera house. The bridge over the harbour. The people taking the bridge over the harbour to get to some of the most beautiful urban beaches in the world. And from here – north and south – beaches radiate out along the length of the coast in ever-more impressive scenes, each one nibbled into the land like a love bite.

The bookends for an east-coast Australia journey are the cities of Cairns and Melbourne. They may be in the same country, but they are worlds apart – tropical to temperate, laid-back to latte-backed, coral to coffee. They are indicative of the variety along this ever-changing coast.

Wherever you travel along the highways, you are never more than about 50km from the coast, and more often you'll be within earshot of the waves. Travel the coast's length and you'll feel as though you've brushed against most of the Australian landscape: beaches, cliffs, eucalypt forest, rainforest, cities, mountains, even the outback as you travel through the open grazing lands between Rockhampton and Mackay. Is it any wonder everyone has chosen to live on this coast?

ESSENTIAL EXPERIENCES

* **Wander along the wild coasts of Wilsons Promontory, one of Australia's finest coastal national parks and among its most popular bushwalking destinations.**

* Climbing the Sydney Harbour Bridge for one of the most gobsmacking city views in the world.

* **Taking the iconic plunge at Bondi Beach or Surfers Paradise, the country's two most famous beaches.**

* Hanging out – that's it, just hanging out – in Byron Bay.

* **Swimming, snorkelling, diving, kayaking or sailing almost anywhere along the length of the Great Barrier Reef.**

* Throwing down a tent and waiting for the wildlife to show up in one of the many coastal national parks.

DISTANCE - 3700KM | **COUNTRIES COVERED** - AUSTRALIA | **IDEAL TIME COMMITMENT** - TWO TO THREE MONTHS | **BEST TIME OF YEAR** - OCTOBER TO APRIL (BRISBANE TO MELBOURNE), APRIL TO OCTOBER (CAIRNS TO BRISBANE) | **ESSENTIAL TIP** - AVOID DRIVING AT DAWN OR DUSK, WHEN WILDLIFE IS ACTIVE AND PLENTIFUL AROUND THE ROADS.

ROO VIEWS

Despite the popular notion, you won't see kangaroos hopping down the streets of Sydney, but the east coast does offer some amazing wildlife experiences. Kangaroos are regularly seen even on the beaches at Cape Hillsborough National Park, near Mackay. Head inland from here, and Broken River, in Eungella National Park, is the place for near-guaranteed platypus sightings. Humpback whales cruise into Hervey Bay's sheltered waters between August and November, while from November to March, female loggerhead turtles haul themselves ashore to lay eggs at Mon Repos, near Bundaberg. Little penguins waddle nightly onto Phillip Island, near Melbourne, and there are hundreds of fur seals on Montague Island, offshore from Narooma.

■ THE JOURNEY TODAY

The northern suburbs of Cairns fade into your rear-view mirror, and across just one headland, you're into Ellis Beach, which seems worlds – not 30km – away from civilisation. World Heritage–listed rainforest already hangs off hillsides, and the Great Barrier Reef lurks over the azure horizon.

Past the resort town of Port Douglas the traffic thins and the road flattens, the highway ending abruptly at the Daintree River vehicle ferry. As it crosses the mud-brown water you scan the banks for crocodiles, which are so prolific here.

The area north of this river has been marketed as 'another world', and you have no argument with that. The road is suddenly encased in rainforest, and there's the trickling sound of gin-clear streams. It feels primeval, a forest as thick and tangled as dreadlocks and filled with strange beasts. The road is lined with signs warning of cassowaries (though you see none) and crocodiles (but who's stopping to look for them?).

For the next 35km the road winds in and out from the coast, though always there's the forest – this is one of the few places in the world where rainforest reaches right to the sea. Through the Noah Range the road descends into Cape Tribulation, a classic castaway-in-the-coconuts kind of town. Here the bitumen road ends and the bitch of a road towards Cape York begins. Here, too, your journey up this amazing coast will end, for you're not geared up for the river crossings, bulldust and corrugations ahead. You step out onto Myall Beach in the gathering sunset. The tide is low and the sand is rippled like an athlete's six-pack. The melon-pink sky looks almost cast in neon, and the coconut palms have darkened to silhouettes. By some miracle there are no high-rise apartments here scratching at the sky, just a cloud of flying foxes.

■ SHORTCUT

If there's a quintessential bit of Australian coastline, it's the stretch of shore between Sydney and Brisbane. Along this 925km section of road you can frolic through the Gold Coast theme parks, drop out in Byron Bay, or burrow into nature at coastal national parks such as Hat Head and Yuraygir.

■ DETOUR

Pick a hinterland. Behind the coast runs the Great Dividing Range, the world's fourth-longest mountain chain, lined with cool retreats that feel a million miles from the baking beaches. Arguably most appealing are the tree-blanketed slopes of northern NSW and southeastern Queensland, which are World Heritage listed as the world's most extensive area of subtropical rainforest. The best hideaways include Dorrigo, Nimbin, Murwillumbah, Tamborine and Springbrook.

OPENING SPREAD What a view: looking out over Leonard Bay and Squeaky Beach, Wilsons Promontory National Park. **ABOVE** Bondi Beach: symbol of Sydney to many. **RIGHT** Are we still on Earth? Luscious Hardy Reef, near the Whitsunday Islands, Great Barrier Reef.

ARMCHAIR

* ***The Fatal Shore*** (Robert Hughes) Richly detailed tale of England's convicts washing ashore in New South Wales.

* ***The Tyranny of Distance*** (Geoffrey Blainey) The most famous book from Australia's most prolific historian.

* ***The Place at the Coast*** (Jane Hyde) Moving novel looking at a woman's aimless life when she returns to her home in a faded coastal NSW town; it was made into the 1987 movie *High Tide*.

* ***Down Under*** (Bill Bryson) An amusing look at the southern nation.

* ***Dancing with Strangers*** (Inga Clendinnen) A wonderful look at the first encounters between Aborigines and European settlers in modern-day Sydney, told from both perspectives.

* ***Chasing Kangaroos: A Continent, a Scientist, and a Search for the World's Most Extraordinary Creature*** (Tim Flannery) The lowdown on the local icon.

GREAT BARRIER REEF

As you travel up the Queensland coast there's one constant: the Great Barrier Reef. The most extensive reef system in the world, it stretches 2000km from the Torres Strait (just south of New Guinea) to just south of the Tropic of Capricorn (near Gladstone). The southern end of the reef spreads itself as far as 300km from the mainland, but at the northern end the reef sits close to the coast in continuous stretches up to 80km wide. The lagoon between the outer reef and the mainland is dotted with smaller reefs, cays and islands. It's said that you could dive here every day of your life and still not see the entire reef.

THE AMALFI COAST ROAD

SNAKING AROUND IMPOSSIBLE CORNERS, OVER DEEP RAVINES AND THROUGH TUNNELS GOUGED FROM SHEER ROCK, THIS ROAD PUTS DRIVING SKILLS AND HUMAN COURAGE TO THE SUPREME TEST, BUT THE REWARD IS ASSURED: SUBLIME, OFTEN HAIR-RAISING VIEWS.

Officially known as the SS163 and colloquially as the 'Blue Ribbon' (or 'Nastro Azzurro'), the Amalfi Coast Road stretches for just 50km. It was commissioned by Bourbon king Ferdinand II and completed in 1853, and it hugs the Amalfi Coast's entire length, dramatically linking all coastal towns along the way. For centuries after Amalfi saw the last of its glory days, which lasted from the 9th to the 12th centuries, the area was poor and its isolated villages were frequently subject to foreign invasion and natural disasters. But this isolation later had a positive side, when it became a drawcard for many visitors in the early 1900s and paved the way for tourism in the area today.

The Amalfi Coast ranks among Italy's finest and most unique destinations, favoured by jet setters, celebrities and ordinary people alike. Everyone finds the coastal road rewarding on many different levels, with those precipitous peaks harbouring a hidden network of ancient paths. Cliffs terraced with scented lemon groves sheer down into sparkling seas, whitewashed villas cling precariously to unforgiving slopes, and sea and sky merge into one vast, blue horizon.

The coastal road is an awe-inspiring feat of civil engineering, and consequently a severe test of driving skill and courage. Knuckles are frequently whiter than sheets as foolhardy drivers pit themselves against the supernatural ability of the local bus drivers. Of course, if they find driving too nerve-wracking, many travellers simply opt out and take the bus, but either way someone has to negotiate the numerous switchbacks and plunging drops to the sea, frequently with only waist-high barriers between living the high life and oblivion.

But relax: there are far fewer accidents than you'd think.

ESSENTIAL EXPERIENCES

* **Driving the coastal road, of course – an experience no guidebook can ever prepare you for.**

* Spotting celebrities relaxing and playing in Sorrento and Positano.

* **Sampling the fine-dining scene in Sant'Agata sui due Golfi, which includes the two–Michelin star Ristorante Don Alfonso, as you sip on a Nastro Azzurro beer, which bears the same moniker as the coastal road's nickname.**

* Spotting classic film locations (see boxed text, p248).

* **Staying in iconic and very view-friendly coastal accommodation.**

* Stopping the car to do the 'Walk of the Gods' trail (see p248) for a different perspective on the famous views.

DISTANCE - 50KM | COUNTRIES COVERED - ITALY | **IDEAL TIME COMMITMENT** - ONE TO SEVEN DAYS | **BEST TIME OF YEAR** - IF DRIVING, TRY THE OFF-SEASON – LESS CROWDS, LESS CARS | **ESSENTIAL TIP** - IF YOU'VE JUST LEARNT TO DRIVE, LET SOMEONE ELSE TAKE THE WHEEL.

AMAZING AMALFI STAYS

Ranging from sumptuous, restored palazzi to superb B&Bs, the Amalfi Coast boasts seriously stylish accommodation should you wish to extend your coastal drive over a longer period. In Positano, Pensione Maria Luisa has five-star sea views and a genial owner. In Amalfi, Hotel Luna Convento, once a monastery, is tranquil and addictive with colourful, large rooms. Near Furore, the farmhouse Agriturismo Serafino features lush views, organic homemade produce and comfortable rooms. Ravello's Hotel Caruso has all the mod cons as well as evocative Moorish surroundings. In Sorrento, Casa Astarita is a relaxing winner with homey warmth, decorative flair and good art.

▨ THE JOURNEY TODAY

Negotiating the coastal road's notorious traffic, you reflect on how amazing the trip has been so far. You started at Sorrento, gateway to the Sirens' domain (see p000) and now you're pulling into Sant'Agata sui due Golfi, where you and your partner admire the spectacular views of the Bay of Naples on one side and the Gulf of Salerno on the other. Although the town is small, you are surprised to find a sophisticated culinary scene. You visit the two-Michelin-starred Ristorante Don Alfonso for lunch, and decide later that you will never forget the heavenly rolls of baby sirloin filled with raisins that were served to you so elegantly.

Further down the road, you pull into Positano, an exquisitely photogenic town and also exquisitely expensive. Your partner pulls out the guidebook and reads aloud a quote from John Steinbeck: 'Positano bites deep. It is a dream place that isn't quite real when you are there and becomes beckoningly real after you have gone.' You can't help but agree as you ponder its preternatural beauty and its hillsides crusted high with beautifully ornate, period architecture.

You've had your fill so you push on to pretty little Amalfi, half an hour away. There, you enjoy the sun-filled piazzas and small beach. You walk from one end of the town to the other and it takes you little more than 20 minutes. Then your partner stuns you with another guidebook fact: tiny Amalfi was once a maritime superpower with a population of more than 70,000!

You're not overnighting at any roadside town, so you hop in the car for one more stop: Atrani, just around the headland, a charming knot of whitewashed alleys and arches surrounding a homely piazza and fashionable beach. As you

ARMCHAIR

❊ **Gran Turismo 4** (2004) Hone your driving before tackling the real thing; this racing game features the road alongside lovingly rendered clifftop views.

❊ **The Talented Mr Ripley** (Patricia Highsmith) This 1955 novel and its film adaptation (1999), starring Matt Damon, take place in 'Mongibello', an imaginary town modelled on Positano.

❊ **Avanti!** (1972) Billy Wilder's comedy-drama stars Jack Lemmon and Juliet Mills, and was filmed in classic coastal locations including Sorrento and Capri.

❊ **Amalfi: Rewards of the Goddesses** (2009) This Japanese thriller, about a mother's search for her kidnapped daughter, makes full use of the coast, coming on at times more like a tourism promo than a feature film.

WALK OF THE GODS

Tired of driving? Stop off and explore the coast's walking trails. One of the best known, the 12km, six-hour Sentiero degli Dei (Walk of the Gods), follows the steep paths linking Positano to Praiano along the pinnacle of the mountains, where caves and terraces plummet from the cliffs to deep valleys framed by the sea's brilliant blue. It can get foggy in the dizzy heights, with the cypresses rising through the mist like dark sword blades. The Comunità Montana Peninsula Amalfitana organises guided walks in the region and can provide information about local trails.

leave, you concentrate on yet another hairpin bend, as your partner exhorts you to look at yet another chocolate-box view...

■ SHORTCUT

If you don't want to stay overnight in the coastal towns, you can easily do the road in one day. Make Sorrento your base and visit Positano and Amalfi for the basic experience. Take detours to tranquil inland towns or stop to hike for a few hours for a more fully rounded trip.

■ DETOUR

The coastal road offers many exciting detours. From Massa Lubrense, follow the road round to Termini. Stop to admire the views before continuing on to Nerano, from where a beautiful hiking trail leads down to the stunning Baia di Leranto and Marina del Cantone. This unassuming village, with its small pebble beach, is not only a lovely, tranquil place to stay but also one of the area's prime dining spots, a magnet for VIPs who regularly boat over from Capri. Bill Gates, Roman Abramovich, Michael Douglas and Catherine Zeta-Jones are just a few of the hobnobbing superstars who have been spotted here abouts.

STEPHEN SAKS | LONELY PLANET IMAGES ©

OPENING SPREAD Typically Amalfi: Ravello's 13th-century Villa Rufolo. **ABOVE** Barely enough room for you, let alone a bus – no wonder cars are small on the Amalfi Coast. **BELOW** See? This is what the fuss is all about: Amalfi and the magnificent coast from afar.

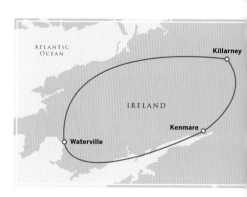

RING OF KERRY

DRIVE AROUND IRELAND'S MOST FAMOUSLY SCENIC ROAD, A JIGSAW OF
IMPOSSIBLY CRENULATED COASTS, ENDLESS GREEN FIELDS CRISS-CROSSED
BY STONE WALLS, ISLANDS WITH ANCIENT HISTORIES, AND THE COUNTRY'S
HIGHEST MOUNTAINS.

250

Of Ireland's three big loop drives (Ring of Kerry, Dingle Peninsula and Beara Peninsula), the Ring of Kerry is the longest and the most diverse. It combines jaw-dropping coastal scenery with more mundane stretches of land that are simply emerald green and sort of blissful. The circuit of the Iveragh Peninsula winds past pristine beaches, the island-dotted Atlantic Ocean, medieval ruins, mountains and loughs (lakes). Even locals stop their cars to gawk at the rugged coastline. And for many, the Ring is simply music to their ears as traditional pubs with music sessions dot the villages.

The road begins in the town of Killarney, its studied twee-ness set in the middle of the sublime scenery of its namesake national park – the first national park in Ireland. From here (heading clockwise), the vista-crazy road to Kenmare winds between rock and lake, the countryside growing hillocky and more rugged as it travels west. Rocks pepper the landscape like a bad case of warts, and with level ground at a premium, even the tiniest flat spots are used to grow potatoes and other crops.

The coast around Derrynane is magnificent, but is just the start of the Ring's true beauty spot. From here the road climbs 200m to Coomakista Pass, and the views over Derrynane National Historic Park (where among the oak woods is Derrynane House, home of 'the Great Liberator' Daniel O'Connell), the harbour and islands are magnificent – even heavenly, if the Madonna statue atop the pass is any indication.

Through Waterville the road crosses to the shores of Dingle Bay, trailing along beside them, and along the foot of the Macgillycuddy's Reeks, as it turns back on itself towards Killarney, re-entering town as you left it: beside the peaty waters of glacial Lough Leane.

ESSENTIAL EXPERIENCES

* **Braving the seas on the boat crossing to Skellig Michael, Ireland's own Mont St Michel, described by George Bernard Shaw as 'the most fantastic and impossible rock in the world'.**

* Playing on the beach at Waterville, with its line of colourful houses strung along the N72.

* **Hiking out in quest of Ireland's highest peak, Carrantuohil, in the Macgillycuddy's Reeks.**

* Kicking back during a trad music session in one of the Ring's many pubs.

* **Contemplating a purchase of Kenmare lace, a famous traditional craft taught by the nuns at Poor Clare Convent in Kenmare.**

DISTANCE - 179KM | **COUNTRIES COVERED** - IRELAND | **IDEAL TIME COMMITMENT** - TWO TO THREE DAYS | **BEST TIME OF YEAR** - MAY, JUNE, SEPTEMBER AND OCTOBER | **ESSENTIAL TIP** - ALL TOUR BUSES TRAVEL ANTICLOCKWISE, SO DRIVE CLOCKWISE TO AVOID THE BUS JAMS.

KERRY WAY

The 214km Kerry Way is Ireland's longest waymarked footpath and pretty much mimics the course of the Ring of Kerry. Usually walked anticlockwise, it starts and ends in Killarney, winding through the Macgillycuddy's Reeks before continuing around the Ring of Kerry coast.

The walk can be completed in about 10 days, provided you're up to a good 20km per day. If you have less time, it's worth walking the first three days, as far as Glenbeigh, from where a bus can return you to Killarney. At the western end it cuts overland towards Waterville, where you can decide between inland or coastal walking to Caherdaniel.

MACGILLYCUDDY'S REEKS

Rising at the eastern end of the Kerry Peninsula, Macgillycuddy's Reeks are Ireland's highest mountain range, containing seven of its highest peaks (including the highest, 1039m Carrantuohil) and nine of its 12 Munros (Scottish name for peaks over 3000ft in height). The name derives from the ancient Mac Gilla Muchudas clan; reek means 'pointed hill'. The red sandstone mountains were carved by minor glaciers into elegant forms, such as Carrantuohil's curved outline – referred to in its name, which translates as 'reversed reaping hook'. The mountains are studded with awesome cliffs, the summits are buttressed by ridges of purplish rock and the cupped valleys between are filled with glittering lakes.

THE JOURNEY TODAY

To be honest, you could easily just stay a few more days in Caherdaniel: it's about as idyllically Irish as you could have imagined. Last night, impromptu trad music flowed from the Blind Piper pub, and you may have had just one pint too many. The car's engine is as sluggish as your head as you motor out of town, grinding up to Coomakista Pass. The wind is doing what it usually does on Ireland's west coast – blowing like a banshee – and below the stone wall and the Madonna, her arms outstretched like guy ropes against the wind, the peninsula slopes down into a foaming, furious ocean. Two fingers of land part the sea and you know that you're looking at a true natural beauty.

To the north is the wide bite of Ballinskelligs Bay and soon you are down on its shores, crossing the outlet of Lough Currane into Waterville. It's a true seaside town – a little charm-challenged. But you've come to see the violent coast, not wallow in ice-cream, so you drive on, undulating overland to Caherciveen, once home to 30,000 people but decimated by the Great Famine in the 19th century. Today, the population is less than 5% of its heyday, and the town still exudes a rawness not found in other parts of this tourism-driven peninsula.

Further along the northern coast you stop at Rosbeigh Strand, a tendril of sand protruding into Dingle Bay like a hair rising from the scalp of the Iveragh Peninsula. You wander along the strand's edges, switching from side to side, amazed by the difference. On the Atlantic side the wind whips the ocean ashore, but on the eastern side it's like a lagoon. And ahead, across the bay, is the Dingle Peninsula, as inviting in its own way as this Ring of Kerry.

SHORTCUT

The Ring can be driven in a day, but if you need to shorten even that, it's the section of road between Waterville and Caherdaniel that has the highest wow value. This 14km stretch, in the southwest of the peninsula, crosses between the area's main seaside resort (Waterville) and a settlement thatbarely qualifies as a hamlet (Caherdaniel), climbing above Ballinskelligs and Derrynane Bays.

DETOUR

The 18km Skellig Ring offers a quiet alternative, looping out through a Gaeltacht (Irish-speaking) area. The area is wild and beautiful, with the ragged outline of Skellig Michael, a World Heritage–listed island, never far from view. The Skellig Ring's narrow roads are also tour-bus free. The road is centred on Ballinskelligs, where the sea and salty air are eating away at the atmospheric ruins of a medieval priory.

MICHAEL ST MAUR SHEIL | CORBIS

OPENING SPREAD A watery view: the lovely Kerry village of Waterville. **ABOVE (L)** A Glenbeigh farmer with his trusty animal crew. **ABOVE (R)** Travellers to Kerry will likely come across a similar scene: Irish musicians in full flight. **LEFT** Some of Kerry's Celtic ruins.

ARMCHAIR

* **Excalibur** (1981) Scenes from this film, starring Nigel Terry, Helen Mirren and Liam Neeson, were filmed around the tiny town of Caherdaniel along the Ring of Kerry.

* **The Iveragh Peninsula: A Cultural Atlas of the Ring of Kerry** (John Crowley & John Sheehan) A comprehensive cultural atlas covering the peninsula from its geography to its centuries of development.

* **Discovering Kerry: Its History, Heritage and Topography** (Tom Barrington) A definitive look at the history, people, music, scenery and more of the region, this book is rich in photographs.

* **Things My Mother Never Told Me** (Blake Morrison) Memoir documenting Morrison's mother's childhood in Killorglin.

* **McCarthy's Bar** (Pete McCarthy) Laugh as loudly as the Irish themselves on this bar-hopping travelogue about self-discovery around Ireland's west coast.

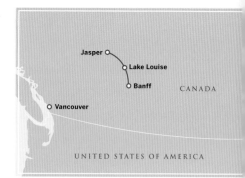

ICEFIELDS PARKWAY

MARKETERS HAVE DUBBED CANADA'S ICEFIELDS PARKWAY THE 'MOST BEAUTIFUL ROAD IN THE WORLD'. IT SEEMS LIKE AN OVERSTATEMENT ONLY UNTIL YOU'VE DRIVEN PAST THE PIN-SHARP PEAKS AND DUCK-EGG-BLUE LAKES THAT DEFINE THIS SLICE OF THE ROCKY MOUNTAINS.

254

Linking Lake Louise to Jasper – and, in effect, a connection between the evergreen resort towns of Banff and Jasper – the Icefields Parkway began as a Great Depression infrastructure project in 1931. Construction crews worked from both ends of the road, finally meeting at Big Bend, below Sunwapta Pass, eight years later. The 230km road opened in 1940 as the unsealed Banff-Jasper Hwy, before being sealed and given its sexier new name in the early 1960s. Early road workers called it 'the road through the clouds', while, soon after its opening, a local newspaper christened it '20 Switzerlands in one', in reference to its wealth of mountain sights.

Threading through creases in the Rocky Mountains, it is arguably the most spectacular mountain road-trip in North America, and high among the finest in the world. It offers the full glossary of mountain features – shapely peaks, glacial lakes, glaciers, copious wildlife, wildflower meadows, open passes, the massive Columbia Icefield – as it crosses between Banff National Park and Jasper National Park.

Today, it's said that around 400,000 vehicles travel the parkway each year. The road transitions between alpine and subalpine zones, with the dazzlingly coloured lakes ever-present, and the icefields sat like frosting across the tops of the mountains. Numerous roadside stops allow you to take in the parkway's natural features and viewpoints. And, though this road takes you about as close as you're ever going to get to the Rockies' craggy summits in a vehicle, you needn't just admire the views from the road. The parkway is stitched with 19 trailheads heading away into various wildernesses and national parks; stop your car and follow one of the walking trails and you'll feel as though you're on top of the world within a matter of hours.

ESSENTIAL EXPERIENCES

* **Sneaking a dawn view of Lake Louise before the daily crowds arrive.**

* Wandering to the Peyto Lake viewpoint for an elevated look across one of the world's most beautiful mountain lakes.

* **Stepping quietly around the Waterfowl Lakes for the rare chance to spot moose.**

* Taking a special bus or a guided hike onto the ice of Athabasca Glacier.

* **Listening to the roar of thundering Athabasca Falls, pouring over a 23m drop.**

* Riding the Jasper Tramway to the summit of Whistlers Mountain for a view that extends up to 75km south along the parkway.

DISTANCE - 232KM | **COUNTRIES COVERED** - CANADA | **IDEAL TIME COMMITMENT** - THREE TO FOUR DAYS | **ESSENTIAL TIP** - DRIVE IN THE EARLY MORNING OR LATE AFTERNOON FOR THE BEST CHANCE OF SPOTTING WILDLIFE.

THE COLUMBIA ICEFIELD

Tourism operators here will tell you that the Columbia Icefield (the main block of ice that gives the parkway its name) is the largest mass of ice south of the Arctic Circle. This tends to overlook a little place called Antarctica, but it is nonetheless an impressive chunk of frozen water. Icing the mountains to the west of the road, it is North America's largest icefield, covering an area of 325 sq km. Its meltwater drains away to three oceans, the Pacific, Atlantic and Arctic, while 11 of the Canadian Rockies' 22 highest peaks rise around the icefield.

THE JOURNEY TODAY

The brilliance of the Rocky Mountains is imprinted onto your windscreen, as it has been for the last couple of hours. You have fuelled up at the Saskatchewan River Crossing, the only petrol stop along the parkway's length, and you are ready for yet more of this mountain march-past.

As you drive upstream, the rock walls close in around the road, and you are reminded of the massive rock faces of Yosemite. Waterfalls drop from the heights but the wind, funnelling through the valley, carries them away before they even reach the ground.

The road climbs towards Sunwapta Pass, and you edge around a pair of cyclists who seem to move as slowly as the glaciers. Atop the pass, 500m above the Saskatchewan Valley, a wind comes from the north, chilled by the Columbia Icefield. Away below, the icefield makes a guest appearance, spilling into the valley in the crumbled shape of the Athabasca Glacier, one of just six glaciers that drip off the edge of the Columbia Icefield.

The descent is intoxicating, but soon you are back into low gears as the road makes the short but steep climb onto Tangle Hill. Tangle Falls lurch down the slopes but the sight that stops the traffic – literally – is the bighorn sheep. Atop the hill, they wander along the road itself and, while the sight is no longer unusual – bighorn sheep are one of 53 mammal species along the road, and you've already been stopped by elk and, most gloriously, a bear sow and cub – you pull off and listen to the tap-dance of hooves on asphalt. It's a classic Rockies' scene, enhanced by the vision across the valley of the multi-layered Stutfield Glacier (another of the Columbia Icefield's arms) gouging its way down 900m of cliff faces. They could easily have called this

ARMCHAIR

❋ **On the Roof of the Rockies** (Lewis Freeman) Classic account of a 70-day trip in the 1920s exploring the region around the yet-to-be-built parkway.

❋ **50 Roadside Panoramas in the Canadian Rockies** (Dave Birrell) A panoramic vision of some classic views, with detailed notes and histories. Icefields Parkway scenes include Sunwapta Pass, Bow Lake and the Alexandra River Flats.

❋ **Bow Lake: Wellspring of Art** (Jane Lytton Gooch) A celebration of Bow Lake's artistic traditions, from the explorer Jimmy Simpson through to the modern artists in residence.

❋ **Jimmy Simpson** (EJ Hart) Biography of the Rockies' legend, whose lodge became the modern-day Num-Ti-Jah Lodge on Bow Lake.

road by any number of names – Wildlife Parkway, Glacier Parkway, Wow Highway – but right now you accept that they might just have it right. This may be the most beautiful road in the world.

■ SHORTCUT

You can barrel along the parkway in a day, snatching a glimpse of the lot, but if you just want to see or touch the main icefield that gives the road its name, you need only drive 100km south from Jasper to the Athabasca Glacier. Here, the Columbia Icefield breaks through a gap in the mountains, spilling down the rocky slopes towards the valley floor, almost to the road itself.

■ DETOUR

Continue south from Lake Louise and you can follow the other parkway – the Bow Valley Parkway – into evergreen Banff. This 65km road parallels Hwy 1, but has fewer cars and more critters. Noted as one of Canada's finest roads for spotting wildlife, it follows the banks of the Bow River beneath the watchful gaze of bald eagles and in the possible company of elk, bighorn sheep and bears. Be sure to wander up into Johnston Canyon to view its waterfalls, which roar in summer and freeze in winter.

JOHN E MARRIOTT | CORBIS

OPENING SPREAD Whiteout! The mountain pass in its winter coat. **ABOVE** In the Rockies, an American Bighorn Sheep surveys its domain. **BELOW** Unyielding, unending and unique: Bow Lake and Crowfoot Mountain, Banff National Park.

CYCLING THE PARKWAY

Cycling the Icefields Parkway has become so popular that, at times, you might even see more bikes than cars on the road. Because of the terrain, it's easier to cycle north. Most cyclists begin in Banff, adding the Bow Valley Parkway to the trip, making for a journey of around 300km. Five days is an ideal commitment – a workable itinerary of nights is Lake Louise, Waterfowl Lakes, Athabasca Glacier, Honeymoon Lake and Jasper. The road has two major climbs, Bow Summit and Sunwapta Pass, both ascending around 500m. The first climb is spread across 40km, while the latter is shorter and sharper, reaching the pass in 15km.

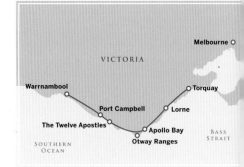

GREAT OCEAN ROAD

AUSTRALIA'S MOST FAMOUS COASTAL ROAD IS WELL NAMED – IT IS A TRULY GREAT ROAD BY THE OCEAN. TAKE A DRIVE THAT'S RELENTLESSLY SCENIC, HUGGING WILD BEACHES, EDGING ALONG SANDSTONE CLIFFS AND BURROWING DEEP IN TEMPERATE RAINFOREST.

258

Australia doesn't lack for great coastline – there's about 60,000km of it all up – but the section of coast followed by the Great Ocean Road has a special place in the nation's heart. It is, quite simply, one of the world's most spectacular seaside routes, and so easily accessed from Melbourne.

Whatever your coastal – or forest – fancy, there's every chance you'll find it here. It might be the stormy backdrop of heaving swells and sunlit sea spray by the ragged Twelve Apostles. Or the storybook wonderland of Apollo Bay's roly-poly hills. Or the walks in the Otway Ranges that reveal eucalypts and myrtle beech of unhuggable girth. Or, at road's end, the annual spectacle as Warrnambool's waters deliver whale babies each spring.

The idea for the Great Ocean Road was floated in 1917 as a way to employ soldiers returning from WW1. The following year the first surveys were completed, and construction began near Lorne on 19 September. It would take 13 years to complete the road and require the labour of around 3000 workers using shovels and crowbars. The road was officially opened on 26 November 1932, running, at the time, from Eastern View to Apollo Bay, and was dedicated to the fallen soldiers of WW1 – look for the memorial plaque and arch at Eastern View. The later extension of the road across the Otways to Port Campbell was originally called merely the 'Ocean Road', even though it contains the natural feature considered the greatest of this coast's many greats: the limestone sea stacks known as the Twelve Apostles.

Today, stretching from Torquay to Warrnambool, the Great Ocean Road attracts around seven million visitors a year.

ESSENTIAL EXPERIENCES

✵ **Watching the sun set over the sea stacks of the Twelve Apostles.**

✵ Catching a wave, or just watching the mayhem, at world-class Bells Beach.

✵ **Heading for the Anglesea Golf Club (if you like birdies, but prefer kangaroos), where the fairways are blithely grazed by roos.**

✵ Cafe-crawling through Lorne, the road's epicurean epicentre.

✵ **Throwing down a tent by the Cumberland River, the prettiest camping ground along the coast, set beneath the craggy, blackened rock face of Mt Defiance.**

✵ Checking out the giant messmate eucalypt, with its trunk 27m in circumference, in Melba Gully State Park; coming at dusk to have your way lit by glow-worms.

DISTANCE - 250KM | **COUNTRIES COVERED** - AUSTRALIA | **IDEAL TIME COMMITMENT** - THREE DAYS TO ONE WEEK | **BEST TIME OF YEAR** - NOVEMBER TO APRIL | **ESSENTIAL TIP** - TRAVEL EAST-WEST TO BE ON THE OCEAN SIDE OF THE ROAD.

THE SHIPWRECK COAST

It's referred to as the Shipwreck Coast, and with good reason. In the days of sailing ships, navigation was a fearsome task along this stretch due to hidden reefs and frequent heavy fog. More than 80 vessels came to grief between Cape Otway and Port Fairy in just 40 years. The most fabled wreck is a Portuguese vessel nicknamed the 'Mahogany Ship', said to have run aground off Warrnambool in the 1500s (which would rewrite the whole story of Australia's discovery). Sightings of the wreck were reported up until 1870, but even a $250,000 government reward for its discovery in the 1990s failed to rustle up more evidence.

GREAT OCEAN WALK

If the drive is great, the walk could well be even better.
Connecting Apollo Bay to Glenample Homestead,
adjacent to the Twelve Apostles, this 91km walking
track was completed in January 2006 and shows off
a section of coast the motorists generally don't get
to see: treats such as wild Milanesia Beach and the
rusted anchors at the appropriately named Wreck
Beach. There are a number of hiker-only camp sites,
while accommodation providers near the track offer
more luxurious stops, usually with track transport.
Allow about five or six days for the entire route, or
simply cherry pick from its many natural features for
shorter day walks.

THE JOURNEY TODAY

The green half is behind, and the yellow half is ahead. Atop the Otway Ranges at Lavers Hill, the drive is about to change in colour and nature. The Great Ocean Road is a journey in two parts and soon the road will be skimming down the western slopes of the range, leaving the teeming rainforest for the bare, windswept cliffs that are such a hallmark of this drive.

After the dampness of the ancient and abundant forest at Melba Gully, it's like dropping into a desert as the road flattens out onto the grassed plain. Except that there really is so much water here, with the Southern Ocean stretching away from the foot of the cliffs towards Antarctica.

Past Loch Ard Gorge, with its heartbreaking shipwreck story, there's the rare chance to wander to the foot of the cliffs, taking the Gibson Steps down onto a typically wild and woolly beach. Waves break over a large rock stack just offshore as a reminder that one of Australia's signature scenes, the Twelve Apostles, is just around the bend.

Back in the car, it's just a couple of minutes' drive to the Apostles where, from the lookout platform, it's worth trying to count the sea stacks. There should be 12, right? But there aren't. Time and the literal tide are slowly taking their toll, eroding these towers towards eventual oblivion. As recently as 2005 one stack here collapsed, reducing the 'Twelve' Apostles to just eight. But still, with the sun setting behind the stacks, and the view along the endless line of cliffs, you'll probably concede that it's a view worthy of a little biblical big-noting. So what if the maths is out.

SHORTCUT

It's possible to drive the length of the Great Ocean Road in a day, allowing time for one beach, one forest and one cliff-top stop. The Twelve Apostles are compulsory, while Lorne and Apollo Bay vie as the top beach spots. If you prefer waves, head for Bells Beach, one of the most revered (and fiercest) surf spots in the world. For a quick, but forest stop, the Maits Rest Rainforest Boardwalk heads through a rainforest gully with some truly giant mountain ash, one of the world's tallest trees.

DETOUR

Somewhere deep inside all the forest that blankets the Otway Ranges, there's a multitude of waterfalls pouring down the hillsides. Deviate even slightly off the main road and you can find that perfectly photogenic blend of cascading water and deep-green rainforest and ferns. Inland from Lorne there's easy access to Erskine, Kalimna and Sheoak Falls, while near to Beech Forest are Triplet, Beauchamp and Hopetoun Falls. Walks to view the falls range from a few hundred metres to 9km.

261

OPENING SPREAD Praise be – it's the Twelve Apostles. **ABOVE** Surf's up, and it's the best, Port Campbell National Park. **LEFT** A fascinating feat of engineering: the road carved into the mountainside.

ARMCHAIR

※ *The Great Ocean Road: A Photographic Souvenir & Traveller's Guide* (Rodney Hyett) This hardback book from a local photographer is the standout photographic souvenir about the road.

※ *A History of the Great Ocean Road* (Peter Alsop) Historical account of the road's construction, written by a former supervising engineer.

※ *The Food and Wine Lover's Guide to the Great Ocean Road* (Max Allen) Graze and guzzle your way along the Great Ocean Road.

※ *The New Shoe* (Arthur Upfield) Detective novel set around the Split Point Lighthouse at Aireys Inlet.

※ *Murder, Mayhem, Fire & Storm* (Max Jeffreys) Boy's Own tales of shipwrecks and maritime disasters around Australia, including the Loch Ard and the Mahogany Ship along the Great Ocean Road.

MILFORD ROAD

PUSHING THROUGH THE MOUNTAINS TO THE SEA, THE MILFORD ROAD IS STUNNING NEW ZEALAND SHOWING OFF – THIS IS THE MOST SPECTACULAR, MOST SCENIC AND MOST INSPIRING OF ALL THE COUNTRY'S ROADS.

262

Though early explorers missed Milford Sound, deceived by its narrow sea entrance (just 600m separates the cliffs at one point), modern-day tourists rarely do. This road, and its conclusion at Milford Sound, is one of the things that brings people to New Zealand, and it's easy to see why.

Interest in the Milford Sound region began with the discovery of Sutherland Falls, the fifth-highest waterfall in the world, and the subsequent construction of the Milford Track in the late 19th century. The road itself began as a Great Depression infrastructure project, employing at first just five men, armed with picks and wheelbarrows and charged with the task of carving a highway into the most famous of New Zealand's fiords. The most difficult section of the construction was around Homer Saddle, the pass discovered by William Homer in 1889. Here, a 1270m-long road tunnel, the Homer Tunnel, was cut through the mountains. Tunnelling work began in 1935 but wasn't completed for almost two decades, being interrupted by WWII and the severity of the conditions – an avalanche in 1945 crushed part of the tunnel, killing several workers (in winter, avalanches remain a threat at the tunnel entrances). The road, Highway 94, was only fully sealed in 1992.

From Te Anau the road enters Fiordland National Park, part of the Te Wahipounamu World Heritage site and the country's largest national park, beside long Lake Te Anau. It climbs gradually to the Divide, threading between the Livingstone and Earl Mountains, before steepening to its highest point at the Homer Tunnel. From the tunnel's western end, the road fishtails steeply down the spectacular Cleddau Canyon, through beech-covered slopes, to the shores of Milford Sound, where 1692m Mitre Peak famously looms over the waters.

ESSENTIAL EXPERIENCES

* **Wandering through Te Anau's glow-worm caves, where said grubs light up the darkness like stars.**

* Stopping at the Divide to hike up to Key Summit, a two-hour return walk that culminates in spectacular views of the three valleys that radiate from this point.

* **Admiring the glassy reflections at the Mirror Lakes – on a calm day the lakes reflect the mountains across the valley.**

* Cruising on Milford Sound for the chance to see seals, dolphins and an almost guaranteed downpour of rain (an average of 7m per year!) that creates a deluge of waterfalls.

DISTANCE - 125KM | **COUNTRIES COVERED** - NEW ZEALAND | **IDEAL TIME COMMITMENT** - ONE DAY | **BEST TIME OF YEAR** - OCTOBER TO APRIL | **ESSENTIAL TIP** - HEAD OUT EARLY (8AM) OR LATE IN THE MORNING (11AM) TO AVOID THE CONGA-LINE OF TOUR BUSES.

HOMER NAKED

The rough-hewn, narrow darkness of the Homer Tunnel might seem confronting in a vehicle, but imagine sprinting through it naked. Held on 1 April each year, the Great Annual Nude Tunnel Run sees around 80 to 100 people shed their clothes (barring running shoes and a head torch) and dash through the 1270m-long tunnel. The event was first run in 1998, and the male and female winners of the race receive a Ken and Barbie doll – naked (of course) – respectively.

■ THE JOURNEY TODAY

It is all so gob-smackingly gorgeous, this tight and twisting drive into the narrowing embrace of the Fiordland mountains. The Eglinton Valley is studded with beech forest, while as you rise to The Divide the roadside seems studded with trampers. From this, the lowest east–west pass in the Southern Alps, some of the country's most famous tramping trails (the Routeburn, Greenstone and Caples Tracks) radiate into the wilderness, and it seems as though every backpack on the South Island might be here, as well as most of the gaiters.

A quick dip off the pass and the climbing begins again: a 13km pull up to the Homer Tunnel. The traffic lights at the tunnel are red, so you sit and wait, the engine idling but the keas are at full acceleration. These birds, the world's only alpine parrot, are notorious here. On tramping tracks their thieving beaks pull at packs and tents; at the entrance to the tunnel they prefer the rubber of windscreen wiper blades. You shoo one bird away and the traffic light finally changes

to green, signalling that it's time to leave this spectacular, high-walled, ice-carved amphitheatre.

There's momentary darkness inside the tunnel, but the light at the end is indeed heavenly. From 940m above sea level, you begin the plunge to the water: 20km of winding, zigzagging, snaking, coiling gloriousness. The alpine lands are suddenly rainforest, the mountain air now salted by the sea. You stop briefly at the Chasm, wandering out to watch the Cleddau River tumbling furiously towards the coast, before finally descending to the shores of Milford Sound. The settlement itself is surprisingly tiny (only about 120 people actually live here) but the

ARMCHAIR

❋ *Men of the Milford Road* (Harold Anderson) Difficult-to-find (published in 1975) account of the construction of the road and Homer Tunnel, written by a paymaster on the project.

❋ *Milford Sound: An Illustrated History of the Sound, the Track and the Road* (John Hall-Jones) An all-in-one history of the region, with chapters on the road, the Homer Tunnel and the Milford Track.

❋ *Below the Mountains: The Diary of Amy McDonald, Milford Road, 1935–36* (Amy McDonald) An account of one girl's time living in a workers' camp during the road's construction.

❋ *The Lord of the Rings trilogy* (2001–03) Middle Earth found much of its home around the Fiordland region; watch the trilogy for a scene-setting intro.

scenery is massive, and you could swear that was a dolphin that just rippled the surface of the sound.

■ SHORTCUT

You can drive the Milford Road in a couple of hours – but why would you? – or you can view the landscape from the top down in even brisker fashion with a flight into Milford Sound. Flights operate out of Queenstown and Wanaka, skimming over the mountains to the sound, and it's possible to return by coach along the Milford Road.

■ DETOUR

It goes without saying that Fiordland is about fjords, and second in the queue to Milford Sound is vast, remote Doubtful Sound. In a wilderness area of rugged peaks, dense forest and thundering post-rain waterfalls, this fjord is three times the length and 10 times the area of Milford Sound. It can only be accessed on tours out of Manapouri. You'll cross Lake Manapouri by boat to the West Arm power station, drive by bus the winding 22km through dense rainforest to Deep Cove (permanent population: one), then head out on Doubtful aboard another boat.

COLIN MONTEATH | PHOTOLIBRARY

OPENING SPREAD A magical, rainfed waterfall near the Homer Tunnel.
ABOVE That's what we're talking about: overlooking the valley from Mackinnon Pass.
BELOW The sheer scope and beauty of the Fiordland National Park.

MILFORD TRACK

More than a century ago a London newspaper described the Milford Track as the 'finest walk in the world'. It's a description that's stuck. Offering a walker's approach to Milford Sound, the track begins on Lake Te Anau and follows the Clinton Valley up to spectacular Mackinnon Pass, before funnelling through the Arthur Valley to Milford Sound. The track predates the road by around 50 years, having been created in the 1880s as a way into 580m-high Sutherland Falls - the fifth-highest waterfall in the world. Hiking the track today is strictly regulated: you must walk it in four days, stopping at designated huts each night.

SOUTH AFRICA

SOUTH AFRICA'S CAPE ROUTE 62

SOUTH AFRICA'S CAPE HIGHWAY IS MORE THAN A MERE ALTERNATIVE TO A BUSY NATIONAL HIGHWAY. IT'S A DESTINATION IN ITSELF, REVEALING LUSH MOUNTAINS AND CRYSTALLINE RIVERS, VINEYARDS, ORCHARDS AND STARK CLIFFS THAT DROP INTO DEEP RAVINES AND SWIRLING SEAS.

266

Enjoy convenient stops where you can dig tribal art and explore game reserves and hiking trails. Maybe you'll paddle a canoe, ride a horse or even an ostrich, or join an expedition into a deep, dark cave. All are possibilities as you make your way out of Cape Town from the Cape of Good Hope on the west coast and into South Africa's famed Cape Winelands, which stretch from Paarl, just 40 minutes from Cape Town, to Ashton. The scene begins to shift from the quilted beauty of vineyards and farms into rockier, wilder climes at Montagu where the scenic heart of Route 62 begins in earnest. Mountains continue to rise and wildflowers bloom in Barrydale on the way to the Tradouw Pass and Ladismith, where the split-peak Towerkop Mountain looms above town. Mountain sports are the main pastime in Prince Albert, just 2km from the foot of the beautiful Swartberg Pass. After navigating Prince Albert Pass the approach to the East Cape takes you through Uniondale, Joubertina, Kareedouw, past Cape St Francis and the epic surf beaches of Jeffrey's Bay and finally, to the one-time family beach getaway that is Nelson Mandela Bay in the growing city of Port Elizabeth.

Just as US Route 66 once both linked and told the story of small town and big time America, Route 62 was an economic and cultural lifeline for South Africa's farming communities. Cape Route 62 was dealt a similar hand as America's Route 66 when federal funding for the national highway system ended after the completion of the N2 Highway in 1958. Thankfully not all of the Cape's villages suffered from the depression experienced by the small towns that live off their end of the US interstate commerce.

ESSENTIAL EXPERIENCES

* **Snapping sunset photos on the cable car up Table Mountain, Cape Town's centrepiece national park.**

* Absorbing the chilly winds of Robben Island history from Mandela's former cell, where he languished for 27 years and wrote his seminal autobiography.

* **Sipping fine wine and nibbling cheese in gourmand Robertson Valley.**

* Rock climbing, mountain biking and hiking amid the red rocks of Ashton, a mecca for some of South Africa's best outdoor adventure.

* **Relaxing into the temperate coastal paradise that is Jeffrey's Bay, where you'll find perfectly formed barrels and a buffer zone of open space.**

DISTANCE - 850KM | **COUNTRIES COVERED** - SOUTH AFRICA | **IDEAL TIME COMMITMENT** - ONE WEEK | **BEST TIME OF YEAR** - SEPTEMBER TO MAY | **ESSENTIAL TIP** - SPEAK WITH SOMMELIERS AND WINE-SELLERS IN CAPE TOWN TO FIND OUT THEIR RECOMMENDATIONS.

A NEW DAY DAWNS

The country's first democratic elections took place in 1994, and across the country at midnight on 26–27 April, 'Die Stem' (the old national anthem) was sung and the old flag was lowered. A new rainbow flag was raised and the new anthem, 'Nkosi Sikelele i Afrika' (God Bless Africa), was sung. In the first democratic election in the country's history, the ANC won 62.7% of the vote; 66.7% would have enabled it to rewrite the interim constitution. The National Party won 20.4% of the vote, enough to guarantee it representation in cabinet. Nelson Mandela was made president of the 'new' South Africa.

THE JOURNEY TODAY

From its signature Table Mountain summit draped with cascading clouds, to the nearby vineyards and golden beaches, there's an incredible array of cultural, culinary and adventure opportunities in Cape Town. For a vital sobering sniff of apartheid, visit Mandela's cell on Robben Island and the District Six Museum then head for the Atlantic Coast for soft-sand beaches and epic surf. Dip your toe then head east to wine country. It begins in Paarl and stretches over nearly half of Route 62. Wellington, with its Stone Age rock art in the mountains and French grapes on the vines, is a nice compact town, with all of the cellar doors a reasonable distance from one another, but the nearby Tulbagh Valley, backed by muscular mountains that get lightly snow-dusted in winter, is home to more well-known vintners. Worcester marks the centre of the Cape Winelands region and is known for its brandy, while the nearby Robertson Valley has some of the Cape's best sips. In Bonnievale, nestled on the banks of the Breede River, locals pair their fine wine with glorious locally crafted cheeses. Rock-climbing, hiking and mountain-biking opportunities abound in Ashton as the topography shifts and the road winds into red-rock canyons. There is more wine, adventure and stunning local flora and fauna in Ladismith. Keep your eyes peeled for kudu, or perhaps a Cape mountain zebra. You can get your fill of ostrich culture in Outdshoorn, and spend the night in a cave in Uniondale, set just inland from Cape St Francis. After buzzing the cape, you'll wind your way to the surf Shangri La of Jeffrey's Bay. Flanked by nature reserves and rivers on both sides, this place is magic, even as development roars from all angles. Make your way to the somewhat rundown city of Port Elizabeth and Nelson Mandela Bay where the beaches are still nice and the waves quite kind.

SHORTCUT

Spend the weekend in Cape Town, then two days exploring the vintners of Paarl, Wellington and Tulbaugh. Or make a beeline from Cape Town to the stunning Robertson Valley, which offers arguably the best of South Africa's winemakers.

DETOUR

You shouldn't miss Kruger National Park, a two-hour flight from Cape Town. In an area the size of Wales, enough elephants wander around to populate a city, giraffes nibble on acacia trees, hippos wallow in the rivers, leopards prowl through the night and a multitude of birds sing, fly and roost. The park has an extensive network of sealed roads and comfortable camps, but if you prefer to keep it rough, there are also 4WD tracks, and mountain-bike and hiking trails.

OPENING SPREAD 'Grandeur', 'majesty', all the superlatives... Table Mountain hogs them all. **ABOVE** Looking out to Cape Town from Robben Island.

ARMCHAIR

* ***Long Walk to Freedom*** (Nelson Mandela) Much of this autobiography by freedom-fighter turned president Mandela was written surreptitiously while he languished on Robben Island for 27 years. His spirit and desire for universal freedom is palpable on the pages even as he describes personal shortcomings.

* ***Cry Freedom*** (1987) A classic Hollywood film about the legendary anti-apartheid activist, Steven Biko, starring a young Denzel Washington as Biko and Kevin Kline as a crusading journalist.

CAPE TIPPLES

Since it made its debut in 1659, South African wine has had time to age to perfection. Dry whites are particularly good, while popular reds include Pinotage (a local cross between Pinot and Cinsaut). Oh, and the brandy is good too. Some of the best is bottled and poured at Worcester's KWV Brandy House. Still, in spite of this, beer (mostly Amstel) remains the national beverage.

WALKS & PILGRIMAGES

GREAT JOURNEYS

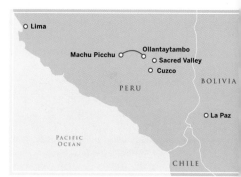

INCA TRAIL TO MACHU PICCHU

THE INCA TRAIL IS A MYSTICAL AND UNFORGETTABLE EXPERIENCE. THINK VIEWS OF SNOWY MOUNTAIN PEAKS, DISTANT RIVERS AND RANGES, AND CLOUD FORESTS ACCENTED WITH ORCHIDS. THAT'S THE BACKDROP AS YOU WALK FROM ONE CLIFF-HUGGING PRE-COLUMBIAN RUIN TO THE NEXT.

270

It's the most famous trek in South America, and is hiked by thousands every year. Although the total distance is only about 43km, it takes four days to navigate this ancient and narrow trail, laid by the Incas, from the Sacred Valley to Machu Picchu. It winds its way up and down and around the mountains, snaking over three high Andean passes en route. Although the journey alone is likely to inspire triumphant and poetic lifelong memories, the destination is equally magnificent.

Blessed with a spectacular location the awe-inspiring ancient Inca city of Machu Picchu, which was hidden from Spanish conquistadores and remained virtually forgotten until the 20th century, is the best-known archaeological site on the continent. Apart from a couple of German adventurers in the 1860s, who apparently looted the site with the Peruvian government's permission, nobody except local Quechua people knew of Machu Picchu's existence until American historian Hiram Bingham was guided to it by locals in 1911. The Machu Picchu site was initially overgrown with thick vegetation, forcing Bingham's team to be content with roughly mapping the site. He returned in 1912 and 1915 to carry out the difficult task of clearing the thick forest, when he also discovered some of the ruins on the so-called Inca Trail. Over the course of his various journeys, Bingham took thousands of artifacts back to the US with him, which remains an international point of contention. Peruvian archaeologist Luis E Valcárcel undertook further studies in 1934, as did a Peruvian-American expedition under Paul Fejos in 1940–41. Although the Inca people laced hundreds of miles of similar trails throughout Andean Peru, the majesty of Machu Picchu, combined with the popularity of the trek to the old city, has led to this route being dubbed 'the Inca Trail'.

ESSENTIAL EXPERIENCES

✳ **Glancing over your shoulder at the icy Nevado Verónica at Wayllabamba.**

✳ Cresting Warmiwañusca pass at 4198m above sea level, the highest point of the trek, with the Río Pacamayo (Sunrise River) snaking far below.

✳ **Descending from the ceremonial baths at Phuyupatamarka ('Town above the Clouds'), into dense and colourful cloud forests.**

✳ Winding through another stand of cliff-hanging cloud forest to reach Intipunku (Sun Gate), where you'll see the sunrise over Machu Picchu.

✳ **Walking in the footsteps of ancient Inca warriors and royalty through South America's greatest archaeological site.**

ORIGINS OF THE CITADEL

Despite scores of studies, knowledge of Machu Picchu remains sketchy. Some believe the citadel was founded in the waning years of the Incas as an attempt to preserve their culture or rekindle their predominance, while others think that it may have already become an uninhabited, forgotten city at the time of Spanish conquest. A more recent theory suggests that the site was a royal retreat or country palace abandoned at the time of the Spanish invasion. The site's director believes that it was an important city, a political, religious and administrative centre. Its location, and the fact that at least eight access routes have been discovered, suggests that it was a trade nexus between Amazonia and the highlands.

SUN WORSHIPPERS

A staircase behind the Sacristy climbs a small hill to the major shrine in Machu Picchu, the Intihuatana. This Quechua name loosely translates as the 'Hitching Post of the Sun' and refers to the carved rock pillar, often mistakenly called a sundial, which stands at the top of the Intihuatana hill. Inca astronomers were able to predict the solstices using the angles of this pillar. Thus, they were able to claim control over the return of the lengthening summer days. Exactly how the pillar was used for these astronomical purposes remains unclear, but its elegant simplicity and high craftwork make it a highlight of the complex.

■ THE JOURNEY TODAY

After crossing the Río Urubamba (2200m), you'll climb gently alongside the river to the trail's first archaeological site, Llactapata (Town on Hillside), before heading south to the hamlet of Wayllabamba (Grassy Plain; 3100m), where you can look over your shoulder for views of the hulking, snowcapped Nevado Verónica (5750m). The trail crosses the Río Llullucha, and eventually emerges on the high, bare mountainside of Llulluchupampa. This is as far as you can reasonably expect to get on your first day. From Llulluchupampa, it's a two- to three-hour ascent to the first pass of Warmiwañusca, also colourfully known as 'Dead Woman's Pass'. At 4198m above sea level, it's the highest point of the trek. From here you can see the ruin of Runkurakay, a basket-shaped building, which you'll visit after a knee-jarring descent and a short climb. Above Runkurakay, the trail climbs past two small lakes to the top of the second pass at 3950m, which has views of the icy Cordillera Vilcabamba. The ecology falls under an Amazonian influence and your surroundings become lush as you descend to the ruin of Sayaqmarka (Dominant Town), perched on a small mountain spur. After another river crossing you'll climb through magnificent cloud forest, and an Inca tunnel carved from the rock, to arrive at the third pass at almost 3700m, which has grand views of the Río Urubamba valley, and where some take in a mind-blowing sunset and spend their final night.

Just below the pass is the stunning, well-named ruin of Phuyupatamarka ('Town above the Clouds'), with a series of ceremonial baths cascading with clear water. From Phuyupatamarka, the trail dives into the cloud forest below, following hundreds of Inca steps to Wiñay Wayna, and continuing through cliff-hanging cloud forest for another two hours to Intipunku (Sun Gate) – where it's

traditional to enjoy your first glimpse of majestic Machu Picchu while waiting for the sun to rise over the surrounding mountains. The final triumphant descent takes less than an hour.

■ SHORTCUT

This 16km version of the Inca Trail gives an indication of what the longer trail is like. It's a real workout, and passes through some of the best scenery and most impressive terraced ruins. It begins with a steep three- or four-hour climb from Km 104 to Wiñay Wayna, and continues another two hours on fairly flat terrain to Machu Picchu.

■ DETOUR

Consider a walk along any of the old Inca routes to Ollantaytambo through the dramatic Lares Valley. Starting at natural hot springs, wander through rural Andean villages, lesser known Inca archaeological sites, lush lagoons and river gorges. Finish by taking the train from Ollantaytambo to Aguas Calientes, the gateway to Machu Picchu. Although this trek is more cultural than technical, the scenery is breathtaking, and the highest mountain pass (4450m) is nothing to sneeze at.

273

OPENING SPREAD Karakoram: a picture tells a thousand stories. **ABOVE (L)** Doing a brisk trade in fruit along the Highway. **ABOVE (R)** 'What's your problem, human?' A snow leopard lays down the law. **LEFT** Yurts at Karakul Lake, with the wonderful Pamir Mountains behind.

ARMCHAIR

✳ **Inca Land: Explorations in the Highlands of Peru** (Hiram Bingham) Bingham's 1922 account of his search for Vilcabamba, the Incas last stronghold, which he thought he'd found at Machu Picchu.

✳ **The Royal Commentaries of the Incas** (Garcilaso de la Vega) The Inca empire's main expansion occurred in the 100 years prior to the arrival of the conquistadores in 1532. When

the Spanish reached Cuzco, they chronicled Inca history as related by the Incas themselves. This, the most famous known account, was written by the son of an Inca princess and a Spanish military captain.

✳ **Porters of the Inca Trail** (2009) A documentary exploring the history and political struggle of the porters as well as cultural and traditional cornerstones of their Quechua heritage.

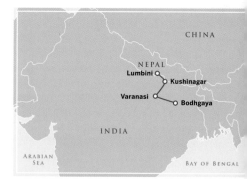

IN THE FOOTSTEPS OF BUDDHA

TRAVEL IN THE WAKE OF A GREAT SAINT WHO WAS BORN A PRINCE, SHED ROYAL CLOAKS AND MUNDANE RESPONSIBILITIES FOR PLAIN ROBES, FOUND ENLIGHTENMENT, TAUGHT THE MIDDLE PATH AND ACHIEVED NIRVANA IN THE WOODED PLAINS OF PRESENT-DAY NORTHERN INDIA AND NEPAL.

274

Siddhartha's journey from palace prince to wandering ascetic to nirvana is the stuff of legend (not to mention classic fiction) and this pilgrimage includes visits to what are considered to be the four holiest sites in Buddhism.

The eventual Buddha was not born in a palace. He arrived while his mother, Maya Devi, was en route to her parents' home in Kapilvastu. The year was 623 BC, the moon was full and Siddhartha was born under a tree in the present-day Nepali town of Lumbini. Court astrologers examined his chart and warned the king and queen that the boy might renounce the world, which is why his parents all but imprisoned the boy prince in pleasure palaces and married him off at a young age. In the end, he did shed the cushy confines and walked the Earth with a band of renunciants before going his own way and resting under a banyan tree on the Falgu River near the city of Gaya. After three days and three nights he became enlightened, which is how Bodh Gaya became the second stop on the Buddha pilgrimage. The Buddha walked to Sarnath, a deer park near the holy city of Varanasi, and delivered his first sermon about the 'middle way' to nirvana. It's commemorated by a stupa built in 234 BC by the Emperor Ashoka, a vicious warlord who turned to Buddhism and spread the message of love and compassion throughout his kingdom.

When Chinese traveler Xuan Zang dropped by in AD 640, Sarnath boasted a 100m-high stupa and 1500 monks living in large monasteries. However, Buddhism soon went into decline in India and, when Muslim invaders destroyed and desecrated the city's buildings, Sarnath disappeared altogether. British archaeologists rediscovered it in 1835.

The Buddha lay down by the Hiranyavati River and announced his coming death in present-day Kushinagar on 543 BC under another full moon. His journey complete, a seven-day ceremony commenced, and his body cremated.

ESSENTIAL EXPERIENCES

✳ **Visiting Buddha's birthplace, and making an offering to his mother at the Maya Devi Temple in Lumbini.**

✳ Chatting with monks, meditating in silence and contemplating life in the shadow of a serene stupa, erected where Buddha was cremated at Kushinagar 2500 years ago.

✳ **Exploring wild Varanasi then hopping on a bus to nearby Sarnath, where Buddha lectured for the first time.**

✳ Considering the incredible global impact of Buddha and the 'ism' he founded, by walking among stupas, pagodas, temples and monasteries erected in the styles of all the different cultures that consider the Buddha (one of) their saint(s).

DISTANCE - 650KM | **COUNTRIES COVERED** - INDIA, NEPAL | **IDEAL TIME COMMITMENT** - FIVE DAYS | **BEST TIME OF YEAR** - OCTOBER TO MARCH | **ESSENTIAL TIP** - VISITING THESE SITES IN CHRONOLOGICAL ORDER IS LOGISTICALLY DIFFICULT; IT'S ALWAYS PLEASANT TO END THE PILGRIMAGE BENEATH THE BODHI TREE.

THE ORIGINAL SUTRA

The Buddha's first known Sutra, known as the Dhammacakkappavattana Sutta, was delivered to five monks in the deer park of Sarnath. In it the Buddha warns against pursuing both worldly sensual pleasures and painful self-mortification. Instead, he advocated a 'middle way' (majjhima patipada) that became forever known as the Noble Eightfold Path (ariyo atthangiko maggo). It includes 'right' (sammā), understanding, intention, speech, action, livelihood, effort, mindfulness and concentration and eventually leads to vision, knowledge, peace, enlightenment and nirvana (nibbana). He went on to delineate the 'Four Noble Truths', suggesting that life is suffering, that suffering is born of desire, that it can be eliminated by liberating yourself from desire and that the only way to do this is by living the Noble Eightfold Path.

▇ THE JOURNEY TODAY

Your journey starts at the place of his birth in the Himalayan foothills of Lumbini. Rising from the forested landscape is the brick Maya Devi Temple complex, complete with sandstone sculpture depicting scenes of the royal birth. South of the temple is Puskarni, a sacred pool where it is thought Maya Devi bathed prior to giving birth. Behind the temple is the half-submerged, 6m Ashokan pillar built by the emperor devotee in 249 BC. From here it is most convenient and oddly poetic to travel over the Indian border and directly to Kushinagar, where the Buddha died in a state of para-nirvana. You can stay in a peaceful, modern temple, chat with monks or just contemplate – historical sights include the serene stupa where Buddha is said to have been cremated and the Mathakuar Temple, where he made his farewell sermon. Next, you'll head south to Sarnath, just outside the entrancing, holy Hindu city of Varanasi. Set in a park of monastery ruins is the impressive 34m Dhamekh Stupa, which marks where the Buddha preached his first sermon. The floral and geometric carvings are 5th century AD, but some of the brickwork dates back as far as 200 BC. Nearby is a 3rd-century BC Ashoka pillar with an edict engraved on it. It once stood 15m tall and had the famous four-lion capital (now in the nearby museum) perched on top of it, but all that remains are five fragments of its base. The large ruined Chaukhandi Stupa dates back to the 5th century AD, and marks the spot where Buddha met his first disciples. You'll notice that incongruous Mughal tower on top. It was built in the 16th century to commemorate the visit of Emperor Humayun. The final, and in many ways the deepest, pilgrimage stop is Bodhgaya, a still serene town where the Buddha became enlightened 2600 years ago. Several Buddhist

ARMCHAIR

❋ **Siddhartha** (Herman Hesse) The tale of a Brahmin who sheds his upper-caste existence, wanders with ascetics, gets roped back into a material world before wandering again and eventually reaching enlightenment during the time of the Buddha.

❋ **Old Path, White Clouds** (Thich Nhat Hanh) Buddhist monk and Vietnamese peace activist Hanh draws from 24 Pali, Sanskrit and Chinese texts, to form an authoritative account of the Buddha's life.

❋ **Buddha: A Story Of Enlightenment** (Deepak Chopra) It's a novel, and as such a relative departure for Chopra. It mostly sticks to the facts of Buddha's life.

❋ **The Buddha** (2010) This PBS documentary, directed by David Grubin and narrated by Richard Gere, tells the story of Buddha's journey while featuring insights from contemporary Buddhists, including his holiness, the Dalai Lama.

stupas, pagodas and monasteries dot the bucolic landscape built in their national style by foreign Buddhist communities. Between October and March, Tibetan monks flock here from Dharamsala and a serene sea of maroon-and-saffron robes rolls beneath the canopy of an auspicious Bodhi Tree.

SHORTCUT

To see one site that encompasses the incredible reach of modern day Buddhism, begin and end your pilgrimage in Bodhgaya. Set amidst a bucolic landscape in the Indian state of Bihar, you'll marvel at Japanese, Thai, Bhutanese, Tibetan, Chinese, Vietnamese, Burmese and Nepalese temples, which stand around the Mahabodhi Temple. Plus, you can attend one of several Vipassana and Tibetan meditation courses on offer.

DETOUR

Varanasi, the gateway to Sarnath, is blindingly colourful, unrelentingly chaotic and unapologetically indiscreet. Also known as Kashi (City of Life) or Benares, this is one of the world's oldest continually inhabited cities, and one of the holiest places in India. Hindu pilgrims come here to the River Ganges to wash away a lifetime of sins in the sacred waters or to cremate their loved ones.

LINDSAY BROWN | LONELY PLANET IMAGES ©

OPENING SPREAD Dhamekh Stupa, Sarnath, India. **ABOVE** Buddhist monks in Nepal, deeply meditative. **BELOW** School girls gather around a bodhi tree, Kandy, Sri Lanka.

THE BODHI TREE

Hard though it is to fathom, the devoted Ashoka's wife killed the original Bodhi Tree, as she was horribly jealous of the emperor's affection for it (looks like someone didn't meditate). Thankfully, before it was killed, someone had carried off one of its saplings and planted it in Sri Lanka, where it thrived. The tree you'll see, snap photos of, and perhaps sit and meditate under in Bodhgaya, started as a cutting from that Sri Lankan descendent. Fear not, these roots are divine. And that red sandstone slab between the tree and the Mahabodhi Temple was placed there by Ashoka to mark the presumed spot of Buddha's enlightenment.

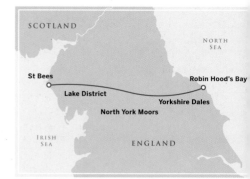

COAST TO COAST WALK

WALK FROM THE IRISH SEA TO THE NORTH SEA UNDER THE AUTHORIAL DIRECTION OF BRITAIN'S MOST REVERED FELL WALKER, CROSSING THROUGH THE LAKE DISTRICT, YORKSHIRE DALES AND NORTH YORK MOORS.

278

The Coast to Coast Walk, beginning at St Bees and ending at Robin Hood's Bay, is one of Britain's most popular long-distance paths, and yet it isn't a national trail and has no official recognition.

It was first described in the near-mythical Alfred Wainwright's *A Coast to Coast Walk*, a hand-printed and illustrated book, published in 1973. Wainwright had taken a year to carefully plan his route, but encouraged readers to make up their own Coast to Coast itineraries: 'There's no end to the possibilities for originality and initiative,' he wrote in the book's introduction. However, most people doing Wainwright's route call it the Coast to Coast, and follow his description very closely. Purists refuse to deviate even a few steps from Wainwright's incredibly precise instructions. Although the route has been realigned in some places (mainly so it now follows legal rights of way), it still keeps pretty much to the original and certainly follows it in spirit.

The Coast to Coast Walk passes through some of England's finest landscape, including three spectacular national parks: the Lake District, Yorkshire Dales and North York Moors. Along its course are disbanded mines and railway lines, reminders of a once-flourishing industrial age; lonely inns on isolated hilltops; historic buildings in bustling market towns; the rugged windswept splendour of both coasts; and drystone walls and barns.

Some sections include several miles of forestry tracks and sealed roads, which are a little tedious at times. However, for the most part it's an inspiring journey though a slice of British geography, history and society.

Wainwright's original itinerary covered 12 days, which is achievable but is tough going. It means walking an average of 25km a day, and most days have some serious ascents and descents. Many people now stretch it out to 14 or 16 days.

ESSENTIAL EXPERIENCES

✳ **Dipping your toe ritualistically into the Irish Sea at walk's beginning, and again into the North Sea at the end.**

✳ Inching your way off Helvellyn along the razor-sharp Striding Edge, one of England's great scrambling routes.

✳ **Enjoying a beverage or bed at the Lion Inn in Blakey, the focal point of this lonely stretch of the North York Moors for centuries.**

✳ Piecing together all that Dales' mining history at the Swaledale Museum in Reeth.

✳ **Admiring the vast views – and the mysterious nine stone-cairns – at Nine Standards Rigg, atop the Pennines.**

DISTANCE - 307.5KM | **COUNTRIES COVERED** - ENGLAND | **IDEAL TIME COMMITMENT** - 12 TO 16 DAYS | **BEST TIME OF YEAR** - JUNE TO SEPTEMBER | **ESSENTIAL TIP** - AVOID STARTING ON A WEEKEND, WHICH IS WHEN MOST WALKERS BEGIN.

ALFRED WAINWRIGHT

When Alfred 'AW' Wainwright wrote *A Coast to Coast Walk* at the age of 66, he was already the doyen of British fellwalking. His seven-volume *Pictorial Guide to the Lakeland Fells*, published in the 1950s and '60s, was so influential it even helped divide the Lake District into smaller regions adhering to his classifications. Wainwright combined a romantic devotion to wilderness and solitude with a scientific attention to detail to produce unique, handcrafted text, maps and illustrations. In all of his guides, the text is (neatly) hand-printed. AW is remembered today by the work of the Wainwright Society and by walkers' attempts to bag 'The Wainwrights', all 214 Lakeland Fells named in the famous guidebooks.

THE JOURNEY TODAY

As walking regimes go, this one is about as good as it gets. In the morning the Packhorse service pick ups your bags and will drop them at the B&B door, waiting for you in the evening. It leaves you walking light and liberated, which is welcome on some of these many climbs. Out of Grasmere, it frees you to climb to Helvellyn, the third highest peak in England, and scramble down the knife-edged Striding Edge for an extra jolt of hiking adrenaline. It's a grand way to say a farewell of sorts to the Lake District.

Some days you don't even need to carry your lunch, as the Coast to Coast is lined with villages, inns and teahouses. It is these, as much as the shared pains and pleasures, that have created one of the things you're enjoying most: the camaraderie shared with fellow walkers – people of all ages and many nationalities. There was the man walking it with his dog. The couple with children in tow. And the friendly local folk. It's been a close-to-perfect way to discovering the wilderness, the space and the sheer beautiful bleakness of the mountains and moors of northern England.

The weather has at times been wild, even though you're walking from west to east so the wind and sun will be mostly behind you, but so is the scenery: the high and harsh Lakeland Fells plunging into satin-smooth lakes; the dales echoing with the ghosts of mining past; and that mist in the North York Moors, as though you've stepped straight from the pages of *The Hound of the Baskervilles*. The most welcome scene of all is the North Sea, as you spend your final hour along the cliff-tops into the walk's end at Robin Hood's Bay.

Here, as is the custom, you remove your boots – bliss – and dip your toe into the sea, a signal that you have indeed just walked from coast to coast.

SHORTCUT

If you can't spare two weeks, and you're geared up for cycle touring, you can always try Britain's most popular long-distance cycling route: the Coast to Coast Cycle. Laid out north of the walking route, it mostly follows minor roads and bike paths between Whitehaven (Irish Sea) and Sunderland (North Sea). Covering 236km, it can be ridden in three days by strong cyclists but can also be stretched satisfyingly across a week.

DETOUR

The allure of the Lake District is such that it can be difficult to leave. If you want some more time here in your hiking boots, swing onto the Cumbria Way, which intersects with the Coast to Coast at Rosthwaite. The 122km path branches north to Derwent Water, Keswick and Carlisle, and south to the Langdale Pikes, Coniston and Ulverston.

OPENING SPREAD The swelling winter beauty of Upper Swaledale, Yorkshire Dales National Park. **ABOVE** Stirring colours mark the palette of North York Moors National Park. **RIGHT** End of the line: charming Robin Hood's Bay.

ARMCHAIR

❋ *A Coast to Coast Walk* (Alfred Wainwright) The classic Coast to Coast resource; the one that began it all. The revised edition, published in 2003, describes alternatives to Wainwright's route where it had strayed from public rights of way, while faithfully keeping the original text.

❋ *A Northern Coast to Coast Walk* (Terry Marsh) Has adjusted the original route in consultation with conservation officials, keeping to rights of way, avoiding eroded areas and reducing time spent walking on roads.

❋ *The Coast to Coast Accommodation Guide* (Doreen Whitehead) A useful booklet about beds along the walk's length; only available online.

❋ *Coast to Coast Cycle Routes* (Mark Porter & John Grimshaw) If you prefer spokes to steps, this book outlines three cross-country traverses.

ROBIN HOOD'S BAY

One thought may strike you while descending the cliffs at Robin Hood's Bay: it's a long way from here to the Sherwood Forest. How this coastal Yorkshire town got its name is a mystery, especially as it's unlikely that the real Robin Hood ever came calling. But that's not to say the town hasn't had its own share of grand stories. In the 18th century it was said to be the biggest smuggling centre on the Yorkshire coast, with a network of underground tunnels supposedly connecting the town's houses. Before the sea wall was built, the storms that flayed the coast once smashed a ship into the Bay Hotel by the slipway.

THE HOLY LAND

IT'S A LAND OF HISTORIC TEMPLES, CHURCHES AND MOSQUES, WAILING
WALLS AND DISPUTED ONES. BELIEVERS FLOCK HERE TO TRACE THE FOOTSTEPS
OF THEIR PROPHETS, TO SEE BIBLICAL RIVERS AND MOUNTAINS WHERE FIRST
ABRAHAM, THEN JESUS AND FINALLY MOHAMMAD CHANNELLED THE WORD.

282

Jerusalem's Temple Mount, known to Muslims as the Haram ash-Sharif, is
truly the beginning of this millennia-old tale. The Talmud states that it was
here that God gathered the earth that was used to form Adam, and that
biblical figures performed ritual sacrifices here. The most well known tells
how Abraham nearly sacrificed his own son Isaac in a test of faith. And it
was here that Solomon built the First Temple, and placed the Ark of the
Covenant inside. The jewel in the Temple Mount crown is the gold-plated
Dome of the Rock (Qubbet al-Sakhra in Arabic), the enduring symbol of the
city and undoubtedly one of the most-photographed buildings on Earth.
The dome covers a stone sacred to both the Muslims and Jews. The famed
Al-Aqsa Mosque stands on what is believed to have been a marketplace on
the edge of the Temple Mount. This might be where Jesus turned over the
tables and drove out the moneychangers. The 200-year-old Western Wall is
the most important Jewish site in Jerusalem. The most important Christian
site is the Church of the Holy Sepulchre, considered by Christians to be the
biblical Calvary, where Jesus was nailed to the cross, died and rose again.
You won't want to leave Jerusalem without visiting St Anne's Church, built
on the site of Mary's birth near the Pool of Bethesda, where the faithful
believe the scene of Jesus' healing miracle took place. Mary was laid to rest
on Mt Zion, where you'll also find the Cenacle, the site of the Last Supper.
From Jerusalem, venture east into the Palestinian Quarter and continue
into Bethlehem where you'll soon arrive at Manger Square and the Church
of the Nativity, the birthplace of Jesus and the oldest continually operating
church (326 AD) in the world. Overnight along the shores of the Dead Sea,
and cross over the River Jordan to Bethany, where Jesus was baptised by
John the Baptist in Jordan. From here it is a smooth ride up the fertile
Jordan Valley into Amman.

ESSENTIAL EXPERIENCES

✳ **Framing a photo of the Dome of the Rock,
where God created Adam from so much dust.**

✳ Touching the holy stone and celebrating
Shabas with the Hasidim at the Western Wall.

✳ **Tracing the *Passion of Christ* to the Church
of the Holy Sepulchre where Jesus was
executed by crucifixion.**

✳ Ducking through the Door of Humility and
glimpsing the grotto where Mary delivered
Jesus to the world.

✳ **Taking a break from holy sightseeing and
exploring outer Jerusalem or heading to
the Dead Sea, slathering yourself with
mineral-rich mud and floating for a while.**

DISTANCE - ABOUT 65KM | **COUNTRIES COVERED** - ISRAEL & THE PALESTINIAN TERRITORIES, JORDAN | **IDEAL TIME COMMITMENT**
- FIVE DAYS | **BEST TIME OF YEAR** - NOVEMBER TO APRIL | **ESSENTIAL TIP** - DRESS MODESTLY: COVER YOUR LEGS, SHOULDERS AND
BACK AT RELIGIOUS SITES.

CONTROVERSIAL CAPITAL

Controversy continues to surround the status of Jerusalem. Both Israelis and Palestinians see the city as their own capital and even though the Palestinian National Authority is based in Ramallah, it hopes to eventually move to East Jerusalem. Israel is determined to never let that happen and has been playing a cautious game of geopolitics to seal the city off from the Palestinian lands. A recent plan to build a new housing block (the Mevaserat Adumim) east of the city that would connect Jerusalem to the Jewish settlement of Ma'le Adumim, sealing the last barrier between Jerusalem and the West Bank has been scuttled, at least for now.

■ THE JOURNEY TODAY

You'll never forget your first taste of Jerusalem. A palpable spiritual energy pulsates through these ancient streets. Temple Mount is a relaxing contrast to the noise and congestion of the narrow streets. It's a flat paved area, fringed with some attractive Mamluk buildings and with the Dome of the Rock positioned roughly in the centre. Line up early for security checks and bear in mind that the Mount closes on Muslim holidays. The area immediately in front of the Western Wall operates as a great open-air synagogue where black-garbed Hasidim rock backwards and forwards on their heels, bobbing their heads in prayer. There are a number of holy sites within the Church of the Holy Sepulchre, including the final five Stations of the Cross. At the entrance to the Franciscan Chapel is the 10th station, where Jesus is said to have been stripped of his clothes. The 11th station, also in the chapel, is where it is said Jesus was nailed to the cross. Look to the right and you'll see a mosaic of Isaac being bound by Abraham. Surrounded by trees and rubble from bygone eras, St Anne's Church looks like a lost archaeological site in the midst of the Old City. Next to the church are the impressive ruins surrounding the biblical Pool of Bethesda. The building is unusually asymmetrical – columns, windows and even steps all vary in size. The Cenacle on Mount Zion is reached via a stairway from the courtyard of King David's Tomb. Many visitors mistake the first large room for the real thing but you need to walk across the hall to enter the much smaller chamber beyond if you wish to see the site of the Last Supper.

The energy on Manger Square and throughout the Old City of Bethlehem on Christmas Eve is electric, but the narrow limestone streets and exotic storefronts charm year-round. The entrance to the Church of the Nativity is a tiny

ARMCHAIR

❋ *From Beirut to Jerusalem* (Thomas L Friedman) This early work of the Pulitzer Prize–winning *New York Times* journalist, who reported from Beirut and Jerusalem, analyses the diplomatic culture clash that is the Middle East.

❋ *Walking the Bible* (Bruce Feiler) Tracing the author's 16,000km trek from Mt Ararat to Mt Nebo, the story is peppered with ruminations on Biblical myth and contemporary politics.

❋ *Religulous* (2008) Revered by atheists everywhere and a dissenting view of all things holy, much of Bill Maher's sharp-tongued documentary was filmed in the holy land.

❋ *Paradise Now* (2005) A brilliant, poignant film about two young Palestinian men who are going nowhere in Ramallah, and are confronted with a choice of life or martyrdom in present-day Palestine.

Ottoman-era front door, aptly named the Door of Humility. At the nave, descend the stairs to enter the Grotto of the Nativity. Lit with lanterns and redolent with mystery, it's where Jesus is said to have been born.

SHORTCUT

Jerusalem has the kind of cultural gravitas and hypnotic buzz to draw you in and keep you for itself. Surrender: visit the main sites in town then wander outside the ancient city walls, where the rest of Jerusalem resembles a collection of 20 small villages stuck together. Little neighbourhoods such as Mea She'arim, the German Colony and Nahla'ot are self-contained units, each with their own character.

DETOUR

Head to St Catherine's Monastery on Egypt's Sinai Peninsula and climb the mountain where Moses received the Ten Commandments. It could take 2.5 hours to reach the summit if you take the less strenuous route. The mosque on the peak is used by local Muslims, and there's a Greek Orthodox chapel here which, though not open to the public, supposedly encloses the very rock, slabbed and inscribed by God, to create the Commandments.

LEE FOSTER | LONELY PLANET IMAGES ©

OPENING SPREAD A sight renowned the world over: the multifaceted Dome of the Rock. **ABOVE** A woman floating in the Dead Sea, feeling very much alive. **BELOW** Prayer time at the Wailing Wall.

CAMINO DE SANTIAGO

GATHER UP YOUR STAFF AND SCALLOP SHELL AND FOLLOW IN THE CENTURIES-OLD FOOTSTEPS OF CHRISTIAN PILGRIMS, DESCENDING FROM THE PYRENEES AND HEADING THROUGH THE FORESTS AND WINE AND WHEAT FIELDS OF NORTHERN SPAIN TO THE TOMB OF THE APOSTLE JAMES.

286

A 13th-century poem from a remote Pyrenean monastery says about the Camino de Santiago (Way of St James): 'The door is open to all, to sick and healthy, not only to Catholics but also to pagans, Jews, heretics and vagabonds.' Not much has changed. The Camino attracts pilgrims from every possible background, age and nationality, those religiously motivated, culture hounds, soul searchers, those longing for a great physical challenge, food and wine enthusiasts, and lovers of natural landscapes and the solitude of back roads.

Its allure dates back to the 9th century, when a religious hermit unearthed the tomb of the apostle James the Greater. The impact was instant and indelible: first a trickle, then a flood of Christian Europeans began to journey towards the setting sun in search of salvation. Santiago de Compostela became the most important destination for Christians after Rome and Jerusalem.

Named as Europe's first 'premier cultural itinerary' in 1987, the Camino experienced a remarkable renaissance in the latter quarter of the 20th century, as people took to re-creating the medieval journey on foot and by bicycle (and, more rarely, on horseback).

The 'trail' is a mishmash of rural lanes, paved secondary roads and footpaths all strung together. Navigation is made easy, with cheerful yellow arrows on everything from telephone poles to rocks and trees. Scallop shells, stuck in cement markers or stylised on blue-and-yellow metal signs, also show the way.

There is no official starting point to the Camino, as over the centuries a web of routes arose across Europe, with pilgrims traipsing from various lands towards Santiago de Compostela and the reputed remains of St James, the first apostle martyred (decapitated) by Herod Agrippa, in AD 44. The most popular route, the Camino Francés – the Camino for most people – begins in Roncesvalles, on the French border and travels for 783km to Santiago.

ESSENTIAL EXPERIENCES

* **Standing on the French border at Puerto de Ibañeta, the same Pyrenean pass that Napoleon used to launch his 1802 occupation of Spain, and thinking about the long road ahead.**

* Sleeping in the *refugios* and *albergues*, operated especially for pilgrims by parishes, local governments, Camino associations and private owners.

* **Getting your Credencial del Peregrino stamped each day as you progress west.**

* Wandering through rolling, expansive stretches of vineyards in Rioja, Spain's best-known wine region.

* **Admiring the sun filtering through the 1800 square metres of stained-glass windows in León's Gothic cathedral.**

* Giving thanks for a safe journey at the altar of Santiago's cathedral.

DISTANCE - 783KM | **COUNTRIES COVERED** - SPAIN | **IDEAL TIME COMMITMENT** - ONE MONTH | **BEST TIME OF YEAR** - MAY, JUNE AND SEPTEMBER | **ESSENTIAL TIP** - WEAR IN YOUR HIKING BOOTS BEFORE SETTING OUT.

PILGRIM HOSTELS

Following the same spirit of charity as the medieval monasteries that gave hospitality to pilgrims, the *refugio* system developed during the Camino's renaissance in the early 1990s. After making the pilgrimage herself, Lourdes Lluch, a Catalan woman, decided that the Camino needed more facilities for pilgrims. During the summer of 1990, she rented a run-down house in Hornillos del Camino – one of the bleakest parts of the Camino – set up a makeshift shelter, and pulled pilgrims in off the street, offering them food, drink and a clean place to rest their weary bodies. The idea took off and there are now around 300 *refugios* along the Camino.

THE JOURNEY TODAY

After almost a month on foot, you are finally here: Santiago de Compostela. Through the Porta do Camiño gateway, you step into the city's historical quarter – just 500m to walk, but now such a massive sense of history all around you. Millions of people have trodden the enormous granite slabs of this street, hemmed in by impressive stone houses and churches.

In the tunnel staircase under the Archbishop's Palace, street musicians play a soundtrack to accompany your final steps into the magnificent cathedral square, the Praza do Obradoiro. You truly look the part, carrying your scallop shell and staff, the age-old symbols of St James that have been adopted by pilgrims. Your staff clicks on the stones as you walk, a sound that reminds you there are rituals to complete.

Inside the cathedral, behind the main altar, you climb to the Romanesque statue of St James – Santiago in Spanish – giving it a hug as so many others have before you. It's like the man himself personally welcoming you to the finish line. Descending into the crypt, you pay your respects to the apostle's relics, the very remains that the Camino is founded on.

You are done, your pilgrimage over, except for that final stamp in your *Credencial del Peregrino* (Pilgrim's Passport) that has travelled with you from Roncesvalles, granting you access to the pilgrims' *refugios* (hostels) these last few weeks. Twice a day you've had this document ink-stamped – at churches, refugios, even bars – and now only one stamp remains to be added. You head for the Oficina de Acogida de Peregrinos, where one final thump of ink confirms it: you are truly a pilgrim, with all the associated pleasure and pain of almost 800km on foot.

SHORTCUT

If you don't have five weeks to walk from Roncesvalles, a very popular alternative is to walk only the last 100km – the minimum distance allowed in order to earn a Compostela certificate of completion given out by the Catedral de Santiago de Compostela – from Sarria in Galicia, winding through rural lanes and villages into Santiago.

DETOUR

Some medieval pilgrims continued trekking from Santiago to the end of the known world, Fisterra, the dramatic, lighthouse-topped cape that juts into the Atlantic on the beautiful, remote Costa da Morte, around 90km from Santiago. They still do today, but most take the bus. Off the end of Fisterra's lighthouse, pilgrims burn stinking bits of clothing while watching the sun set over the endless blue abyss – there's nothing between here and America except ocean.

OPENING SPREAD Divine inspiration can be found at León's Gothic cathedral, Santa Maria de Regla, which dates from 1199. **ABOVE (L)** The scallop shells carried by pilgrims along the way. **ABOVE (R)** An idyllic scene, direct from Roncesvalles. **LEFT** Pilgrim Heaven: the Castle of Clavijo, Rioja.

ARMCHAIR

❋ *Pilgrim Stories: On and Off the Road to Santiago Analysis* (Nancy Frey) An anthropologist explores the pilgrimage's modern resurgence.

❋ *A Practical Guide for Pilgrims* (Millán Bravo Lozano) Provides great maps and route descriptions.

❋ *Walk in a Relaxed Manner* (Joyce Rupp) A compelling account of an inner journey along the Camino.

❋ *The Pilgrimage* (Paulo Coelho) A mystical journey is described in this international bestseller, recounting Coelho's life-changing Camino walk in 1986, which led to a spiritual awakening (and future mega-sellers such as *The Alchemist*).

❋ *A Food Lover's Pilgrimage to Santiago De Compostela* (Dee Nolan) A big walk works up a big appetite, and this personal account explains the food traditions along the route.

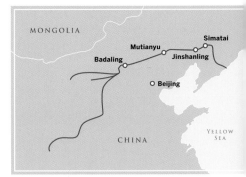

THE GREAT WALL OF CHINA

THE ULTIMATE EXPERIENCE TO LIVE AND PERHAPS DIE FOR. HORDES HAVE HIT THE GREAT WALL OF CHINA, THE SYMBOL OF THE COUNTRY, FOR CENTURIES. SAVOUR THE MONUMENTAL SCOPE OF THIS MAN-MADE PHENOMENON WHICH MEANDERS ITS WAY ACROSS CHINA FOR AN UNBELIEVABLE 8850KM.

290

The Great Wall of China, or at least sections of it, stretches from Xinjiang in the far west to as far east as the border with North Korea. Aside from its obvious awe-inspiring, aesthetic qualities, the wall is also a potent and visible reminder of China's incredibly turbulent history. The ancient Chinese always fortified their cities and states with enormous walls, and by 290 BC China's northern frontier was riddled with defensive structures. In 224 BC, when Mongolian nomads came knocking on China's doorstep, some of these structures were linked together to form one huge mega-structure. Thousands of workers were put to the task, ensuring China had the mightiest military barrier in the world. After falling into disrepair by the time of the Sui dynasty (AD 589-618), the wall was rebuilt, although it failed to repel the Mongols as they swept into China. While it didn't stop invading forces, its role as a signal post was beyond compare. Sentries on the watchtower warned the capital about enemy movements with the aid of smoke signals produced by burning – as you do – wolf dung.

Today, much of the wall is again in disrepair. Lengthy sections have disappeared altogether and the entire structure may have gone the same way if it weren't for the tourism industry. Several important sections have been rebuilt and opened to the public, coming complete with souvenir shops, restaurants and amusement-park rides. The most touristed area is at Badaling. Also renovated but less visited are Simatai and Jinshanling. Despite the government's attempts to implement conservation programs, in remote areas sections of the wall are plundered by farmers, who pillage its earthen core for use on the fields, and developers who strip the wall's bountiful supply of shaped stone from the ramparts for use in road and building construction.

ESSENTIAL EXPERIENCES

* **Escaping the crowds to visit Mutianyu, the 2250m-long granite section of wall, 90km northeast of Beijing, with its Ming dynasty guard towers and stirring views, and breathtaking cable-car journey.**

* Going with the flow at Badaling, the most popular section of wall.

* **Testing your mettle with the rugged Simatai section of wall.**

* Detouring to the Ming Tombs for yet another iconic experience.

* **Taking a break from the Wall to visit the Forbidden City, the Summer Palace, the Buddhist magnificence of the Yungang Caves and the Longmen Caves, and the Army of Terracotta Warriors.**

DISTANCE - 8850KM | **COUNTRIES COVERED** - CHINA | IDEAL TIME COMMITMENT - ONE TO TWO DAYS | **BEST TIME OF YEAR** - NOT ON WEEKENDS, ESPECIALLY IN SUMMER | **ESSENTIAL TIP** - THE EARLY MORNING OR LATE AFTERNOON MEANS AVOIDING CROWDS, AND BEST LIGHT FOR PHOTOGRAPHS.

HARD LABOUR

Construction of the 'original' wall began over 2000 years ago during the Qin dynasty (221–207 BC). The task was to link together separate walls that had been constructed by independent kingdoms to keep out marauding nomads. This Herculean effort required hundreds of thousands of workers – of course, China had a vast store of political prisoners who could be 'recruited' for the task. It's estimated that 180 million cu metres of rammed earth was used to form the core of the original wall, and among the many legends surrounding it is the one the about the bones of workers who had died on the job being used as building materials.

▣ THE JOURNEY TODAY

Your first encounter with the Great Wall is northwest of Beijing. You're at Badaling, the most-photographed manifestation of this most famous artefact. You were told that Badaling was commercialised, but still you went, after reading that it has much to offer the traveller hungry for experience. You are not disappointed: the raw scenery is amazing, and you are impressed with the archetypal views of the wall snaking into the distance over undulating hills. That's what it's all about, but all the same, it's a deeply strange experience, as you realise that Badaling has been heavily renovated and consequently overrun with hawkers, vendors and snack stands, a massive disjunction between present and past. On the other hand, the repairs have made it one of the wall's best sections for older travellers, children and anyone else put off by the crumbling stonework and sheer drops found elsewhere. Good for them you think, and an interesting experience all round, but the next day you're ready for something different again, so you travel to Simatai, 110km northwest of Beijing.

Your shoes, like Run DMC, are tougher than leather and they have good grip – you know you're ready for Simatai. Less packaged and more dramatic, you find Simatai totally exhilarating, befitting its status as one of the wall's steepest points. Partially renovated, some parts of the 19km section are rough and rocky with startling dips and rises, and you find the eastern section the most treacherous, with its 16 watchtowers and dizzying ascents. You concentrate with all your might. Before setting off, you stuffed all your belongings into a day pack for maximum manoeuvrability, and this proves to be mightily effective. What a relief to have your arms free of distractions while you scramble up and down Simatai's precipitous length!

ARMCHAIR

✳ **The Great Wall is a Great Wall** (1996) This was the first American film to be shot in China, and is about a Chinese–American couple and the cultural differences between them. The title refers to Richard Nixon's famously banal comment upon seeing China's greatest attraction for himself: 'This is a great wall' was all he could muster.

✳ **The Karate Kid** (2010) In this remake of the 1984 film, the eponymous kid is seen training at locations including the Great Wall.

✳ **The Emperor and the Assassin** (1999) The epic tale of the First Emperor of Qin and his lust for power. Woven with murder, love and political intrigue, this film is beautifully shot and a must see whether you're a history buff or not.

HEADLESS AT JIANKOU

Lord Cai masterminded the building of Jiankou, Beijing's most spectacular section of the wall, exercising the strictest quality control: every inch of masonry represented a whole day's work for one labourer. But the Ministry of War wasn't impressed by such extravagance, and beheaded him. Legend has it that Cai's decapitated body stood erect for three days before toppling, perhaps a reference to the fact that this section of the wall was the only one to successfully repel the invading Mongols, a successful defence that resulted in Cai becoming posthumously honoured. But what good is rehabilitation when you don't have a head?

You made it.

You're staring into the mist-shrouded valley way, way down below, and one thing's for sure: all your physical exertion has been more than worthwhile, because that right there is the view of a lifetime.

SHORTCUT

Suitable for a more condensed experience, the 3km-long section of wall at Mutianyu, 90km northeast of Beijing, is renowned for its Ming-dynasty guard towers and rousing views. With 26 watchtowers, it's manageable for most travellers, and hawking is kept to the lower levels. If time is pressing, take the cable car up and walk down.

DETOUR

Ming emperors did things in style – even death. The Ming Tombs, 50km northwest of Beijing, are the final resting place of 13 of the 16 Ming emperors alongside their wives, concubines, treasures and lots of ceremony. Three of the tomb grounds are open to the public. At first glance, the tombs don't seem that impressive. It's the stories that make them come 'alive', so consider a guide or an English-speaking tour group.

JAMES GRITZ | PHOTOLIBRARY

OPENING SPREAD So what if it can't really be seen from space, like the legend says? You won't find a finer sight than the Great Wall. **ABOVE** An unflinching gaze: terracotta soldiers outside the Wall. **BELOW** Simatai under snow, even more beautiful than usual.

THE HAJ

THE MASSIVE SWIRLING WAVES OF SPIRITUALISED HUMANITY THAT WASH OVER THE SAUDI DESERT, AND SATURATE THE TWIN HOLY CITIES OF MEDINA AND MECCA DURING THE LAST MONTH OF THE ISLAMIC CALENDAR, FORM WHAT HAS BECOME PERHAPS THE GREATEST PILGRIMAGE ON EARTH.

294

One of the Five Pillars of Islam, the pilgrimage to Mecca (known as the Haj) is a duty every Muslim must perform at least once, a journey that cleanses them of sins, reaffirms their faith, and brings a new meaning and direction to their lives.

The rituals and route are based on the trials of the prophet Ibrahim who took his wife, Hajar and infant son, Ishmael, to Arabia where Allah instructed him to leave them in a dry valley. As supplies wore mortally thin, Hajar prayed to Allah, while Ishmael cried of hunger and thirst, and when the baby stamped his foot on the ground a wellspring shot up. The family named the spring Zamzam and around it the desert city of Mecca grew. Pilgrims commemorate that search for water by performing the *sa'ee*, walking seven times between the two hills of Safah and Marwah. Ibrahim's greatest trial was when Allah instructed him to carry his son to the mountains and sacrifice him. On his way there, Shaitan (the devil) tempted Ibrahim to disobey, and Ibrahim threw stones to chase him away, ritualised by the stoning of the *jamrah* (pillars) in Mina. At the sacrificial site, Allah spared the child and instructed Ibrahim to slay a ram instead, the origins of the Haj's Eid al-Adha (Festival of Sacrifice).

One day, Allah commanded Ibrahim to build a house of worship in Mecca. After the death of his father, Ishmael continued to maintain the cubic Kaaba. After a prolonged rise in paganism, a man by the name of Mohammed ibn Abdullah was born in Mecca in AD 570. For 23 years, the Prophet Mohammed spread a message of obedience to Allah and a law of peace and order in Arabia. He purified the Kaaba and rededicated the house for the worship of Allah alone. Thousands of followers gathered to hear his sermon at the Haj.

The Haj has historically played a key contribution to the social cohesion of one of the world's great religions. Mecca, and nearby Medina – which many pilgrims also visit – are considered Islam's two holiest cities.

ESSENTIAL EXPERIENCES

✳ **Exploring the streets of Jeddah, crowded with pilgrims turned merchants from many of the 160 countries represented.**

✳ Shopping for camels or parrots, textiles or pistachios for a song at the Jeddah bazaar.

✳ **Dressing in the same, simple white cloth (the *ihram*), performing the same rituals and making the same challenging and exhausting journey (sleeping on the ground, eating from a common dish): enjoying the equality of being a participant within the surrounds of the holy cities.**

✳ Viewing the deeply transporting sight of the massive, robed, praying flock from the Mount of Mercy at Arafat.

DISTANCE - APPROXIMATELY 482KM | **COUNTRIES COVERED** - SAUDI ARABIA | **IDEAL TIME COMMITMENT** - ONE WEEK | **BEST TIME OF THE YEAR** - TWELFTH MONTH OF THE MUSLIM CALENDAR | **ESSENTIAL TIP** - ORGANISE YOUR VISA AND FLIGHT FAR IN ADVANCE.

STAR PILGRIMS

The Haj holy cities have seen many rich-and-famous faces pass through their gates. Past pilgrims include Ibn Battuta, one of history's greatest travellers, the lyrical American heavyweight champion Muhammad Ali, British pop singer Yusuf Islam (aka Cat Stevens), King Abdullah of Jordan, President Nasser and Pakistani cricketer Imran Khan. One such personality who famously wrote about his experience was a certain 'Al-Haj Malik el-Shabazz', otherwise known as Malcolm X, the American civil rights activist. Writing a letter to his followers back in Harlem, he declared: 'Never have I witnessed such sincere hospitality and overwhelming spirit of true brotherhood as is practiced by people of all colours and races here in this ancient Holy Land.'

RULES ARE RULES

Sure, there are positives – like possible eternal salvation, peace, balance and a divine connection in life, but religions (Islam in particular) are sticklers for their rules, and if you break one of the rules of *ihram* during the Haj, you must pay a kaffarah. Depending on which rule you've broken, there are three ways to redeem yourself: by offering a sacrifice; by feeding six impoverished people; or by fasting for three days. At or near the top of the verboten list: drinking, adultery (read: sex) and theft. These have punishments far worse than a mere kaffarah.

THE JOURNEY TODAY

These days the Haj is much more accessible. While 50 years ago there were less than 10,000 pilgrims annually, in 2010 that number had skyrocketed to nearly three million. Book one of the hundreds of flights that touch down in Jeddah nearly every minute as the Muslim calendar approaches the seventh day of the 12th month. Once you disembark in Jeddah, on *yawm at-tarwiyah*, the day of reflection and the first day of the Haj, called '8th Dhul Hijja', you will don your *ihram*, white robes fashioned from two sheets of unsewn cloth, and make your way to Mecca, 80km away.

Pilgrims perform the *tawaf al-qudum*, the circling seven times of the Kaaba, inside the walls of the Great Mosque – the largest in the world. After praying between the Black Stone and the door of the Kaaba, pilgrims head to the Station of Ibrahim for more prayers. Next, they drink from the holy waters of Zamzam, before proceeding to the ritual *sa'ee*. This is the famous running and walking seven times back and forth between the two hills of Safa and Marwah.

On the second day (9th Dhul Hijja), named the *yawm al-wuquf* (the day of standing), you'll travel among the pilgrims to Arafat where you will recite the solemn *talbiyah* (words attributed to Ibrahim when he first summoned mankind to Mecca) for hours. If you climb the Mount of Mercy (Rahmah), you'll have a bird's eye view of the millions praying together.

The stoning of jamarah, and the required animal sacrifice happen on the third day (10th Dhul Hijja), or *yawm an-nahr* (the day of sacrifice). During the final three days, or *ayyam at-tashriq* (the days of drying meat), you'll remain in Mina, casting seven stones at the three symbolic stone pillars, then leave Mecca on 14th Dhul Hijja.

SHORTCUT

The *umrah* ('lesser pilgrimage' or 'visitation') or Little Haj is a short version of the Haj. It can be carried out in around two hours at any time of year, except during the Haj itself. Umrah pilgrims wear the *ihram* and perform the *tawaf al-qudum* and the *sa'ee*. Many pilgrims say that the umrah experience is a much quieter, more peaceful and contemplative experience than the Haj.

DETOUR

Though not a requirement of the umrah or the Haj, pilgrims often visit the Prophet Mohammed's tomb and that of his daughter, Fatima, in Medina. On a more secular track, remember there is no value-added tax in the Kingdom, and after the pilgrimage, many hajis (one who has made the haj) remain in Medina to go shopping for luxury goods that they can't afford at home. Apparently, faith does have its earthly rewards.

OPENING SPREAD A Kenyan pilgrim comes to pay his respects at Mecca. **ABOVE** Incredible scenes: evening prayer at the Mosque of the Prophet, Medina. **LEFT** A congregation of Muslim Haj pilgrims on the Mount of Mercy, Arafat.

ARMCHAIR

✳ *Travel of Ibn Jubayr* (Ibn Jubayr) The 12th-century courtier from Arab Spain performed the Haj and stayed in Mecca for a period of eight months. His book is considered the first traveller's diary written and published in Arabic.

✳ *Personal Narrative of a Pilgrimage to Al-Madinah and Mecca* (Sir Richard Francis Burton) A travel memoir written by a religious sceptic and one of England's most intrepid 19th-century writers and explorers.

✳ *The Autobiography of Malcolm X* (Malcolm X & Alex Haley) The seminal work of one of America's greatest civil rights activists who shed his own reverse racism while making the Haj.

✳ *Religulous* (2008) The Haj makes an appearance in this anti-religion documentary that verges on the kind of atheist propaganda hovering in Leftist comic, Bill Maher's wheelhouse.

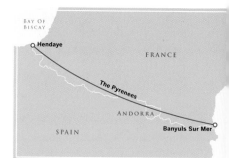

HAUTE PYRENEAN ROUTE

EUROPE'S OTHER GREAT MOUNTAIN RANGE ALSO OFFERS ONE OF THE
CONTINENT'S MOST INCREDIBLE WALKING ADVENTURES, TRAVERSING THE
ENTIRE PYRENEAN RANGE FROM SEA TO OCEAN, BALANCING ATOP
ITS HIGHEST RIDGES AND PEAKS.

298

Like a chain of castles protecting Spain from the advances of the rest of
Europe, the Pyrenees burst out of the waters of the Mediterranean, climb to
the heavens and then sink, Atlantis like, into the deep cold of the Atlantic
Ocean. From beginning to end they span a distance of around 435km,
straddling the Spain-France border as they go (and incorporating Andorra
in its entirety) and rising to a high point of 3404m at Pico de Aneto.

It is a mountain range that offers myriad challenges, but none more
demanding or enticing than the Haute Pyrenean Route (Pyrenees High
Level Route). The Haute Pyrenean was the brainchild of Georges Veron,
considered the granddad of all Pyrenees walkers. His 1968 French-
language *La Haute Route des Pyrénées* detailed a route across the tops
of the Pyrenees. Not bothered with beginners or even intermediate
walkers, this master of navigation, with an unparalleled knowledge of
the mountains, gave route descriptions that were often minimal and
frequently just struck out where no path existed.

As such the walk has always been more a concept than a track. It's not
waymarked (though it does at times merge with the marked GR10) and
numerous variations are possible. All it takes is beginning at Hendaye and
finishing at Banyuls-sur-Mer (or vice versa), keeping as high as you can.

Despite this lack of formality and familiarity on the ground, the Haute
Pyrenean Route rings out like a siren call to hikers across the world.
There's an extensive network of mountain refuges, taking away the need
to camp if you so desire, and whatever routes you choose will invariably
take you through Spain's two Pyrenees national parks: Parc Nacional
d'Aigüestortes i Estany de Sant Maurici and Parque Nacional de Ordesa y
Monte Perdido.

ESSENTIAL EXPERIENCES

✳ **Border-hopping between Spain and France
as you follow the high tops of the range.**

✳ Looking over all of Andorra from the narrow
spine, at times no more than 2m wide, of
Cresta de l'Estanyo.

✳ **Spending hours or days in the company
of nothing but marmots and chamois in
remote areas of the range.**

✳ Being greeted by the Pyrenees' highest peaks
as you rise onto the Col de Mulleres.

✳ **Staggering to the sea edge after a month
and a half on foot in the Pyrenees.**

DISTANCE - APPROXIMATELY 800KM | **COUNTRIES COVERED** - SPAIN, FRANCE, ANDORRA | **IDEAL TIME COMMITMENT** - 45 TO 50
DAYS | **BEST TIME OF YEAR** - JULY AND AUGUST | **ESSENTIAL TIP** - MAP AND COMPASS SKILLS ARE VITAL.

THE CYCLISTS' HAUTE PYRENEAN

If hikers have the Haute Pyrenean, cyclists have the Raid Pyrénéen, offering a very similar challenge: to traverse the Pyrenees from Hendaye to Cerbére. The idea for such a cycling challenge was first raised in 1912, though a definitive route and a successful attempt on it wasn't completed until 1950. It takes cyclists up 28 significant climbs, ascending 16,000m in roughly 800km, and is officially classified as *hors categorie*, meaning it's so difficult it is beyond classification. Riders who preregister with Cyclo Club Béarnais, obtain the *brevet* (route card) and have it stamped at nominated checkpoints while riding the route within 10 consecutive days, qualify for a medallion.

■ THE JOURNEY TODAY

The shrill call of a marmot scratches the air and a vulture coils about on the thermals...just another day in the high Pyrenees. You have been in these mountains – and, more to the point, on these feet – for three weeks now but still the sounds and sights are the most blessed of wake-up calls. You are halfway to the Atlantic Ocean and, right now, you don't want it to end. You have a big day planned, perhaps the biggest of your journey, crossing two high passes to the distant refuge at Renclusa. It feels appropriate that you are setting out from a 'hospital'. The stone Hospital de Vielha (named for the original meaning of the word: a place where hospitality is offered) dates back to the 12th century and, with its bar and restaurant, felt almost more like a Spanish roadside inn than a mountain refuge.

The pass ahead, the Col de Mulleres, is the highest of the high. At 2928m it's the highest crossing you'll make – just 500m shy of the highest peak in the range – and it sure feels it. It's been a two-hour walk to the Refugio de Mulleres and here the real work begins. The ascent from here is entirely over rock. Sometimes you're on huge slabs, sometimes on slippery scree. And all the while you are trying to beat the inevitable cloud to the pass, which is up there somewhere, though it's difficult to distinguish it against the skyline, even now that you're so close.

You follow footsteps through a narrow snowfield and then the final sting in the tail: a grunt of a scramble that makes you wonder what on earth you have in this suddenly so-heavy backpack. But that's it. Gasping for breath, you are here on the pass, presented abruptly with a stupendous view of Pico de Aneto, the Pyrenees' highest mountain and your planned excursion for tomorrow. But tomorrow's another day.

ARMCHAIR

❋ *La Haute Route des Pyrénées* (Georges Veron) When only the original will do (or opt for the out-of-print, abridged English translation, called Pyrenees High Level Route).

❋ *Pyrenean Haute Route* (Ton Joosten) Comprehensive guide to the trail, deviating from Veron's original in places to improve on the route.

❋ *Plant List for the Pyrenees* (Lance Chilton) Hard-to-find guide to those flowers you'll be passing.

❋ *Through the Spanish Pyrenees GR11: A Long Distance Footpath* (Paul Lucia) A guide to one of the alternative, lower Pyrenees traverses.

❋ *Backpacks, Boots & Baguettes* (Simon Calder & Mick Webb) Tale of two mates walking the Pyrenean high passes, albeit along the GR10.

SHORTCUT

More low-cuts than shortcuts, the GR10 and GR11 walking trails also offer Pyrenees traverses, but are waymarked and often lower down the mountain slopes. The GR10 is the classic Pyrenees hiking route, sticking just to the French side of the border, and while it may be lower, don't expect anything much easier – it climbs almost 50,000m across its course. The GR11 sticks to the Spanish side, with a comparatively modest 40,000m of ascent.

DETOUR

If you're spending weeks with your head and boots in the Pyrenean clouds, you'll probably be more than a little tempted by Pico de Aneto, the range's highest peak and the second-highest in Spain. The classic route, with a climb of 1265m, leaves from Refugio de la Renclusa. It's a strenuous day walk and an early morning start is essential – allow 4½ hours for the ascent and, given the rough terrain, don't count on the descent being all that much shorter. The challenge shouldn't be underestimated: you'll need crampons and an ice axe – or walking poles at the very least – for the glacier crossing.

IAN CUMMING | PHOTOLIBRARY

OPENING SPREAD Sky high and guaranteed to blow your mind: Mallos de Riglos, Aragon, Spain. **ABOVE** Hiking through the Ordesa Canyon in the Pyrenees. **BELOW** A sweeping view of the La Maladeta massif.

THERE'S A BEAR IN THERE

No-one seems to know exactly how many bears there are now living in the Pyrenees, though estimates suggest it's no more than 24. What is certain, though, is that the original population is effectively extinct. The last surviving female Pyrenean brown bear died in 2004, leaving only two males from a population that not so long ago numbered over 200. In an attempt to 'restock' the mountains in the last decade, 'immigrant' brown bears from Slovenia have been introduced and they have been successfully breeding. The bears are understandably timid, not dangerous to humans, and you're extremely unlikely to encounter one, although you may see tracks or droppings.

SHIKOKU PILGRIMAGE

FOR OVER 1000 YEARS PILGRIMS HAVE WALKED CLOCKWISE FOR 1400KM AROUND WILD, BEAUTIFUL SHIKOKU, IN THE FOOTSTEPS OF THE BUDDHIST SAINT, KŌBŌ DAISHI (774–835). KNOWN AS THE '88 TEMPLES OF SHIKOKU', THIS IS JAPAN'S BEST-KNOWN PILGRIMAGE AND ORIGINAL BACKPACKER TRAIL.

302

The *henro* (pilgrim) is the most ubiquitous sight on the island of Shikoku. Trudging through shimmering heat, or biblical monsoons, they are easy to spot, dressed in their *hakue* (white garment) to symbolise purity of mind, sheltered beneath a *sugegasa* (straw hat) that has protected pilgrims from the sun and rain since time immemorial, and tapping their *kongozue* (colourful staff). Pilgrims believe the *kongozue* to be the embodiment of long-gone, enlightened Kōbō Daishi, who is said to accompany all pilgrims on their journey, hence the inscription found on so many backpacks: dogyo ninin, meaning 'two people on the same journey'. The routine at each temple seldom varies. There's a chime of a bell, the chanting of the Heart Sutra at the Daishi-do (one of the two main buildings in each temple compound), before checking in at the *nokyosho* (desk) where the resident monks inscribe the pilgrims' books with beautiful characters detailing the name of the temple and the pilgrimage date.

The quest traditionally begins in Tokushima-ken, home to the first 23 of the 88 temples along with the powerful, entrancing whirlpools of the Naruto Channel, and the dramatic mountain scenery and deep gorges of the Iya Valley. Remote landscapes such as this explain why before the days of reliable maps and guidebooks, pilgrims frequently faded away into Shikoku's interior never to return, like so much mist. The most desolate section is along the rugged Pacific Coast in the Kochi-ken prefecture, which covers one-third of the mileage but includes only 16 temples. The 75th and largest temple of all, Zentsu-ji, is special because this is the saint's birthplace, and the mossy camphor trees surrounding the five-tiered pagoda are said to date back to before Kōbō Daishi was born.

ESSENTIAL EXPERIENCES

* **Strolling into 8th-century Ryozen-ji, its lanterns flickering, as you pray in the first of 88 temples.**

* Navigating the rugged, and somewhat desolate, Pacific Coast in Kochi-ken

* **Staring out to sea, just like the statue of the great saint, at Hatsumisaki-ji on Muroto-misaki, one of the islands' southern capes and one of the wildest places in all of Japan.**

* Taking in the natural beauty of Setonaikai National Park on the north coast.

* **Paying your respects at Zentsu-ji, the 75th and largest temple, where Kōbō Daishi was born.**

DISTANCE - 1400KM | COUNTRIES COVERED - JAPAN | **IDEAL TIME COMMITMENT** - 30 TO 60 DAYS ON FOOT | **BEST TIME OF YEAR** - SEPTEMBER TO NOVEMBER | **ESSENTIAL TIP** - THE HEAT IN SUMMER CAN BE UNBEARABLE; GO DURING SPRING OR AUTUMN.

SANUKI UDON

People in Takamatsu are serious about their udon (delicious, thick white noodles made from wheat), and no trip here would be complete without at least one bowl of the famous speciality, Sanuki udon. Why 'Sanuki'? It's the old name for the province that's now modern Kagawa-ken. As with most things in this part of Japan, there is a Kōbō Daishi connection: according to tradition, the great saint was the first to bring the noodles to Japan when he returned from Tang China 1200 years ago. There are udon shops on just about every corner, and you don't have to stay here long before you start to recognise the characters for the words te-uchi udon, meaning 'handmade noodles'.

TAGA-JINJA & SEX MUSEUM

Once upon a time, many Shintō shrines had a connection to fertility rites. Of those that remain, Taga-jinja, in Uwajima, is one of the best known. The grounds of the shrine are strewn with tree-trunk phalluses and numerous statues and stone carvings, but the star attraction is the three-storey sex museum. It's packed floor to ceiling with explicit Peruvian pottery and Greek vases; an illustrated Kama Sutra, Tibetan tantric sculptures, South Pacific fertility gods, and a showcase of S&M gear from the Victorian age to now. There's a decent collection of porn rags too.

THE JOURNEY TODAY

Flanked by mountains and cantered on a palm-line promenade, the bustling city of Tokushima is the jumping-off point for your pilgrimage. The mode of travel is almost as diverse as the *henro* community itself. Some are students on a lovers' spin, others weekender professionals nibbling at a handful of temples at a time, and retired wise ones who fit the pilgrim archetype perfectly. The minority carve out 30 to 60 days and do it all on foot. Most travel by bike, motorcycle or car. The first five temples are near the whirlpools of Naruto. The first, Ryozen-ji, is the most stunning, built in the 8th century and lit by hundreds of lanterns. Kōbō Daishi spent several weeks in meditation here. Moving out of the city swirl, life still moves at a slower pace. Single carriage trains trundle through rice fields and sheer valleys. Lonely rugged capes witness only the rhythm of wind and sea. The most gruelling country will be Kochi-ken, as there are only 16 temples to visit and more than one-third of the island to cover. But there are rewards. Muroto-misaki, the first of two great capes on the south coast is one of the wildest places in Japan, and it is here, where Kōbō Daishi achieved enlightenment. A huge white statue stares out into the sea just north of the cape at Temple 24, Hatsumisaki-ji, which he founded in the early 9th century. Kongofuku-ji, Temple 38 on Ashizuri-misaki, the other cape, is likewise blessed with sublime Pacific views. The westernmost region of Ehime-ken has 27 of the 88 temples, and when you reach Matsuyama, Shikoku's largest city, you'll know the toughest country is behind you. From here, hug the stunning coastline, along the remarkable Inland Sea National Park, pay your respects to the saint's birthplace at Zentsu-ji, go surfing in Shikoku, explore a 300 year old market in Kochi, sea kayak along Ashizuri-misaki, or dip into the Dongo Onsen, one of the oldest hot springs in Japan. It's all part of the path to enlightenment.

SHORTCUT

If time is short you can get a taste by completing a *henro*-for-a-day mini-circuit. The first five temples, from Ryozen-ji to Jizo-ji, are possible to visit on a day trip from Tokushima to Naruto. While Temples 41 and 42, Butsumoku-ji and Ryuko-ji, are separated by just 5km of picturesque rice fields and stone staircases in Uwajima.

DETOUR

In the Iya Valley, just inland from Tokushima, you'll find superb hiking on 1955m Mt Tsurugi, and white-water rafting through the stunning Oboke and Koboke Gorges. After a chilly hike or paddle, warm up with the locals by dipping into top-notch natural onsen (hot springs) followed by a bowl of the locals' beloved Iya soba (buckwheat noodles). Slurp, smile, repeat.

JTB PHOTO | PHOTOLIBRARY

OPENING SPREAD A veritable blanket of snow covers a typical Kagawa landscape. **ABOVE** Pilgrims clad in white doing what pilgrims do best: paying homage. **LEFT** A scene to make a believer out of you: Kongofuku-ji, temple 38.

ARMCHAIR

✻ **Japanese Pilgrimage** (Oliver Statler) The grandfather of all English language books about the pilgrimage, the author spent about three months on the Shikoku trail in 1971.

✻ **Neon Pilgrim** (Lisa Dempster) The author covered the trail in 2009, camping most of the way. She started out as an unemployed, overweight and depressed *henro*, hoping the trail would work its magic and change her life.

✻ **The 1918 Shikoku Pilgrimage of Takamure Itsue** (Musume Junreiki) Essentially a young woman reporter's pilgrimage journal, this is a compilation of 105 newspaper articles she wrote and filed while on the trail in the early 20th century. At times she was regarded as a deity and asked to heal the sick. At other times she endured unbearable heat and mythic typhoons. She will forever be groundbreaking.

INDEX

INDEX

INDEX

INDEX

INDEX

INDEX

GREAT JOURNEYS

TRAVEL THE WORLD'S MOST SPECTACULAR ROUTES

IST EDITION
Published August 2013

Publisher Piers Pickard
Associate Publisher Ben Handicott
Project Manager Jane Atkin
Written by Andrew Bain, Sarah Baxter, Simon Sellars, Adam Skolnick
Copyeditors Victoria Harrison, Paul Harding, Jocelyn Harewood
Art Direction & Design Mark Adams
Layout Designers Seviora Citra, Lauren Egan, Yvonne Bischofberger,
Mazzy Prinsep, Wendy Wright, Nicholas Colicchia
Image Research Sabrina Dalbesio, Kylie McLaughlin, Aude Vauconsant
Pre-Press Production Ryan Evans
Thanks Helen Christinis, Jane Hart, Indra Kilfoyle, Tracey Kislingbury, Yvonne Kirk,
Nic Lehman, Lucy Monie, Susan Paterson, Sally Schafer, Rebecca Skinner,
Marg Toohey, Stefanie di Trocchio, Juan Winata

PUBLISHED BY

Lonely Planet Publications Pty Ltd ABN 36 005 607 983
90 Maribyrnong St, Footscray, Victoria 3011, Australia
ISBN 978 1 74321 718 4
Text & maps © Lonely Planet Pty Ltd 2013
Photos © as indicated 2013

Printed in China
10 9 8 7 6 5 4 3 2 1

AUSTRALIA (HEAD OFFICE)
90 Maribyrnong St, Footscray, Victoria, 3011
Phone 03 8379 8000 **Fax** 03 8379 8111

USA
150 Linden St, Oakland, CA 94607
Phone 510 250 6400 **Toll free** 800 275 8555

UNITED KINGDOM
BBC Worldwide, Media Centre, 201 Wood Lan
London, W12 7TQ **Phone** 020 8433 1333

FRONT & BACK COVER IMAGES **Front** (top) Men leading camels in Lybian desert (Frank Lukasseck / Corbis); (bottom) Jiankou Great Wall blanketed in snow (Fotosearch / Photolibrary); **Back** Road to Monument Valley (Corbis) FRONT MATTER IMAGES **Pages 2–3** Gornergrat Ridge and Mt Matterhorn, Zermatt, Switzerland (Daniel Schoenen / Photolibrary) **Page 4** Bavarian fields and country roads, Germany (Gerald Nowak / Photolibrary) **Pages 6–7** Monument Valley, USA (Alan Copson / Photolibrary) **Page 8** Desert (Ingram Publishing / Photolibrary)